TWO NATIONS INDIVISIBLE

The Council on Foreign Relations (CFR) is an independent, nonpartisan membership organization, think tank, and publisher dedicated to being a resource for its members, government officials, business executives, journalists, educators and students, civic and religious leaders, and other interested citizens in order to help them better understand the world and the foreign policy choices facing the United States and other countries. Founded in 1921, CFR carries out its mission by maintaining a diverse membership, with special programs to promote interest and develop expertise in the next generation of foreign policy leaders; convening meetings at its headquarters in New York and in Washington, DC, and other cities where senior government officials, members of Congress, global leaders, and prominent thinkers come together with CFR members to discuss and debate major international issues; supporting a Studies Program that fosters independent research, enabling CFR scholars to produce articles, reports, and books and hold roundtables that analyze foreign policy issues and make concrete policy recommendations; publishing *Foreign Affairs*, the preeminent journal on international affairs and U.S. foreign policy; sponsoring Independent Task Forces that produce reports with both findings and policy prescriptions on the most important foreign policy topics; and providing up-to-date information and analysis about world events and American foreign policy on its website, www.cfr.org.

The Council on Foreign Relations takes no institutional positions on policy issues and has no affiliation with the U.S. government. All views expressed in its publications and on its website are the sole responsibility of the author or authors.

TWO NATIONS INDIVISIBLE

MEXICO, THE UNITED STATES, AND THE ROAD AHEAD

SHANNON K. O'NEIL

A Council on Foreign Relations Book

OXFORD

UNIVERSITY PRESS

Oxford University Press is a department of the University of Oxford.
It furthers the University's objective of excellence in research, scholarship,
and education by publishing worldwide.

Oxford   New York
Auckland   Cape Town   Dar es Salaam   Hong Kong   Karachi
Kuala Lumpur   Madrid   Melbourne   Mexico City   Nairobi
New Delhi   Shanghai   Taipei   Toronto

With offices in
Argentina   Austria   Brazil   Chile   Czech Republic   France   Greece
Guatemala   Hungary   Italy   Japan   Poland   Portugal   Singapore
South Korea   Switzerland   Thailand   Turkey   Ukraine   Vietnam

Oxford is a registered trade mark of Oxford University Press in the UK
and certain other countries.

Published in the United States of America by
Oxford University Press
198 Madison Avenue, New York, NY 10016

Library of Congress Cataloging-in-Publication Data
O'Neil, Shannon K. (Shannon Kathleen)
Two nations indivisible : Mexico, the United States, and the road ahead / Shannon K. O'Neil.
p. cm.
Includes bibliographical references and index.
ISBN 978–0–19–989833–6
1. United States—Foreign relations—Mexico. 2. Mexico—Foreign relations—United States.
   I. Title.
E183.8.M6O54 2013
327'.73072—dc23   2012034521

ISBN 978–0–19–989833–6

9 8 7 6 5 4 3 2 1
Printed in the United States of America
on acid-free paper

CONTENTS

MAP

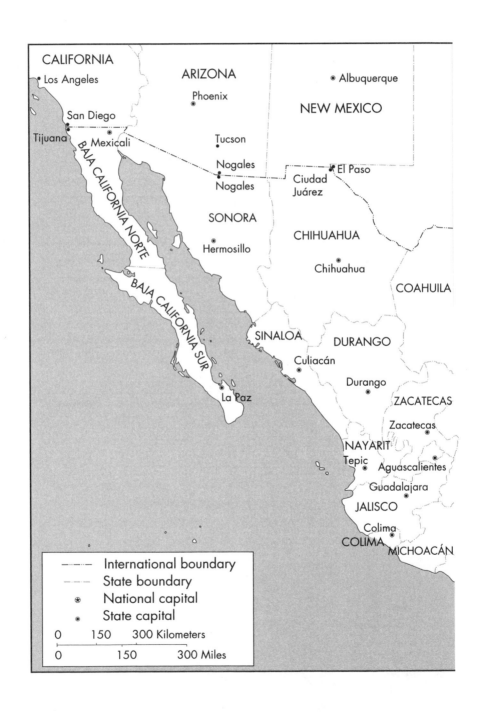

CALIFORNIA
• Los Angeles

ARIZONA

• Albuquerque

Phoenix

San Diego

NEW MEXICO

Tijuana

Mexicali

Tucson

Nogales

El Paso

BAJA CALIFORNIA NORTE

Nogales

Ciudad
Juárez

SONORA

Hermosillo

CHIHUAHUA

BAJA CALIFORNIA SUR

Chihuahua

COAHUILA

SINALOA

DURANGO

Culiacán

Durango

ZACATECAS

La Paz

Zacatecas

NAYARIT

Tepic   Aguascalientes

Guadalajara

JALISCO

Colima

COLIMA   MICHOACÁN

—··—··—   International boundary
— · —   State boundary
⊛   National capital
⦿   State capital

0   150   300 Kilometers
0   150   300 Miles

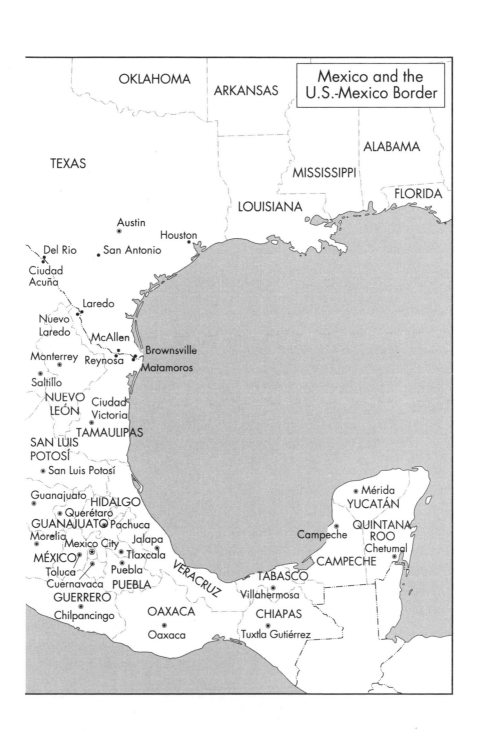

Mexico and the
U.S.-Mexico Border

OKLAHOMA
ARKANSAS
ALABAMA
MISSISSIPPI
FLORIDA
TEXAS
LOUISIANA
Austin
Houston
Del Rio
San Antonio
Ciudad
Acuña
Laredo
Nuevo
Laredo
McAllen
Monterrey
Reynosa
Brownsville
Matamoros
Saltillo
NUEVO
LEÓN
Ciudad
Victoria
TAMAULIPAS
SAN LUIS
POTOSÍ
San Luis Potosí
Guanajuato
HIDALGO
Mérida
YUCATÁN
Querétaro
GUANAJUATO
Pachuca
QUINTANA
ROO
Morelia
Mexico City
Jalapa
Campeche
Chetumal
MÉXICO
Tlaxcala
CAMPECHE
Toluca
Puebla
Cuernavaca
PUEBLA
VERACRUZ
TABASCO
GUERRERO
Villahermosa
Chilpancingo
OAXACA
CHIAPAS
Oaxaca
Tuxtla Gutiérrez

ACKNOWLEDGMENTS

This book has been a long time in the making, drawing on my days in investment banking, in academia, and now in the policy world at the Council on Foreign Relations. In each place, so many people have shared with me their time and insights, educating me, at times arguing with me, but all the while improving my understanding of Mexico and U.S.-Mexico relations. Though too numerous to name, I greatly appreciate their generosity, as it has informed the analysis of this book.

I will always remember with great fondness my first stint living in Mexico, and those with whom I first explored its cities and countrysides, Bradley Tirpak, Caroline Whitehorn (Butler), and Alex Hayek. When I returned several years later as a researcher at the Autonomous Institute of Technology (ITAM), Alejandro Poiré, Gabe Aguilera, Eric Magar, Federico Estévez, Jorge Buendía, Memo Rosas, and Isaac Katz made my time both fruitful and fun. I learned perhaps as much during our lunches as I did through my archival work and interviews. During this time I also met Claudio X. González, and have had the pleasure of talking about Mexico and U.S.-Mexico relations with him for now over a decade.

At Harvard, Steven Levitsky, Paul Pierson, and especially Jorge Domínguez helped me hone my intellectual, analytical, and teaching skills, making me a much better scholar, as did my graduate student colleagues Hillel Soifer, Magda Hinojosa, Mark Copelovitch, Casey Klofstad, Fiona Barker, and Annie Stilz. They also supported me in making the jump from academia to policy. Now at the Council on Foreign Relations (CFR), I have been lucky enough to work for Richard Haass, who has been unfailingly supportive of my work over the last five years and of the fact that Mexico does matter for the United States. As head of CFR Studies department, Jim Lindsay has both pushed me and helped me carve out the time to finish the manuscript. The *Consejo Mexicano de Hombres de Negocio*, Tinker Foundation, and Ford Foundation have all supported my work at CFR, for which I am truly grateful.

This book wouldn't have come into being without David Miller's and Lisa Adam's patient guidance through numerous book-proposal drafts and then with the manuscript itself. It wouldn't be as well researched without the great efforts and abilities of Sebastian Chaskel, Dora Besterczey, Dave Herrero, Charlie Warren, Natalie Kitroeff, and especially Stephanie Leutert, who crossed the finish line with me. I look forward to watching each of their careers develop, and hope they hire me one day.

I am humbled by the incredible kindness—and incisiveness—of the many who offered their time, reading a part or whole of the manuscript. Jorge Domínguez, Steven Levitsky, Noel Maurer, Susan Gauss, David Ayón, and Carlos Pascual read significant parts, and Andrew Selee, Hillel Soifer, Magda Hinojosa, Gabe Aguilera, Ken Greene, Francisco González, Enrique Hidalgo, James Taylor, Alfredo Corchado, Jamie Trowbridge, Dedee O'Neil, and my CFR colleagues Julia Sweig, Ted Alden, Liz Economy, Jim Lindsay, and Richard Haass read it in its entirety. Two anonymous readers also provided useful feedback. I have incorporated as many of their suggestions as I could, and they have definitively made this book much better.

As I made the transition from writing to editing and marketing, I benefited greatly from the insights of David McBride and the enthusiasm of the Oxford University Press team. I received extensive support within CFR as well, from Trish Dorff and Lia Norton in publications, Lisa Shields and the communications team, Leigh Gust and Michelle Baute in our library, Nancy Bodurtha and Stacey LaFollette in meetings, and Irina Faskianos and her team in national outreach.

Everyone says writing a book is a lonely process, but looking back I will remember best the friendships that formed and blossomed throughout. My early morning chats with Liz Economy both focused and distracted me when needed, as did those with other Fellows Michael Levi, Adam Segal, Micah Zenko, Isobel Coleman, Laurie Garrett, Benn Steil, and Jagdish Bhagwati. I've greatly benefited from their smarts and have been honored by their friendship over the last five years. Andrew Selee, Eric Olson, David Shirk, Chris Sabatini, Iván Rebolledo, Juan Pardinas, Alejandro Hope, Ana Paula Ordorica, Rafael Fernández de Castro, Carlos Pascual, Emilio

Carrillo Gamboa, Alfredo Corchado, and James Taylor helped put it all in perspective, as did Sarah Drummond, Jim Neidert, and Melissa Wolff. I greatly appreciated the encouragement of the O'Neil and Trowbridge families. I also couldn't have written this without Silvia Pérez de Martinez, as knowing that my daughters were in her loving hands made it much easier to head off each day.

Throughout it all, I relied on the unwavering support and love of my husband, Jamie Trowbridge, and the patience of my girls, Lillias and Beatrice. I am happy to be home again with them in the mornings.

PREFACE: THE "REAL" MEXICO

I arrived at Benito Juárez airport in Mexico City around four o'clock in the afternoon on a full direct flight from New York's John F. Kennedy airport. With two large suitcases I pushed my way through the Mexican families waiting for their sons and daughters and past numerous porters wanting to assist the *güera* with her bags. Forty-five minutes later, I met two strangers—my new Mexican roommates. The three-room railroad apartment in Anzures, adjacent to the tonier Polanco, was too small for the three of us and, as I discovered over time, we had little in common. But at that moment I was happy not to be alone facing my first days in one of the world's largest cities.

I came to begin a job as an equity analyst at a boutique investment bank. I was an unconventional hire, somehow convincing my soon-to-be boss that a good liberal arts education, passable Spanish, and a stint at a human rights organization in New York City would translate well into analyzing retail, food, and beverage companies on Mexico's expanding stock market.

The fact that Mexico was booming helped. In March 1994, NAFTA was three months under way, and a pervasive optimism filled Mexico City's taxis, streets, and neighborhoods. Sure, there was talk about the Zapatista uprising, but it was mostly gossip about the group's mysterious green-eyed leader Subcomandante Marcos and the wave of Hollywood celebrities heading to meet him in the Chiapas jungle. The poverty and pain of southern Mexico seemed otherworldly in the streets of Polanco, Mexico City's financial hub. Our traders worked the phones all morning, selling hundreds of millions of dollars of *cetes* and *tesobonos*—Mexico's treasury bonds—to French millionaires, Scottish pension fund managers, American institutional investors, and each other. Our corporate finance guys joked between client calls, gossiping about Morgan Stanley's newly rented space down the street, and whether an upcoming high-society wedding would lead to a corporate merger. Hermès tie wearing businessmen (and just a few women) filled the serene courtyard bar and restaurant of the newly opened Four Seasons Hotel, business lunches often extending into the twilight hours. Long meals, bookended by small glasses of Don Julio tequila, were part of the normal business schedule. Political heavies gravitated toward Casa Bell, the also new gardened courtyard restaurant—complete with songbirds—just a few blocks away. At the ivory-clothed tables, the seating chart was always meticulously curated. Avid watchers of the ruling political party's smoke signals could discern the current hierarchy of power and favor from the subtle positioning of advisors and aides at the tables radiating out from a prominent minister, or on some days even the president himself.

Within days of my arrival, this balance briefly foundered with the assassination of Luis Donaldo Colosio, the dominant Institutional Revolutionary Party's (PRI) presidential candidate. Still finding my feet, I didn't understand its significance for Mexico. But, it turns out, neither did anyone else. After initial market jitters, President Carlos Salinas and his world-renowned finance minister, Pedro Aspe, reassured the markets and kept the party going through the July 1994 presidential election. Even after a second political assassination—of José Francisco Ruiz Massieu, secretary general of the PRI—prominent investment firms and voices shook off any worries that Mexico might be on the edge of yet another economic crisis.

In October I temporarily joined our trading desk, filling the seat of a honeymooning colleague. For the next three weeks I took orders from foreign clients and negotiated with my Mexican counterparts, cajoling them to go easy on the newbie gringa. As I (gladly) returned to my research reports in early November, my bosses, veterans of the 1982 Latin American debt crisis, sold all their Mexico positions, fearful of a peso decline with the presidential transition on December 1. Going against the markets, they were in rarified company. Over the course of 1994, Carlos Slim, at the time Mexico's wealthiest man (later the world's wealthiest), converted into pesos over $1 billion of dollar-denominated debt owed by his various companies.

History did repeat itself on December 19, 1994. His hand forced by dwindling international reserves, newly installed President Ernesto Zedillo initially devalued the peso by 15 percent. A bewildered and betrayed market then pummeled the currency, which quickly tumbled past six pesos to the dollar—erasing half of its value in the following weeks.

Inflation rose, stores and restaurants closed, and millions lost their jobs. Even Mexico City's main volcano, Popocatepétl, reacted, spewing ash across the capital's beleaguered residents. Daily life as a foreigner became more difficult; while my compatriots and I were somewhat less affected by the economic crisis, crime quickly worsened. The often entertaining rides in Mexico's Volkswagen Bug taxi cabs turned menacing, as stories of "express kidnappings"—forcing passengers to withdraw the maximum from ATM machines before dumping them in outlying, sketchy neighborhoods— spread through the expat community. Like others I knew, I was held up at gunpoint outside my apartment. After almost three years, I decided to return to New York. While I and others didn't realize it, we were experiencing the lethal blow to Mexico's political system. Once all-powerful, the PRI could not control the economic, political, and social changes that would follow.

I returned to live in Mexico City in 2002 at a very different moment. Having left the investment banking world for academia, I came on a Fulbright grant as a visiting researcher at the Autonomous Institute of Technology, or ITAM, one of Mexico's most prestigious private universities located on the edge of San Ángel, a cobble-stoned neighborhood in the south of the capital.

Much had changed in my absence. Immediately noticeable was the air. Economic shifts and government regulations that pushed factories out of the city and limited car use meant one could finally see, even on bad pollution days, at least a block ahead. The city too had expanded. Just a mall, movie theater, and a couple of apartment buildings in the mid-1990s, the far western end of Reforma Avenue had become a city unto its own. Dubbed Santa Fe, it made one feel transported to a Houston suburb, the landscape dominated by sleek glass office buildings interspersed with residential high-rises and gated communities. With so many multinational corporations headquartered in the new neighborhood, many—mostly Mexico's rich—rarely headed into the city's downtown anymore, their world now centered on the westward edge, halfway to Toluca. The city stretched farther to the east as well, creeping out past the airport to the toll booths on the highway to Puebla, where miles of neatly appointed starter houses trailed off toward the horizon.

Even as the upper classes and newly middle classes pushed out and filled in the city's edges, Mexico's central neighborhoods made a full comeback. Condesa and Roma—once home to bookish immigrants and the bohemian set—now attracted the chicer Lomas and Polanco crowd. The incessant hammering of construction workers slowly erased the 1985 earthquake scars, sleek apartment buildings popping up next to stately belle époque and art deco jewels.

In the 1990s we had made the culinary trek to the few Condesa outposts: Fonda Garufa for its huitlacoche pasta, or next door to the newly opened Café la Gloria for bistro-style fare. Nearly a decade later, these stalwarts were surrounded by dozens of competitors, diners spilling over the sidewalks and onto the streets. The arrival of Mexico's young, hip, and moneyed changed the feel of the leafy neighborhoods.

These welcome shifts were just one part of a larger transformation. Ubiquitous shopping malls, internet cafés, and Walmarts fed the consumption habits of Mexico's expanding middle class. Mexicans reveled in their newfound democracy, with debates over issues large and small covered in the now fiercely independent press. The country began to reenvision its ties north, with politicians referring to migrants as "diplomats" and even "heroes" rather than implicit traitors to their country.

But even as the old system faded, new problems appeared. Political competition brought legislative deadlock, delaying necessary reforms. Free elections did little to create strong independent public institutions or widespread accountability—frustrating citizens and international observers alike. International competition and Mexico's own failings meant only slow (if stable) economic growth, which was unable to provide opportunities for many Mexicans at home. Workers and their families continued to migrate north, despite the increasingly hostile reception from U.S. policymakers, media, and a number of communities.

Some things hadn't changed. Crime, which spiked during the 1995 economic crisis, never subsided. Drug-related violence rose, spurred by changes in the global narcotics industry as well as the side effects of Mexico's democratization. The vacuum left by the retreating autocratic power of the PRI had yet to be filled by a far-reaching democratic rule of law.

While starting the century on its most promising note ever, by 2003 Mexico's relationship with the United States had again stumbled, falling back into traditional patterns of mutual suspicion and vocal recriminations in the raw days following September 11 and in the subsequent lead-up to the war in Iraq.

In the capital, the green Volkswagen Bug taxis had been mostly replaced by more sedate maroon and gold Nissan Tsurus and Volkswagen Jettas, though the passive-aggressive driving style of the *chilangos* remained the same. Even as Mexicans added the local Sam's Club and Superama supermarkets to their shopping circuit, vendors still did a swift business at the city's stoplights and major intersections—hawking newspapers, phone cards, gum, "Japanese" peanuts, oranges, and even coat racks. Still ubiquitous, too, were the weekly *tianguis*, or open-air markets, where Mexicans of all stripes bought fruits, vegetables, and meats, as well as flowers, pots, pans, and even electronics in the temporary maze of stalls and stands set up under bright red, pink, and blue tarps, shielding the overloaded wooden pallets from the sun.

As I finished my research at the ITAM, I again left Mexico, though this time with a greater appreciation of the country's challenges, opportunities, and its incredible importance for the United States. Since then, I have remained a frequent visitor to Mexico. Each time I return, I see a sharp contrast between what I read and hear in the United States about our southern neighbor and what I experience on Mexico's streets. Mexico faces serious challenges, but it is also committed to addressing them, working to enlarge its middle class, open its political system, and provide for its citizens. What is true is that the future of its economy, its democracy, and its society hangs on the many choices being made today.

What is also more apparent, whichever side of the border I am on, is that the United States' future will be highly influenced by these outcomes next door. As one of the United States' largest sources of trade, oil, people, culture, and illegal substances, what happens in Mexico no longer stays in Mexico. The stakes for U.S. economic growth, social cohesion, and basic security are high.

Unfortunately, U.S. policy toward its neighbor hasn't caught up. The old mindsets and approaches are now exacerbating the challenges facing both countries, as we obstinately try to solve alone the many issues permeating official boundaries. Mexican and American individuals and communities span the border, flouting outdated and counterproductive immigration laws. Decaying border infrastructure limits North American competitiveness, hitting the bottom lines of both U.S. and Mexican companies. Mexico's economic struggles lead many into illegal trades—including drugs and contraband—and crime more generally, which can then spill over the border. Even as the United States spends billions to support democracy in faraway places like Iraq and Afghanistan in the search for world stability, it overlooks the related struggles next door. Instead, the United States' reaction—committing billions of dollars toward a border wall—hasn't stopped illegal migration, trafficking, or, in the end, made America safer.

Resolving these problems, as well as taking advantage of these opportunities, requires a new approach to our neighbor. It requires a rethinking of the United States' understanding of Mexico, and the forces that have shaped it and that will shape its future. It requires us to understand those problems from Mexico's perspective as well as our own, and to put U.S. interests front and center. Perhaps most of all, it means understanding the implications of the United States' continued thinking that we can wall Mexico off, or the idea that we would ever want to do so.

MEXICO AT THE CROSSROAD

Once a sleepy border town known best for creating the burrito, Ciudad Juárez is now one of Mexico's fastest-growing cities. Hundreds of new buildings and factories fill the city's streets, affixed with large signs announcing the presence of world-class companies: Boeing, Bosch, Lear, Delphi, and Siemens. Dozens of construction sites signal that the steady stream of *maquila* factories and jobseekers is not about to end. From the twelfth floor of the Torres Campestre building, you can see downtown El Paso, Texas, now the smaller of the two connected cities.

In 2008 Juárez was named the "City of the Future" by *Foreign Direct Investment* magazine, a trade journal of the Financial Times Group. Per capita incomes surpassed Mexico's average, and Juárez's expansion spurred the biggest housing boom in the nation. New cars filled the streets, dozens of stores and restaurants opened, and the city boasted eight universities.

On a normal day at the Juárez–El Paso border crossings, some eighty thousand people come and go.[1] In the morning, children line up with backpacks, ready for school. Later on, drivers carry shopping lists or business leads as they pass through checkpoints to the other side. At night, couples, families, and friends visit relatives or head to bars and parties in the neighborhood (and often country) next door.

But open a newspaper or turn on the television, and a very different image of Juárez emerges. Each morning, numbed reporters recount the previous night's murders. In 2009, Juárez's death count topped 2500—the highest in Mexico. Juárez set another macabre record in 2010, surpassing 3000 drug-related killings, making it by many measures the most violent city in the world. The bloodshed of 2011 brought the cumulative five-year total to more than nine thousand souls.[2] Teenagers, with little else to do, hang around gawking at bloodstained sidewalks. Close to half of Juárez's youths do not work or attend school, setting themselves up for a life on the margins. Even in the strong midday sun, the unlawful menace is palpable, leading residents to scurry between their houses and work, to resist lingering in the open air, to duck when a car backfires. Whole neighborhoods have emptied out, as the residents, driven by fear, have made the heartbreaking decision to walk away from their homes. In 2009, the government sent in seven thousand military troops and federal police to patrol the streets in face masks and bulletproof vests, carrying automatic weapons at the ready. This only temporarily quelled some of the bloodshed.

The extent of today's violence is unparalleled, but crime is hardly new to Ciudad Juárez. Drug-related violence first exploded in 1997 when the Juárez cartel leader died while undergoing plastic surgery to change his identity. What began as intracartel fighting escalated as the Tijuana and Sinaloa drug trafficking organizations entered the fray in an attempt to gain control of the city's lucrative border crossings. Ciudad Juárez is also infamous for the violent deaths of hundreds of young women—most workers in the international *maquila* factories. Their murders remain unsolved, the law enforcement system being too weak, too incompetent, or too complicit to delve into the deep underworld of this burgeoning Mexican city.

Juárez today mirrors Mexico's—and the United States'—larger dilemma. Can it realize its potential and become a hub of North American competitiveness and interconnectedness? Or will it succumb to inept government, weakened communities, and escalating violence, walled off rather than embraced by its neighbor next door?

Turn on U.S. cable news and story after story recounts gruesome beheadings, spectacular assassinations, and brazen prison-breaks, painting Mexico as a country overrun by drug lords and on the brink of collapse. More evenhanded news outlets aren't far behind. The *Los Angeles Times* boasts a whole section entitled "Mexico under Siege." If this threat was not enough, pundits and politicians alike conjure up images of vast waves of humanity pouring over the nearly two-thousand-mile border— illegal aliens flooding U.S. schools and hospitals and taking Americans' jobs. Whether by lost jobs, illegal immigrants, or thugs and drugs, Mexico's downward spiral is portrayed as imperiling the American way of life. But this conventional wisdom about Mexico is incomplete. Worse, the response—walling off the United States—is counterproductive and even harmful to U.S. national interests. Paradoxically, such efforts make the doomsday scenario next door that we so fear only more likely, directing billions of dollars away from policies that could actually improve U.S. security and prosperity.

Overlooked, underreported, and at times even blatantly ignored in the United States is the positive side of what is happening in Mexico. Yes, the Mexican government faces significant challenges—the most urgent being security. But as dismal as the current news is, Mexico stands on the cusp of a promising future. Mexico's real story today is one of ongoing economic, political, and social transformation led by a rising middle class, increasingly demanding voters, and enterprising individuals and organizations working to change their country from the inside.

Mexico has come a long way. Three generations ago, the vast majority of Mexicans lived in semifeudal conditions, tied to the land and political bosses. Two generations ago, Mexican students were massacred for their political beliefs by the authoritarian PRI government. Today, Mexico is a consolidating democracy, an opening economy, and an urbanizing society. Mexico is less a problem and more an answer for the economic, security, and international diplomatic challenges the United States faces today.

This isn't the first time that the United States has misunderstood its southern neighbor or that its misguided actions have exacerbated the problems plaguing both countries. What is different now is how important the outcomes in Mexico are for America's future. Over the last few decades, through the movement and integration of companies, products, and people, Mexico and the United States have become indelibly intertwined in ways that most Americans do not see or understand. What happens in Mexico today has ramifications for towns, cities, and states across the United States; this reality has yet to sink in, at least on the northern side of the border.

Policies such as the border wall assume that the challenges both countries face can be solved unilaterally. This too is wrong. Instead of clinging to the myth of autonomy, we must find a better way to work with Mexico for our own well-being. If we don't, the consequences will be far worse than we imagine.

Mexico's Crossroads

After nearly three transformative decades, Mexico is still in the midst of change, still forging its global political, economic, and social identity. Pushed there by the challenges of massive emigration, political and economic opening, and widespread insecurity, it has come to a crossroads. Mexico can follow a path that makes the most of its opportunities, or it can be consumed by its problems. The country faces two extreme potential futures: it could evolve into a highly developed democracy such as Spain, or it could deteriorate into a weak and unreliable state, dependent on and hostage to a drug economy, an Afghanistan.

It is not fantasy to suggest that Mexico has the opportunity to become the Spain of the western hemisphere. Under the tight political reins of General Francisco Franco, Spain began its transformation in the late 1950s. Long the poor cousin to its northern European neighbors—with per capita income at the time on a par with Mexico, not France—Spain slowly emerged from its post–World War II shell. From a base in a new economic planning office, savvy technocrats wrestled back policy control from the Falangist old guard, laboring to reverse years of self-enforced economic isolation and lingering suspicions of its pro-Axis past.

Initially bypassed by the Marshall Plan, the country received substantial foreign aid and investment in the 1960s. Tourists returned to Mallorca's beaches, Granada's Moorish palaces, and Madrid's cafés. Combined with the remittances of the million Spaniards abroad, the influx spurred a decade of unprecedented industrialization and economic growth, dubbed the "Spanish miracle." It drove internal migration from the countryside to the cities and created a large new middle class. Just as these changes threatened Franco's conservative reign, the Generalissimo died. A peaceful transition to democracy and Spain's accession to the European Common Market followed. Flash forward three decades, and Spain—even with its current problems—is now an advanced economy, a middle class society (with per capita incomes averaging US$30,000 a year), a strong democracy, and a respected nation on the world stage.

Mexico could follow a similar path. It is already situated firmly in the top tiers of nearly every comparative international democracy index.[3] Since NAFTA, Mexico has been a darling of the foreign direct investment crowd—receiving a quarter of all investment bound for Latin America—equal to and often surpassing Brazil's share. Add in the billions in remittances from its migrants, and the test becomes turning Mexico's resource base and its links to the world's largest economy to true advantage. Sharing much more than a common language, Mexico today holds many of the same opportunities—and faces many of the same challenges—that its colonial forbearer confronted with such aplomb.

Leveraging these benefits and broader U.S. ties, per capita income could increase and Mexico could become a top-ten world economy. Supported by migrants residing in the United States and a growing middle class at home, Mexico's democracy could thrive. Already afforded a prominent platform as a G-20 country, Mexico could emerge as an important diplomatic voice around the world.

A Spain next door would bring astonishing benefits for the United States. An established democratic rule of law would dispel many of today's security worries. A strong Mexican economy would boost our own far into the future—as the flow of goods and people south could easily rival those headed north. Given our already close family, community, economic, and political ties, a thriving Mexico could be a much-needed ally at a time when the United States is in need of multilateral support. A Spanish-style transformation would finally fulfill a decades-long U.S. foreign policy goal of surrounding our nation with strong, stable, and prosperous democracies.

That scenario isn't guaranteed, however. Mexico could also fall into a drug-driven downward spiral of violence and instability; there is a chance it could descend into a narco-state, where basic security and any semblance of the rule of law remain elusive outside the few larger cities. Drug cartels could overwhelm Mexico's emerging democratic government, thoroughly corrupting state institutions at every level. The lack of basic public safety would send the legal economy into a tailspin, destroying the foundations of the country's growing middle class. Mexico would become the subject of, rather than participant in, multilateral meetings, as other nations tried to limit the international fallout.

Mexico today is nowhere near this worst-case scenario, but traces of growing disorder are there. Criminal gangs cull the poorer neighborhoods for recruits, pulling in youth devoid of other opportunities or of hope. Drug lords leverage familial ties to build multinational illegal enterprises, supplying the vices of the West. These criminals are already testing the vulnerabilities of Mexico's democratic politics—bribing some officials, threatening others, and weakening local political and social structures.

A descent into anarchy next door would come at a steep cost to the United States. A devastated Mexican economy and society would push waves of citizens north, searching for work and basic safety. The troops and resources required to secure the U.S.-Mexico border from drug traffickers, migrants, and terrorists would far outstrip those sent to Afghanistan or Iraq. More damaging, shutting the border would change our way of life. A sustained threat so close to home would militarize U.S. society, economy, and politics in ways unseen before. The costs in terms of treasure, manpower, and the U.S. national ethos would be enormous.

Yet as much as we fear this outcome, it isn't inevitable. It is not even the most likely. Mexico has changed in recent years, largely for the better. For all the worry, the United States is lucky to have Mexico next door. There is likely no border between such economically asymmetrical nations that is as cooperative and peaceful.

What Mexico will never be is far away. And the ties today between the United States and Mexico go far beyond sheer geography. While the moniker "distant" may once have been apt, it is no longer the case.[4] Bound by economic, environmental, cultural, familial, security, and diplomatic bonds, perhaps no other country is as intertwined with the United States as Mexico.

Building an impenetrable wall—if that were even possible—won't solve the problems, as U.S. ties to Mexico will not stop with a line on the map. Mexico's future is permanently linked to our own. The deepening of business, personal, and community relations has drawn the United States and Mexico much closer than ever.

Mexican migration, always part of the bilateral relationship, skyrocketed over the last three decades as, each year, hundreds of thousands of Mexican citizens headed north. Some twelve million Mexicans and over thirty million Mexican Americans now call the United States home and are a permanent part of America's social fabric. Less visible is the fact that a million Americans have moved south, creating the largest U.S. community abroad in the world.[5] Mexico's workers fueled the U.S. economy during years of record low unemployment rates. And they hold the promise of mitigating the next economic challenge on the horizon: the retirement of the oversized baby-boomer generation.

NAFTA-led economic integration has been a success not just for Mexico, but for the United States. Trade between the nations has tripled, as Mexico rose from middling partner to the second-largest export market after Canada for U.S. goods. Each month, Texas exports over US$7 billion and California over US$2 billion in products to their neighbor. But this bonanza isn't limited just to border states. The economies of states such as South Dakota, Nebraska, and New Hampshire now send roughly a quarter of their total exports to Mexico as well.[6] Products range from electronic equipment, motor vehicle parts, chemicals, and household appliances to paper products, red meat, pears, and grapes. Many of the United States' flagship industries depend on Mexico for their survival and success. Integration with Mexico has allowed giants such as General Motors, Johnson & Johnson, General Electric, and Hewlett Packard to lower costs and compete in global markets where they would otherwise be excluded—creating more exports and jobs for both the United States and Mexico in the process.

All of these links mean that the impact of Mexico's collapse would reach far into the heartland. Decimated trading ties would threaten millions of U.S. (not to mention Mexican) jobs. And it would tear apart U.S. families and communities.

The exchange isn't always positive. It is the U.S. demand for drugs that has funded and U.S. guns that have armed Mexico's drug cartels. These increasingly sophisticated criminal organizations now operate in over one thousand U.S. cities.[7] Closing the border will not end their dominance in Phoenix, Atlanta, or Stark County, Ohio. Instead, it would limit the intelligence gathering and international law enforcement cooperation necessary to take the cartels down and to protect America's streets in the process.

U.S. and Mexican diplomacy and policies lag far behind these deepened ties, based as they are on an understanding of our southern neighbor that is increasingly disconnected from reality. This gap has become not just unfortunate, but downright dangerous. Our misperceptions and misguided policies have and will have real consequences as Mexico faces its future.

Creating a New Partnership

Working with Mexico—for the good of both countries—will require not just a new set of policies (though these too are needed), but a larger conceptual shift toward forging a true partnership. We can work with

Mexico to form this connection only if we know the forces that shape it. It is vital that the United States understands the post-PRI, post-NAFTA, post-9/11 global Mexico to strengthen the good and limit the bad in such a close, but still unequal relationship. By continuing to misunderstand or ignore the goings-on south of our border, we are leaving America's fate in part in Mexican hands. I argue that we should determine it ourselves, but that we can do so only through active efforts based not on conflict but on cooperation.

A new partnership should start by creating an environment that understands how highly interconnected the two nations are and supports rather than shuns the binational people, families, and communities already existing in and between us. This means rethinking immigration and border policies to encourage, not hinder, the legal movement of Mexican workers and their families.

Upending the current thinking, Americans may soon come to see immigration as the answer to—not the cause of—many of the United States' woes. Under the current radar are ineluctable demographic shifts happening on both sides of the border. Changed family patterns mean that fewer Mexicans will be coming of age and needing jobs. In the United States, the eighty-million-strong baby-boomer generation is beginning to retire, leaving more openings than the smaller "Generation X" could hope to fill. This combination may lead to a rapid turnaround on this hot-button issue: desperate to close the gaps in America's workforce, in the next decade we may be urging Mexicans to come to the United States.

Diplomatically, we also need to rethink the United States' approach in light of Mexico's ongoing political transformation. A stronger partnership provides the best platform for a prominent U.S. twenty-first century foreign policy priority: democracy promotion. Despite frequent misunderstandings our long shared history, intertwined economies, and strong personal and community links provide the constant multilayered interaction necessary to work together toward the complex goal of strengthening democracy. Joint economic development initiatives, support for local citizen organizations, and efforts to increase transparency and strengthen courts and police forces will all benefit from the strong links that already exist between our two nations.

Mexico, not the Middle East, should be the test case for solidifying market-based democracy. It is not only much more likely to succeed, but also arguably much more likely to hurt the United States if it fails. Mexico's success is more probable because it has already taken many tough steps, all on its own. After seventy years of one-party rule, Mexicans used their votes to usher in an opposition party president. Abandoning a long history of ballot-box stuffing, Mexico's parties now compete in quite clean and transparent elections. The country's over 100 million citizens dream of—and are already working hard to create—a vibrant and prosperous political system where their voices can be heard and their hard work rewarded. If successful, Mexico would provide a positive example of a newly consolidated democracy, offering lessons for others worldwide.

Nevertheless, it still faces considerable challenges. Many in fact worry that Mexico's democratic gains may be lost, overcome by political bosses, special interests, and drug-related violence. And Mexico's failure would lead to disastrous consequences for U.S. foreign policy, not to mention America's economic, political, and social well-being at home. The United States' focus elsewhere—particularly in Asia and the Middle East—has distracted us from the game-changing importance of political choices being made just next door.

A better partnership also requires rethinking U.S.-Mexico economic relations—in particular moving beyond the prejudices and misinformation that have grown up around NAFTA. In the United States, the great sucking sound of American jobs going south didn't happen. Instead, with nearly half a trillion dollars' worth of goods flowing back and forth each year, Mexican consumers and companies support over two million U.S. workers directly and four million more indirectly—as the earnings from exports cascade down into local economies.[8] Though the benefits spread unevenly, by spurring and reinforcing economic opening NAFTA transformed Mexico and helped secure the economic underpinnings of today's broadening middle class. It also encouraged (albeit unintentionally) Mexico's democratization.

But for all this, the agreement itself and more importantly the concept of a North American economic platform has fallen into disfavor. Few in Des Moines, St. Louis, or Atlanta, much less in Washington, see Mexico as part of the solution to the United States' current struggle to become more economically competitive. Recognizing the benefits of cross-border production is an uphill but necessary battle if the United States wants to boost exports, jobs, and overall economic growth.

Partnership, too, is the only way to stop the current bloodshed since the cause—drug-fed organized crime—thrives on both sides of the border. Given increasingly sophisticated criminal networks spanning the globe, intelligence gathering, analysis, and operations cannot stop with a line (or wall) in the sand. What Mexico needs is to firmly establish a democratic rule of law. Without clean cops and clean courts, the insecurity will never end. And the United States needs to grapple with its own role in supplying the money and the guns that fuel the violence. Together, the two nations can be more successful taking on the corruption and impunity that permit and perpetuate violence.

Increased cooperation means leaving behind the isolationist tendencies of both nations. But this more ambitious framework will be the best (and perhaps only) way to ensure a safe, stable, and prosperous future on both sides of the border.

Despite today's resounding negativity, transforming U.S.-Mexico relations is not only important but also possible. Economic, demographic, and security developments in both countries are providing and will provide opportunities to push for new and better approaches. Those most closely tied to Mexico—U.S. companies and their workers, border communities, Mexican American voters—have yet to make their quite powerful voices heard. An opening for debate and the opportunity to change the United States' approach is coming. For our own sake the shift needs to be for the better.

This book provides a roadmap for understanding and addressing the biggest overlooked foreign policy challenge of our time—U.S. relations with its southern neighbor. Overturning the conventional wisdom and condemning the efforts to try and wall ourselves off (literally and figuratively) from our neighbor, it argues for prioritizing and expanding bilateral ties.

Presenting a picture of a very different Mexico than most Americans see and read about, the following chapters trace the complex and intertwined issues of immigration, political change, economic opening, and rising violence, illuminating how much Mexico has changed over the last thirty years, and how these transformations influence how Mexico—and the United States—will navigate the current crossroads.

Mexico today boasts a vibrant (if imperfect) democracy and a growing middle class, and it is on the verge of becoming an important international player and an easy ally for the United States. Mexico can be a solution, rather than a problem, for its northern neighbor. But this positive outcome cannot be taken for granted. Mexico still faces stark challenges on the road to democratic stability and prosperity.

In the end, Mexico's path, of course, depends on Mexicans. No other nation can decide its future. But, through our actions or inactions, the United States can either support Mexico or throw further obstacles in its way. And whichever path Mexico takes will have far-reaching repercussions for the United States.

REENVISIONING U.S.-MEXICO DIPLOMATIC RELATIONS

With a heavy heart U.S. ambassador Carlos Pascual handed his resignation letter to Secretary Hillary Clinton in March 2011. Though she had urged him to stay and ride out the diplomatic storm, in the end the pressure became too great. He worried that President Calderón would never get beyond his now open animosity, and that it would spread and threaten the larger U.S.-Mexico relationship.

Things had started out quite well. On a hot August day less than two years before, Pascual had descended the stairs of Air Force One with President Obama in Guadalajara. With Mexico playing host, the newly confirmed ambassador sat in on meetings among the U.S., Mexican, and Canadian presidents at the annual trilateral summit.

A few weeks later he headed to Mexico's capital, receiving warm welcomes as he began the rounds of meeting government ministers, opposition leaders, academics, business owners, civil society activists, and journalists. Energized by the ambitions on both sides of the border to deepen cooperation, he spent long days working with his Mexican counterparts to expand and reenvision bilateral security ties. He also labored in Washington, visiting, discussing, at times cajoling dozens of officials in nearly as many agencies and departments, working to weave together the broad-based support necessary for this more complex vision of bilateral collaboration.

As he neared his first anniversary, optimism prevailed. The revamped Merida Initiative (a U.S.-Mexico joint security plan) would move beyond taking down drug kingpins to strengthening Mexico's law enforcement and justice institutions, and even to addressing deep social challenges in places such as Juárez. The bilateral vision was so broad that the two governments set about building a new office to house members from U.S. and Mexican security forces alike, working side by side. All the while Ambassador Pascual kept crisscrossing the country, shaking hands, cutting ribbons, and working with his Mexican counterparts to advance the shared agenda.

The first cracks in this new bilateral edifice began to show during the fall of 2010. Though the new security vision had always been jointly trumpeted, on-the-ground efforts were coming up short. However hard Pascual and his team pushed for change, Mexico's federal government and bureaucracy dragged their feet, seemingly unwilling or unable to move beyond military and federal police raids. Reports back suggested that not only were government ministers not putting their full force behind the efforts, but that the ambassador's consistent pressure irked the president.

Pascual's personal life too was creating problems. His deepening relationship with the ex-wife of the president's former chief of staff, the daughter of a prominent PRI leader, was said to also bother the president, who saw the political in the personal.

These tensions overflowed with the release of several confidential cables by WikiLeaks that winter. Signed by the ambassador and his deputy chief of mission, John Feeley, they presented unfiltered assessments of the strengths and weaknesses of the Mexican government's security efforts, pointing to a hidebound Mexican army, infighting between Mexico's various security institutions, and worries about corruption and human rights abuses. While in line with the views of numerous independent analysts—as well as many security officials in their more candid moments—the leaks embarrassed the Calderón government, and provided fodder for rival politicians as the Mexican electoral arena heated up for 2011 gubernatorial races and the 2012 presidential contest.

In response, Calderón turned to the press. In a wide-ranging and sensational interview in *El Universal*, one of Mexico's leading newspapers, he vented his anger. He accused the U.S. diplomats of "laying it on thick," distorting and exaggerating their analyses for ulterior motives. He went further, saying the lack of coordination and rivalry was not on the Mexican but on the U.S. side, among the Immigration and Customs Enforcement, the Drug Enforcement Agency, and the Central Intelligence Agency. The vitriol was so strong that U.S. Homeland Security head Janet Napolitano formally responded the next day, asserting that not only did U.S. agencies work well together, they also worked closely with their Mexican counterparts.

In March 2011, just a few weeks later, Calderón headed to Washington to meet with Barack Obama, and address a joint session in Congress. Though the private discussions between the two leaders ranged widely, it was Calderón's public comments to the *Washington Post* that defined the visit, and in these he again skewered the U.S. ambassador. Two weeks later, Mexico lost an important interlocutor and champion for the U.S.-Mexico relationship and the ear of many in Washington.

For decades, the bilateral relationship has had fits and starts—beginning with expansive promises from new presidents and ending with bitter divisions. Domestic politics were often behind the fracture, as Mexico's ruling PRI painted the United States as the great imperialist to rationalize its own heavy political hand and U.S. administrations often changed course at the first hint of domestic opposition to more expansive and cooperative approaches. Personal differences and real or perceived affronts also at times played a role in sinking once-promising bilateral ties.

This latest episode highlighted that though both countries stress their interdependence and the need to transform the way the bilateral relationship figures in the public debate in the United States and in Mexico, they are still quite distant from achieving this goal.

America's Strong Arm

During the nineteenth and early twentieth centuries, conflicts between the United States and Mexico often were resolved with guns, nearly always to Mexico's detriment. When Mexico finally gained its independence in 1821, its dominion over New Spain brought vast territories but very little control. The patchwork of understandings and treaties relinquished by retreating Spanish, French, and British colonialists left the actual borders unclear and insecure and North America up for grabs.

Though the United States was of a similar size and population, and had less than a half-century head start on Mexico, it gelled as a nation much more swiftly. Having asserted authority over its own territory, it quickly began to covet more. Packaging its voraciousness as "manifest destiny," the budding republic pledged to answer the call to spread progress and democracy to new lands, from sea to shining sea. Its gaze turned quickly south and west—to what today are Texas, Arizona, New Mexico, and California. While technically Mexican lands, all parties knew that possession (through settlement) was at least nine-tenths of frontier law. In the 1820s only a couple of northern Mexican outposts existed in what would become Texas—today's San Antonio and Goliad. The few thousand Mexican natives lived in a state of virtual siege, threatened by rumors of Spanish and British expeditions and preyed upon by marauding bands of Comanche Indians.[1]

The Mexican government—suffering from a perennial shortage of cash, battles between political factions (leading to thirty-six governments in twenty-two years), and no national spirit—struggled to develop a coherent policy for its borderlands and even to protect its few pioneers. Desperate, the government turned to colonization, granting large tracts of land to those willing to swear fealty to the Mexican flag. For Mexico and its territorial integrity, this turned out to be a grave mistake.

That call was answered mainly by settlers from U.S. territories. In the first ten years the invitation brought in some twenty-five thousand newcomers—overwhelming the few thousand original Mexicans. Some of them, such as Stephen Austin, went by the book. Austin worked his way through the internecine factions and bureaucracies to obtain legal rights to the lands he and his brethren inhabited. But many more flooded in without the legal niceties and then bristled at Mexico's tepid attempts to assert its authority. The volatile combination of U.S. expansionism and Mexico's chronic instability came to a head in 1836. The imposition of a new constitution (that moderately raised taxes and tariffs and enforced basic citizenship rules) pushed the settlers over the edge.[2]

With the Texans in full revolt, General Antonio López de Santa Anna (serving the fourth of his eleven turns as president) set off eagerly from Mexico City with a few thousand troops to teach them a lesson and to burnish his name, bolstering his political support through military victory. In late February the force arrived in San Antonio—home to a small fortress, the Alamo.

When Americans "remember the Alamo" today, it conjures up images of James Bowie, Davy Crockett, William B. Travis, and two hundred other Texans fighting bravely against impossible odds. For Mexico, the story is of radical American immigrants threatening national sovereignty. Though the Texans lost the battle—and nearly all of them their lives—Santa Anna's brutality galvanized their resolve. A month later Texan forces caught the Mexicans by surprise and captured Santa Anna, effectively ending the war. While the Americans celebrate the surrender as a victory against tyranny, Mexicans view the seccession of Texas as a case of might triumphing over right.

Just ten years later, the border again erupted in battle. After the Mexican government rejected a U.S. offer for what is today Arizona, New Mexico, California, and parts of Colorado, Utah, and Kansas, President James Polk decided to take the land by force. Provoking a skirmish along the disputed Texas-Mexico border, the United States quickly declared war on May 13, 1846. Some seventeen months later, General Winfield Scott raised the American flag over Mexico City's Chapultepec Castle to the refrains of "The Star-Spangled Banner." Santa Anna—again president—had fled, leaving the chief justice to negotiate yet another humiliating surrender.[3] The 1853 Gadsden Purchase added insult to injury, as the United States used coercive diplomacy—through a thinly veiled threat of military intervention—to force the Mexicans into parting with yet another chunk of territory, this time to satisfy U.S. transcontinental railroad ambitions.

During the nearly decade-long conflict starting in 1910 that became known as the Mexican Revolution, U.S. troops and cavalry crossed into Mexican territory repeatedly, often pushed by U.S. business and other interests and at times pulled by various Mexican political and military factions hoping to gain an advantage over their rivals. In 1913 the U.S. ambassador became complicit in the plot that killed democratically elected President Francisco Madero. Yet in the political and military chaos that followed his death, the United States soured on his successor, General Victoriano Huerta.[4] President Woodrow Wilson, with the pretense of teaching Mexicans to "elect good men," sent some eight hundred marines and sailors into Veracruz to seize a shipment of guns and then the port itself from Huerta loyalists.[5] Many believe the United States was decisive in turning the tide first against Madero, then against Huerta, and finally in grudging support of Venustiano Carranza. In fact, some see the Mexican Revolution as an "intervened civil war," pointing to the meddlesome role of the United States throughout.[6]

U.S. military interference didn't stop there. In 1916, U.S. troops crossed the border again, this time to chase—though never quite to catch—Pancho Villa through the Sierra Madre Mountains. Infuriated that the United States had sided with his once friend and now archenemy President Carranza, the Durango-born cowboy goaded the U.S. government into battle. He killed sixteen Texan mining engineers—pulling them off a North western Railway Company train—and then raided Columbus, New Mexico, killing seventeen before the local cavalry drove him and his *pistoleros* back across the border.[7] The United States responded with the so-called Punitive Expedition, sending a force of nearly five thousand troops in retaliation. Though a ruthless killer and notorious bandit, Villa also was a hero to Mexico's poor, an avenger for the downtrodden. With few locals willing to guide U.S. troops through the labyrinthine hills and canyons against a favorite son, Villa and his army deftly avoided General John Pershing's advances. After several months the two governments negotiated a peaceful resolution, and the United States left empty handed.

The bilateral sparring didn't end with the physical fighting. U.S. economic interests in Mexico only deepened during the years of turmoil. In fact, many U.S. businesses flourished with the upheavals, emerging from the revolutionary period more powerful and wealthy, holding the lion's share of Mexico's natural resources. The U.S. government was not shy about defending its citizens and companies, threatening to withhold diplomatic recognition or to suspend U.S. treasury purchases of Mexican silver at the first hint that their freewheeling rights might be threatened.[8] These tensions continued throughout the 1920s and 1930s.

The most inflammatory fight occurred over oil. The revolutionary years were very good to Mexican oil—and the American companies that dominated the sector.[9] Investment poured in and output boomed, increasing from fewer than 4 million barrels a year on the eve of the revolution in 1910 to over 150 million in 1920.[10] Mexican oil production grew to fill over a quarter of the world's oil needs.[11] Companies such as the Mexican Petroleum Company of Delaware and Standard Oil of New Jersey ruled as virtual states within a state, arrogantly flouting the fledgling postrevolutionary government's new laws, regulations, and taxes.

The fiercest dispute was over subsoil rights—who actually owned the oil below. In the colonial times the monarch retained full control of the oil reserves, but in 1887 the Porfirio Díaz regime handed the rights to private—and mostly foreign-owned—companies. The 1917 revolutionary constitution took back ownership of Mexico's natural resources, limiting foreign companies to concessions.[12] But U.S. companies—backed by the State Department—demanded the Mexican government respect their previous deals.

In 1938, these simmering disputes reached a final dramatic showdown between the oil magnates and the Mexican government.[13] Standoffs between workers and owners escalated, leading to massive strikes. Rejecting government arbitration, the disputes finally ended up in front of Mexico's Supreme Court. When the oil companies refused to comply with the verdict against them, President Lázaro Cardenas nationalized the sector, to recover not just oil, but "the dignity of Mexico." Unable to convince President Roosevelt to intervene, the slighted companies engineered a widespread boycott, leading to shortages throughout the Mexican economy.[14] These tensions ended only with Pearl Harbor and the U.S. entrance into World War II.

AMERICA'S HELPING HAND

This narrative of threats, intimidation, and intervention dominates standard historical recaps of U.S.-Mexico relations.[15] Yet not all bilateral interactions were violent, abusive, or even strained. Often forgotten is the substantial cooperation and even camaraderie between both peoples and countries since their foundings. The first flickers of cross-border friendship emerged in the 1820s. Mexican federalists warmly welcomed the first U.S. ambassador (then called minister), Joel Roberts Poinsett, and even modeled their 1824 constitution after ours.[16] In the decade after the Gadsden Purchase, the United States kept alive Mexico's dream of becoming a republic by sheltering the exiled Benito Juárez, among the most beloved of Mexico's presidents, in New Orleans. During the 1860s the United States went further, providing Juárez with arms and even troops in his successful overthrow of the French-backed would-be emperor, Ferdinand Maximilian Joseph. Later, the United States would protect Francisco Madero, the Coahuilan whose reformist movement ended Porfirio Díaz's reign.

Cordial, even close, economic relations developed in the latter half of the nineteenth century. Once back in office, President Benito Juárez continued to look north, creating the first official free trade zones along the border. General Porfirio Díaz expanded and deepened these ties during his twenty-seven-year reign (1884–1911), which became known as the Porfiriato.[17] Guided by his motto, "Order and Progress," Díaz focused his considerable energies and power on modernizing Mexico. Through concessions, preferential tariffs, subsidies, and even outright grants, he courted foreign individuals, money, and know-how. U.S. entrepreneurs, corporations, and speculators responded enthusiastically.

The influx of foreign capital—combined with political stability—led to rapid economic growth. The external funds helped build hundreds of factories, lay thousands of miles of railway, construct countless docks, expand telegraph lines, set up electricity grids, and pave streets. Mexico became a top world producer of gold, copper, zinc, iron, and lead, as well as an exporter of coffee, livestock, and beans.[18] Internally, Mexico began producing its own steel, cement, and dynamite, and expanding production of basics such as tobacco, beer, and textiles.[19] The speed and breadth of Mexico's modernization would have been impossible without its northern neighbor's support.

These bonds reshaped bilateral relations. Mexico became the first foray abroad for U.S. businesses, a testing ground for domestic companies with dreams of becoming multinationals. Even as the more developed countries of the day—Britain, France, and Germany—invested in the United States, American investors flocked south, sending over $1 billion (some US$25 billion in today's terms) to Mexico around the turn of the twentieth century.[20]

Joining hundreds of lesser-known investors were some of America's best-known titans. William Randolph Hearst amassed nearly seven million acres of land. The American Smelting and Refining Company (ASARCO)—owned by the Guggenheims—quickly became the largest privately owned company in Mexico, dominating silver, lead, and copper production through its mines, smelters, and refineries.[21] Companies such as Phelps-Dodge and Standard Oil also invested heavily and profited handsomely.[22]

These investors became integral to—and at times leaders of—U.S. foreign policy. William Randolph Hearst probably saw the Mexican president more often than the U.S. ambassador did, as he routinely lunched with Díaz, who affectionately referred to him as a son.[23] The Guggenheims and Rockefellers, among others, directly pressed their cases and concerns with Mexican secretaries, ministers, and the president himself—with the implicit and often explicit power of the U.S. government behind them. The inverse was also true—the Mexican government leaned on these moguls for targeted investment and even advanced tax payments when government coffers were empty.

Yankee money was not necessarily benign. American investors were by no means socially responsible (to use today's jargon). In an age of robber barons and bare-knuckled capitalism, child labor, health, and safety regulations were few and discrimination between U.S. and Mexican workers stark. The economic benefits didn't trickle down beyond a small elite. Rather than diminishing, poverty worsened in the years leading up to the Mexican Revolution. The poor had so little that a 1904 uptick of corn prices—the staple of a working-class diet—wiped out the domestic textile industry, as the average Mexican could no longer afford cotton cloth.[24]

In their role as pseudo-emissaries, U.S. businessmen often pressured the Mexican government for their own narrow interests, threatening Mexico with U.S. tariff hikes if the government raised taxes or tried to enforce less than industry friendly rules.[25] The rapaciousness of some, and their dominance of Mexico's vital infrastructure and extractive industries, made even Porfirio Díaz begin to worry about the concentration of power and the asymmetric nature of the U.S.-Mexico relationship and to seek out European investors and allies. For good and bad, this de facto diplomacy continued through and after the revolution, with American companies and magnates often defining U.S. interests and actions.

THE BORDER

The push and pull of early U.S.-Mexico relations were no more emblematic than at the border. For decades neither central government knew much about, much less controlled, its frontiers. The travails of successive surveyors show the immensity of the task of just defining the line, something that wasn't fully resolved until the 1960s.[26]

In the beginning people, cattle, communities, and commerce routinely crossed the border, hardly recognizing their daily patterns as "international relations." Ranches, farms, and towns regularly spanned the international line. The distinctions between American and Mexican blurred. Mexicans became Americans when the border moved, and American settlers, including former president Vicente Fox's grandfather, rode down to make a new life for themselves in the south. It was also open enough that

Mexican political leaders of all stripes jumped back and forth as they went in and out of exile, the United States becoming an equal opportunity safe haven.

With the central governments far removed, it was left to locals to define and develop these vast lands. With few highways or even adequate roads, the frontier remained open, arid, sporadically inhabited, and poorly policed. In this truly wild west, Mexicans and Americans as often worked together as apart to face mutual challenges: threats from raiding Apache or Comanche Indians or the more mundane needs for supplies, news, and community.[27] Border settlements shared fire departments, police, trading posts, churches, and often social clubs, all integrated across international lines.

This autonomy began to wane by the turn of the twentieth century. The arrival of the railroad transformed the hinterlands. In October 1882, crowds amassed along the border to cheer the inauguration of the first major cross-border rail line, connecting the Sonoran port of Guaymas to Arizona through the border at Nogales.[28] Thousands more miles were soon added, connecting nearly all of Mexico's major cities and mining centers to each other and up to the main U.S. east-west rail arteries. Linked for the first time to far-off populations and ports, the north's empty prairies and isolated foothills became active ranches and mines, and small settlements blossomed into full-fledged cities.

As tens of thousands flocked to this land in between, the frontier slowly hardened into a border. The frenzy of activity drew the attention of national governments interested in taxing expanding trade and commerce. The first fence was built in 1909 between California and Baja California to stop tick-infested cattle, but during the 1910s the idea of fences to control human crossings quickly spread.[29] The Mexican Revolution and World War I deepened worries on both sides of the border, and during the Great Depression the United States added Mexican immigration to its concerns and tasked the newly formed Border Patrol with stanching the flow. By the eve of World War II, the federal governments had reined in the border's freewheeling autonomy, asserting the primacy of national agreements and agendas.

During their first century, bilateral relations veered from monumental highs to incredible lows. When working together, U.S. and Mexican governments and investors helped transform and modernize Mexico for the better. But when at odds, the United States managed to appropriate half of Mexico's physical territory, and at times manipulate the politics and economics in what remained. But through all the ups and downs, the flow of people, money, and goods never stopped.

Diplomatic Distance

By the mid-twentieth century, the tension between deep embraces and abrupt separations gave way to a Prozac-induced foreign policy—that for nearly forty years studiously avoided the previous highs and lows. In part, the lack of interest and intensity reflected the fundamental asymmetry in the relationship. After World War II, Mexico's importance diminished, as the country became a sideshow in the Cold War showdown. But the detachment also reflected Mexico's wariness and its active efforts to keep the United States at arm's length.

Mexican leaders had always been cautious of a U.S. embrace. But these sensitivities were cultivated and amplified by the long-ruling political party, the PRI. The PRI mythologized Mexico's past and its relationship with its larger neighbor. Wrapping itself in the Mexican flag by adopting the colors and symbols of Mexico as its own, the party cloaked its every move in heightened patriotism. This is not to say the United States hadn't frequently overstepped its bounds and meddled in Mexico's political and economic life. But the PRI also justified its own excesses as necessary for defending the nation against the "Yanquis" next door. This "looming threat" narrative— endlessly repeated in political speeches, news editorials, and grade-school textbooks—guided Mexico's foreign policy in the postwar period.[30]

Mexico steered clear of U.S.-led regional economic projects, pointedly rejecting aid through the Alliance for Progress (though it received billions in funding from the World Bank, IMF, and less high-profile U.S. agencies such as the Export-Import Bank). Diplomatically, Mexico hid behind a veil of sovereignty and nonintervention. While asserting autonomy on issues near home—Cuba, Central America, or voting within the Organization of American States (OAS)—Mexico steered clear of getting involved in broader U.S. foreign policy issues. It steadfastly avoided membership in multilateral organizations, declining to join the General Agreement on Tariffs and Trade (GATT), staying away from Organization of the Petroleum Exporting Countries (OPEC), and rarely taking a seat on the United Nations Security Council. In the early 1950s, it was one of the only Latin American countries that didn't negotiate a bilateral defense treaty with the United States.

In general, Mexico and the United States avoided creating new institutions that would tie the countries together. There were few new bilateral trade agreements, defense pacts, or border commissions. The only significant policy for nearly a half-century was the Bracero program, begun at the height of World War II to address U.S. labor shortages (and at the behest of large farmers and ranchers who worried about organized labor making inroads with U.S. agricultural workers).[31] It ended in the 1960s, leaving yet another void in formal ongoing relations. Overall, the PRI cultivated cordial but distant ties, encouraging investment while pushing back against any real or imagined "Yankee imperialism."

Accepting the reign of the PRI, the United States appreciated Mexico's newfound order while it privately disapproved of the antidemocratic and often corrupt means to this end. Overall, Mexico's political stability—and its firm anticommunism at home—gave U.S. cold warriors the luxury of focusing on farther away locations: Korea, Vietnam, China, and Afghanistan. Instead of interfering in Mexico, the United States chose largely to ignore it.

Brief episodes would catapult Mexico to the top of the U.S. agenda, but without the urgency—or combativeness—of the past. In 1968, months of student-led street demonstrations—demanding greater autonomy, openness, and transparency—seemed to threaten the PRI's firm grip. With several tanks, thousands of troops, and even some equipment provided by the CIA, the Mexican government responded with brutal force during a rally in Mexico City's historic Tlatelolco area. Though officially there were just thirty deaths, most historians count the number of protesters who died in the hundreds. As Mexican authorities cleaned up the day's blood, the United States remained noncommittal and turned back to other foreign policy concerns.

A decade later, oil finds would again attract U.S. attention, coming when the United States was searching for relief from the worldwide oil shock. As Americans waited for hours at the gas pump and President Jimmy Carter—donning a tan cardigan—implored his fellow citizens to turn down the thermostat to save energy, Mexico's massive Cantarell oil field was just coming on line. By the late 1970s millions of barrels of oil flowed north and billions of dollars south, rebalancing, if only briefly, the bilateral relationship. But when oil prices declined and an economic recession in the United States lessened demand, U.S. interest in Mexico again waned.

Despite the shared border, Mexico through much of the twentieth century remained a middling trading partner, just one of many sources of migrants, a modest energy source, a peripheral world power, and a Cold War backwater. Mexico held little interest in a tighter embrace, pushing back whenever the United States stepped closer or offered any opinion (much less a criticism) on matters to its south. Bilateral rhetoric often talked about a "special relationship," but actual policy initiatives were scarce. This detachment, while decidedly second best to actual engagement, allowed the two nations to muddle through many years without real trauma.

Ever-Deepening Ties

The on-the-ground reality was different, one of intensifying integration. U.S. companies never left Mexico, and any lingering hard feelings over oil were forgotten when Mexico became a World War II ally and a vital economic link in the war supply chain. After the war, as Mexico's PRI worked to build a modern industrial state, it embraced U.S. businesses, and they responded in kind, investing roughly $1 billion a year for decades.[32] Whether with local partners or alone, the U.S. corporations that entered the Mexican market benefited from high tariff walls and generous government subsidies, reaping huge profits selling cars, tractors, tires, sodas, soaps, and cigarettes. Without blinking, Mexican customers drank Coca-Cola, brushed their teeth with Colgate toothpaste, washed their dishes with Palmolive, and, if well-to-do, bought their clothes at Sears Roebuck.[33] U.S. manufacturers such as Westinghouse, Dow Chemical, Ford, and General Motors set up shop, supplying Mexico's growing needs and linking industry back north.

What did change was corporate America's diplomatic role. U.S. businesses, no longer on the frontlines, accepted Mexico's rules of the game. Instead of pressuring the Mexican government, they often supported it. For instance, during the 1980s debt crisis, U.S. banks leaned on the International Monetary Fund to help bail out the nation (and themselves). In fact, U.S. and Mexican businesses were so enthusiastic about their shared prospects that they tried to lead Washington and Mexico City into a NAFTA-style agreement a decade earlier.[34]

The back and forth of people also intensified in the postwar period. While migration was a centuries-old reality, the Word War II Bracero program quickened the pace. Over its twenty-plus years, some five million Mexicans came to the United States legally, and perhaps another two million or so followed more surreptitiously in their footsteps.[35] These active networks of workers and employers continued long after the government pulled the policy plug. Reagan's 1986 immigration reform inadvertently reinforced these bonds, cementing cross-border families as some two million Mexicans became permanent residents or citizens.

DIPLOMACY CATCHING UP

In the 1980s and 1990s, the diplomatic modus operandi began to change. The end of the Cold War refocused U.S. foreign policy interests, no longer dividing the world (at least for a decade or so) into those with and against us. Yet even as the threat of communism faded, that of global economic competition rose. Fears of Japanese, European Union, and later Chinese economic ascendency led the United States to search for economic allies to counter the rise of regional trading blocs, opening the doors to its neighbors. Domestic concerns—in particular migration and the war on drugs—also raised Mexico's profile.

Mexico too was changing. The 1982 debt crisis left the country's inward-looking and state-heavy economy in shambles. As Mexico began a wrenching reorganization, it worked to prove its free trade bona fides by opening up its markets and finally joining GATT. An influx of Harvard-, Yale-, and Chicago-trained Mexican technocrats into high-level government positions reduced the anti-U.S. rhetoric within the PRI. As Mexico visibly democratized, U.S. congressional resistance to closer relations also diminished.

The final years of the twentieth century would again be a time of cooperation, even camaraderie, as Mexico and the United States faced the post–Cold War world together.[36] The most concrete and ambitious project was NAFTA, a comprehensive free trade and investment treaty linking the economic fortunes of the two nations (along with Canada). In its wake, the United States and Mexico set about creating a host of bilateral commissions to address topics ranging from transportation and trade disputes to labor and the environment. For the first time in decades the two countries arranged to sit face to face and hammer out issues large and small on a regular basis.[37] Discussions and consultations spread to encompass the border, drug trafficking, and even immigration.

Working to catch up with the intensifying rhythm of relations, the United States amplified its presence in Mexico. The multifaceted and expanding ties led departments and agencies to either send or enlarge on-the-ground staff, making the Mexico City Embassy one of the largest in the world. The consulate network within Mexico grew too, canvassing the country by the late 1990s as officials struggled to keep up with the rising demands of U.S. businesses, travelers, and hundreds of thousands of citizens living in Mexico. And they were dealing with a growing number of visa applications; by the late 1990s, Mexico's consulate network was issuing a quarter of all U.S. nonimmigrant visas each year.[38]

The Mexican diplomatic and consular transformation was perhaps even more revolutionary, as the country came around to embracing its diaspora. Throughout the twentieth century, Mexico had no policy toward its millions of migrants. Even as so many at home depended on their paychecks, immigrants remained invisible to politicians. Colloquially, Mexicans dismissed migrants as *pochos*, or "rotten fruit"—insinuating that they had betrayed their homeland by searching for a better life to the north.

The diplomatic shift began in the aftermath of the controversial 1988 Mexican presidential election. As Salinas assumed the presidential mantle, Mexican migrants led passionate anti-PRI protests in front of the Los Angeles and San Diego consulates, shouting "Death to the PRI!" and "Viva Cuauhtémoc Cárdenas!"[39] Stung by the vehemence—and the widespread coverage by U.S. Spanish-language television—Salinas began studiously courting Mexico's citizens abroad.

By the 1990s, a cornerstone of Mexico's foreign policy became turning *pochos* into *paisanos*, or countrymen.[40] Through a reinvigorated and expanded consulate network and a series of high-level visits, the Mexican government showered attention on its sojourners, listening to their grievances, supporting their leaders, and working to better their lives in the United States and strengthen their ties back home. Channeling migrants' energy toward development, the Mexican government collaborated with its citizens abroad to build roads, schools, and community centers back in their hometowns. In subsequent years, President Ernesto Zedillo continued to reach out, and Vicente Fox went even further, calling migrants "ambassadors," and even "national heroes" as he campaigned around the United States.

While these efforts were initially designed to polish the PRI's tarnished image and undermine political opposition, Salinas also hoped to create an ethnic lobby in the United States along the lines of the Israelis, Greeks, and Irish—to influence U.S. policy toward Mexico. Zedillo made this goal even more explicit, telling a group of Mexican American leaders gathered in Texas in 1995 that he hoped they would pressure U.S. lawmakers on matters affecting U.S.-Mexico relations.[41] He also pushed through a dual-citizenship law, ensuring that Mexicans would not lose their ties to home, even as they gained potential weight—as citizens and voters—in the United States. This grand vision fizzled, as no ready-made lobby existed. But the outreach took on a life of its own, reengaging migrants and strengthening cross-border bonds.

THE MOMENTUM STALLS

In the twenty-first century, Mexico hasn't changed its tune about the United States. Public opinion surveys show an abundant goodwill.[42] Members of Mexico's middle class are drawn to the United States, admiring and emulating—rather than fearing—their northern neighbors. A Pew Research Center 2009 poll found that over two-thirds of Mexicans viewed the United States positively. In 2010, this warmth diminished for several reasons, most noticeably the passage of Arizona's SB 1070 law that empowers local and state police to check immigration status. Even so, a majority of Mexicans still viewed the United States favorably, believing people enjoy a better life up north.[43] Other surveys show that Mexico's northerners—those in closer proximity and with more exposure to America—are more favorably inclined than their southern compatriots.[44] Perhaps more telling than what Mexicans say to pollsters is what they choose to do at one of life's biggest moments: naming their children. There are now more Jonathans and Abigails born each year in Mexico than there are Rafaels and Gabrielas.[45]

Mexico's elites are more wary of the United States than the average citizen. But nationalistic outbursts in the political arena are far fewer than in the past. Instead, driven by the economic, political, and societal changes of the last thirty years, Mexico has come around and embraced the United States and North America as its home.

The United States, in contrast, has become less receptive. Polls throughout the 1970s, 1980s, and 1990s reflected Americans' genuine bonhomie toward their southern neighbor. Americans were consistently more open to Mexico than to any other developing country, and felt as fondly toward their neighbor as we did toward many European nations, and even Israel. U.S. political leaders were also more engaged, coming to see Mexico as second to none in terms of America's vital interests. But by the mid-2000s public opinion tumbled, and Mexico's perceived importance among decision makers faded dramatically.[46]

The media too turned decidedly negative. A study of the *New York Times* and the *Wall Street Journal* shows the stark swing in Mexico news coverage. During the mid-1990s, the reporting was intense, with most of the articles focused on economic and political relations between Mexico and the United States.[47] Generally optimistic, even encouraging, these newspapers of record weighed the pros and cons of NAFTA and told stories of Mexico's political opening. Yet in the last ten years, the focus and tone changed. Immigration, drugs, and corruption replaced economics and politics in the headlines, with Mexico becoming little more than a crime story.[48]

These shifts reverberated in the halls of government, affecting bilateral relations. Mexico and the United States have continued to work together, it is true, but often without the earlier enthusiasm or optimism. After a tough fight in 2007, a comprehensive immigration reform failed. It would have created a guest worker program, provided a path for legalizing undocumented immigrants already in the United States, and increased resources for workplace and border enforcement.[49] Economic issues too became seemingly untouchable, as Mexico was blamed for factory closings and job losses. Only in security did the relationship advance, as the United States and Mexico joined together to take on the drug cartels. But even here, the money tells the story: as the United States invested roughly US$300 million a year in cooperative security aid, it spent more than triple that expanding a border fence, and some US$3 billion more a year on the Border Patrol.[50] It is safe to say that the restrictionists have won the resource battle.

Bilateral tensions, inflamed by populist rhetoric, made it a heavy lift to get even small things done—such as finally resolving the lingering trucking dispute between the two countries (fulfilling U.S. commitments under NAFTA by allowing certified Mexican truck drivers onto American highways). The political climate also makes it difficult to imagine more transformative policies that would truly enhance both countries' economies, security, and communities.

* * *

As the diplomatic relationship stagnates, nonofficial links continue to deepen. American brands increasingly depend on Mexico to satisfy customers and shareholders alike. U.S. companies—Ford, Whirlpool, Lear, Dell, and hundreds of others—have upped their global game through cross-border supply chains. Walmart—now Mexico's largest private sector employer—has delighted Mexicans with its "everyday low prices," and in the process made Arkansans (and Walmart owners) happy too. Citigroup was arguably kept afloat during the depths of the 2008 financial crisis not just by U.S. tax-payers but by the profits of its Mexico division, Banamex. And today businesses are no longer only moving north to south. The United States' largest baker (Bimbo), top cement supplier (Cemex), and fastest-growing luxury movie theater chain (Cinépolis) are Mexican transplants.[51] From what we eat to what we drive, to how we celebrate birthdays or spend our free time, America is increasingly linked to Mexico.

Personal ties are deepening too. An estimated twelve million Mexicans live in the United States, roughly 10 percent of Mexico's total population. Regardless of their official status, millions of Mexicans are now part of binational families and communities, with ties too deep to break. They are parents to some ten million American kids.[52] Millions more are tourists, retirees, students, patients, shoppers, workers, business owners, bankers, entrepreneurs, artists, authors, journalists, worshippers, teachers, as well as gang members, smugglers, and drug traffickers, linking the two nations and shaping de facto relations.

The border again is emblematic, illustrating the true benefits—and the challenges—of closer bilateral ties. Today it is the densest part of both nations. Border states, now the most urban of areas, are home to roughly one in five Mexicans and Americans.[53] Once an economic backwater, the border is now a powerhouse, growing at a faster clip than any other part of the United States or Mexico. Each day thousands of trucks and a billion dollars of wares cross, the physical manifestation of the back and forth of people, goods, investment, and know-how that fuels both economies.

Yet for all its frenetic development, the border faces significant challenges. Its communities remain some of the poorest in the United States, with decaying schools, inadequate health care, and in more than a few places, no water or sewage.[54] A concentrated microcosm of U.S.-Mexico relations, the border represents the good and the bad, the cooperation and the conflict between our two nations. Former Arizona governor Janet Napolitano often said she had a closer day-to-day working relationship with the governor of Sonora than the governor of New Mexico, while her successor, Jan Brewer, has vehemently called for hardening the border and building the wall. Though starkly different reactions, both reflect the inexorable reality of interdependence.

Whether we like it or not, Mexico is now part of the U.S. economy, people, society, security, and world. To catch up to this reality, the U.S. government must move beyond repeating that Mexico is the most important relationship it has to actually acting as if this were true. This in turn requires a better understanding of Mexico today and the evolving forces that continue to influence the mutual future of the two countries. The next four chapters turn to these issues—immigration, political opening, economic change and integration, and interlinked crime and violence—and how they have transformed Mexico and its ties to the United States.

IMMIGRATION'S BINDING TIES

Maria came to visit me, despondent. I had met her three years before when, as a sophomore, she moved into my entryway in Winthrop House, one of Harvard's dorms. Growing up on Chicago's South Side, her hard work, academic talent, and sunny personality had brought her to Cambridge's brick-lined arches and walkways. As her resident tutor and departmental advisor, I watched her through classes, papers, and exams; dates, sorority pledges, and black-tie formals. She excelled academically, as a political science major (government concentrator in Harvard's lexicon), and also socially, developing a tight group of friends.

But now, having earned her crimson diploma, her troubles were about to start. She had no legal job prospects. Her parents had arrived in the United States in the late 1980s, missing the amnesty window. To legally live and work in the United States, she would have to return "home" for ten years, separated from her family and friends. Having left Mexico when she was seven years old, she had little recollection of her homeland—just pictures of distant family and stories of a life before—of the political and economic system that left those like her and her kin always near the bottom. Her parents preferred to talk about their new life in America, and their happiness in providing the best for their four children. Here she was, having exceeded their wildest expectations but caught in the contradictions of U.S.-Mexico relations.

Though of course not all attend Harvard, there are estimated to be over one hundred thousand undocumented students who have already completed two years or more at U.S. universities, and over a million more undocumented youths poised to follow this path into higher education.[1] Like Maria, these young people are deeply rooted in American society, and mostly in good ways.

The Obama administration's 2012 decision to halt deportations and grant work visas to those who were brought illegally as children (before they were sixteen) will allow some to come out of the shadows. But their paths would be more secure with the congressional passage of the DREAM Act, a bill that would provide legal status as well as a path to citizenship for these youths, provided they graduate from high school and do not have a serious criminal record.[2]

Overlooked or misunderstood in today's immigration debates and surrounding vitriol are the real makeup and motives of the people who come to the United States from Mexico. These youths are just perhaps the most poignant example. Others are workers, customers, church members, and volunteers, as well as friends, family, and moms and dads. The current approach misses the complex causes that brought so many to the United States. Economic needs, demographic trends, and deep family and community connections on both sides of the border all led to the wave of Mexican immigration over the last thirty-plus years.

Despite the often bitter tone of debates, this wave is already receding, and is unlikely to ever rise again.[3] Migration from Mexico has declined since 2005, to the point that in 2011 it reached a "net zero"—a roughly equal number coming and going. At the 2006 movie premiere of *The New Los Angeles*, mayor Antonio Villaraigosa cautioned supporters and critics alike about assuming today's reality will be tomorrow's as well. Deftly summing up the U.S. experience, he reminded the crowd that while today Latinos are ascendant—signified by his own political success—in the future it may be the Chinese, and that too will be okay for Los Angeles and the United States. Not only will America survive, it can thrive with change.

Transitory demographic dynamics aside, today's punitive unilateral policies overlook not just the inescapability but also the real benefits of such a close connection with Mexico through our mutual peoples, families, and communities. As the United States confronts the challenge of growing economically while growing older, its neighbor can and should play an integral part in the solution.

Economics, Demographics, and Policies Lead Mexicans North

The years leading up to Maria's family's flight represented the heyday of the old PRI system. Earlier episodes of student unrest had all but disappeared. President José López Portillo was presiding over an oil boom. The PRI had easily "won" the 1979 midterm elections, granting only a quarter of the four-hundred-seat Congress to its cowed opposition and reaffirming its control over nearly every governorship, mayorship, and local legislative body in the nation.

But plunging oil prices in the early 1980s quickly shrank the government's slush fund. U.S. interest rates spiked to record highs, slamming shut the doors of the international banks to Mexico and other sovereign borrowers. By February 1982, massive capital flight pressured the Mexican currency. In an interview with foreign press correspondents, López Portillo famously promised to defend the peso "like a dog." Despite his rhetoric, the currency quickly devalued by some 40 percent, pushing Mexico's economy into recession. In August, Mexico stopped paying interest on US$80 billion of foreign debt, and the peso plummeted even further. At his final State of the Union on September 1, 1982, López Portillo stopped the central bank from selling dollars and nationalized the banking system. He then skulked into retirement at his four-mansion estate on the edge of the capital city, still referred to today as the Dog's Hill. With the livelihoods of millions destroyed, Mexico's "lost decade" had begun.

The prolonged economic crisis set off what would become an unprecedented, long-lasting wave of migration north. To be sure, Mexicans were already on the move, relocating from the farms to the cities. Searching for work, many hadn't stopped at the border, continuing north to U.S. fields and factories. But with the onset of the debt crisis—bringing skyrocketing inflation, plummeting wages, and millions of lost jobs—a desperate population set its sights on the United States.

The economic crisis coincided with a growing demographic bubble. While Mexico's mortality rates began to decline in the 1950s and 1960s with better health care, birth rates took a while longer to slow down. Through the 1960s and 1970s women still had on average over six children each—a figure that has fallen to just over two today. By the mid-1980s, in the depths of the economic crisis, these "extra" youths began hitting the streets in search of work. U.S. policy decisions and choices also played an important role in creating the current "immigration problem." For decades the United States either explicitly or implicitly promoted Mexican migration. Strict immigration laws passed in the 1920s set quotas on Chinese and Eastern European immigrants but exempted Mexicans. This encouraged their movement north. The United States officially opened the door in 1942 with the creation of the Bracero guest worker program (*bracero* roughly translates as "strong arm"). The program expanded with the U.S. economy during the postwar boom, bringing hundreds of thousands of immigrant workers each year to America's fields, orchards, and rails.

Over its twenty-two years, the Bracero program brought nearly five million Mexicans to the U.S. heartland, establishing well-trodden paths between the two nations and a mutual dependence between Mexican and U.S. communities.[4] After its end, the flows didn't stop; only their legality changed.

Economic ties between the United States and Mexico indirectly set the stage for mass migration as well. Mexico's 1965 Border Industrialization program developed special preferential tariff regimes for several miles on either side of the U.S.-Mexico border, creating the *maquila* industry. The idea behind these assembly factories was to enable companies to take advantage of U.S. capital and Mexican labor, playing to each country's strength. But it was also a response to the unilateral end to the Bracero program, as Mexico struggled to employ the multitude of workers forced home.

When the 1980s economic crisis hit Mexico, and the peso cheapened, these border-based textile and manufacturing shops became Mexico's one economic bright spot. Factory after factory opened, luring foreign capital with the promise of cheap wages and few tariffs. The possibility of work drew thousands from their rural villages, small towns, and even large cities to Mexico's north. Already uprooted, many continued to the United States.

This influx coincided with the U.S. economic recovery. The tough interest rate medicine prescribed by chairman of the Federal Reserve Paul Volcker was finally taking effect, beating back the 1970s' stagflation, the deep recession, and the near-double-digit unemployment that plagued Reagan's first two years in office. Just a few years later, economists began referring to the "great American job machine," and businesses eagerly welcomed millions of Mexicans in the scramble to find workers.

While Mexico's economic catastrophe pushed and the U.S. economic recovery pulled, the 1986 immigration reform in the United States changed the nature of the game. The Immigration Reform and Control Act (IRCA) granted a path to citizenship (dubbed "amnesty" by some) for over two million undocumented Mexican immigrants. This, in turn, created a whole new base of relatives willing and able to sponsor their spouses, children, parents, and siblings for U.S. residence, or to help friends and former neighbors get settled, fueling further migration north in the years to come.

With snowballing economic pressures and policy incentives, Mexicans were on their way to becoming the United States' predominant immigrant group. Their numbers grew during the 1970s, then more than doubled during the 1980s. They doubled again during the 1990s. By the mid-1990s, the Mexican immigrant population was growing by nearly five hundred thousand a year. A mix of documented and undocumented alike, many headed to live and work in traditional border and gateway states: California, Texas, and Illinois. But they also ranged much farther—doubling the Mexican immigrant populations in states as far-flung as Louisiana, South Dakota, Ohio, and Alaska.[5] The trend continued into the twenty-first century, and since 2000 over seven million Mexicans have come north to live and work.[6]

Today nearly a third of all U.S. immigrants come from next door—some 10 percent of Mexico's total population (and 15 percent of working-age citizens).[7] Polls show that over half of Mexicans today have a close family member or friend in the United States. Even Presidents Felipe Calderón and Vicente Fox have cousins in "el norte."

BORDER BUILD-UP

Ignoring the multiple and wide-ranging factors behind rising Mexican immigration, the United States fixated on the border. Throughout the 1990s, operations Hold the Line (El Paso, Texas), Gatekeeper (San Diego, California), Safeguard (Nogales, Arizona), and Rio Grande (southeast Texas) poured billions of dollars into fences, lights, surveillance cameras, and manpower to stop these sojourners. After September 11, 2001, the federal government struggled to expand these local lockdowns along the entire border. The new U.S. Department of Homeland Security whisked the Immigration and Naturalization Service (INS) away from the Justice Department and rechristened it the U.S. Citizenship and Immigration Services (USCIS). This functioned alongside an ever-growing Immigration and Customs Enforcement (ICE) and Customs and Border Protection (CBP). The 2006 Secure Fence

Act promised literally to steel the line for some 700 border miles, while the Secure Border Initiative pledged sophisticated technology to defend the other roughly 1300 miles. The same year, Operation Jumpstart sent six thousand National Guard members to the southwest. Over the next four years, U.S. Border Patrol agents more than doubled to twenty thousand, and the annual budget rose to over US$3 billion.[8] By 2010, the federal government even deployed Predator drones—the type used in Iraq and Afghanistan—to patrol the southern frontier.

What have been the results of all these actions? Apprehensions along the southern border rose in absolute terms—to a high of 1.6 million in 2000.[9] Government officials heralded the success, but interviews showed that, at this peak, four out of every five migrants still made it across—pretty good odds.[10] Those that got caught the first time usually just tried again. Starting in 2005, the number stopped at the border began to fall. By 2010, apprehensions were less than half the 2000 peak, matching numbers last seen in the early 1970s.[11] Again the Border Patrol touted the achievement, citing the deterrent effect. Yet the decline seems to match just as directly to the shifts in the U.S. and Mexican economies and societies. Surveys of crossers suggest that those who try to get across generally do, even with the surge in manpower, technology, and steel.[12] David Aguilar, former head of the Border Patrol, admitted that the fence only slows illegal immigrants by three or four minutes.[13] Interviews show that aspiring crossers—well aware of the increased dangers—rarely change their minds. Even those who knew someone who died crossing were not deterred.[14]

In the rush to harden the border, the heartland was largely forgotten. It remained business as usual in the strawberry fields of California, apple orchards of Washington state, meatpacking plants of Marshalltown, Iowa, carpet mills of Dalton, Georgia, construction and landscaping businesses in Phoenix, Arizona, hotels in Las Vegas, Nevada, and restaurants in New York City. While immigration reform had created a mechanism to match up names and social security numbers and outlined punishments for employers who knowingly hire undocumented migrants, the rules were rarely enforced, with the government conducting no more than a smattering of workplace raids. None of these new measures made a dent in the ubiquitous and increasingly diverse migratory paths to communities large and small, old and new.

Feeling overwhelmed, local governments waded into the political fray. In Beaufort County, South Carolina, Cherokee County, Georgia, and

Mission Viejo and Escondido, California, deputized local police officers began enforcing immigration laws on their beats. Towns such as Hazleton, Pennsylvania, and Riverside, New Jersey, passed ordinances to punish landlords and businesses that rented to or hired illegal immigrants. Some sixty other cities—including San Francisco, New York, Washington DC, Houston, and Philadelphia—went the other way, designating their metropolises as sanctuaries, prohibiting police officers from inquiring about immigration status without a criminal cause.[15]

States took up the call—most vocally in Arizona. Facing a tough reelection fight in 2010, Governor Jan Brewer did not hesitate as she signed the Support Our Law Enforcement and Safe Neighborhoods Act, or Arizona SB 1070. The law required police officers to check people's immigration status if there was a "reasonable suspicion" that they might be here illegally, and made it a crime not to have official identification on hand. In defending the bill, Brewer assured constituents that it would protect U.S. citizens "against a relentless and daily barrage of narco-terrorist drug and human smugglers."[16]

Public outrage immediately spilled forth. Rallies around the country denounced the bill, with protesters carrying signs saying "Stop the hate" and "What does illegal look like?" Opponents warned that now WWH— "walking while Hispanic"—would be a crime. Yet counter rallies also occurred, with placards declaring "Arizona got it right" and "Adiós illegals." Opinion polls revealed strong backing for the law, and similar initiatives began to work their way through other state legislatures across the country, passing in Georgia, Alabama, Indiana, and South Carolina.[17]

In June 2012, the U.S. Supreme Court struck down the Arizona provisions that made it a state crime for immigrants not to carry papers at all times and for illegal immigrants to work, as well as the provision allowing state police to arrest suspected illegal immigrants without a warrant. But it upheld what many see as the most controversial part of the law—requiring law enforcement officers to check the status of anyone they stop or detain if they suspect them of being in the United States illegally.[18]

Less heralded or vilified were those choosing a different path, most notably Utah. Alongside greater enforcement measures, the Republican-dominated state legislature passed a bill granting work permits to undocumented workers.[19] It even planned to create a pilot program with the Mexican state of Nuevo León to bring guest workers north legally.

Proponents of border protection and stricter internal laws—including many politicians up for reelection—say we need more money, more fences, more boots on the ground. Yet the incremental benefit of further boosting border resources is questionable. Since 1998, the Border Patrol has tripled in size and its funding has risen 800 percent. Apprehensions have not kept pace, instead falling fivefold. Some see the declines as part of the deterrent effect of a harder border. This is likely true. But the escalating costs of each apprehension also highlight the diminishing returns of more money at the border.

Part of the issue is that the southern crossing is just one of many routes into the United States. At least 40 percent of the unauthorized population entered legally and then just never left.[20] Prioritizing defensive measures on the southwest border will do nothing to affect this illegal migrant flow. The question, then, is really how best to spend U.S. government resources (taxpayer dollars in the end) to ensure the safety and enhance the prosperity of America. Here the other costs beyond public funds need to be considered.

The Fallout of a Harder Border

Hardening the border has had other unintended but still destructive consequences. Illegal migration has become more and more dangerous. Pushed away from the big cities, most border crossers now come through the punishing desert, facing rattlesnakes, scorpions, and hundred-degree heat on a cool day. Border crossing deaths doubled in the last fifteen years—at times claiming over sixty souls a month during the summer heat.[21] The Pima County, Arizona morgue has borne the brunt of these macabre increases. Stretched beyond capacity with Juan and Juana Does, chief medical examiner Dr. Bruce Parks has had to rent refrigerated trucks to house the overflow. With the bodies (and sometimes just bones) come the remnants of family photos, voter registration cards, telephone numbers, and rosaries—often the only hints to past and now extinguished dreams.[22]

Immigration laws—and the unselective enforcement—created new and highly profitable markets for illegal papers. In the downtowns of Los Angeles, Denver, Atlanta, and Houston, document vendors do a brisk business in social security cards, green cards, passports, and driver's licenses—any official paper necessary to apply for a job or make one's life here.[23] Vendors openly pass out flyers heralding their services, priding themselves on their swift customer service as they are able to fill most orders in just a few hours. With start-up costs of little more than a camera, printer, and scanner, the profits are large, and it is easy to blend back into the woodwork and start up again elsewhere if and when the authorities get suspicious.

By driving up the crossing costs, the hardening border has also attracted organized crime. In small towns such as Sasabe or Agua Prieta, Sonora, the change is palpable.[24] Slick-looking men wearing large belt buckles idle outside the bus station, awaiting the arrival of today's *pollos*, or "chickens"—those needing passage north. These intermediaries chat up the disembarking passengers, delivering them to coyotes—smugglers—who will take them over the border and into Phoenix, Los Angeles, Chicago, or beyond. Once shared by mom-and-pop operations, locals hoping to earn a few extra dollars on the weekends or at night, the border is now dominated by toughened criminals moving their wares—men, women, and often small children. They travel well armed, to fend off attempts by rival gangs to steal their living merchandise and to better control their charges. With violence always lurking, crossers worry that even at exorbitant rates of US$3000 apiece they might face extortion, beatings, rape, or even worse. Yet still they come.

These barriers and dangers, while not necessarily discouraging migration, are fundamentally altering its rhythm. Instead of going north for several months and then returning home—dubbed "circular migration" by scholars—most migrants now stay, or at least stay longer. Before the U.S. border build up, roughly one of every two migrants would return home within a year; 75 percent left within two years. The vast majority of Mexicans did not come to settle, but to earn enough money to better their and their families' lives at home. But starting in the late 1980s, this pattern began to change as the costs of crossing back and forth rose. Now only one in five immigrants return each year to Mexico.[25] Even as the U.S. unemployment numbers rose after the 2009 financial crisis, the number of Mexican immigrants voluntarily heading home continued to drop.[26]

Instead, many sent for their spouses, kids, and other family members, reluctantly making their home here. A telltale sign of this shift is the thousands of unaccompanied children stopped every year at the border.[27] Ranging from infants to teenagers, many travel to reunite with family members already on the other side. When they get caught, parents, cousins, or other family and friends scramble to come up with enough money to try again.

Under current laws, sponsoring children and relatives through legal channels is unrealistic. The wait time for legal entry numbers not months but years, even for those with close relations—parents, spouses, children, siblings. Many Mexican immigrant parents face the heartbreaking dilemma of bringing their young children illegally or letting them grow up far away, waiting for a family visa. Millions more mothers and fathers confront an equally agonizing catch-22—having no way to fix their immigration status without leaving the country for a decade or more. As a result, the parents of an estimated 5.5 million youths, 4.5 million of them U.S. citizens, have to hide in the shadows in order to stay together in the United States. These kids live in daily fear of losing their mom, dad, or both—likely for decades— and with good reason. According to the Homeland Security inspector general, over one hundred thousand parents of U.S. citizens were sent home between 1998 and 2007 (a rate that then accelerated under the Obama administration).[28]

Leslie, Marcos, and Adeline are just three American citizens caught in this web. Their parents, Abel and Zulma, left Mexico twenty years ago to try to save their first baby from leukemia. Rather than leave the United States after his death, they overstayed their temporary permits. Abel landed a job as a landscaper and butcher, and then later as an electrician. By 2007, Abel and Zulma were the proud parents of three Californians—sixteen-year-old Leslie, thirteen-year-old Marcos, and eight-year-old Adeline. They paid taxes, attended church, volunteered at the kids' schools, and owned their San Diego home. Yet they could never reconcile their own unlawful immigration status. In February 2007, federal agents arrested and later deported them. Not wanting to uproot their children from their home and country, they signed over custody to a relative.[29]

The children still live in their parents' house, though life has never been the same. With Abel and Zulma stuck in Tijuana, Leslie acted as a surrogate mother, cooking and caring for her siblings and making sure they finished their homework. To pay the mortgage and buy food, she and her brother both got jobs, and then struggled to stay in school. Both made it, but their high school graduations were bittersweet—the elation tempered by the absence of their parents' proud faces among the crowd of well-wishers. Given the tough reentry rules, Abel and Zulma will not be eligible to even apply to return the United States until 2017, perhaps to see their youngest walk across the stage in cap and gown.

Rounding up all of the estimated eleven million undocumented individuals—while appealing to the law and order folks—is extremely costly.

A report by the Center for American Progress conservatively estimates that the costs to find and deport these people would top US$57 billion a year for five years—approximately the entire budget of the Department of Homeland Security, or roughly US$23,000 per deportee.[30] This doesn't consider the disruptions to the workplace: factories, restaurants, hotels, construction sites, laundromats, farms, and ranches could all shut down, rippling through the economy.

This approach is also directly at odds with the United States' history of generosity and its self-image. Thomas Jefferson wrote in 1801, "Born in other countries, yet believing you could be happy in this, our laws acknowledge, as they should do, your right to join us in society."[31] Just over 150 years later President John F. Kennedy noted,

> The contribution of immigrants can be seen in every aspect of our national life. We see it in religion, in politics, in business, in the arts, in education, even in athletics and in entertainment. There is no part of our nation that has not been touched by our immigrant background. Everywhere immigrants have enriched and strengthened the fabric of American life.[32]

Forgotten in the heated debates over "illegals" is who these people are. Their undocumented status aside, most are hardworking and law-abiding individuals, embodying the very traits we prize. These millions are already part of the United States' society, deeply tied through work and family. Today's rigid rules are un-American in that they give no second chances, no way to make good here.

The farther-flung economic consequences are also perverse. Immigration rules have helped change the structure of the U.S. job market, in many instances hurting those it was designed to protect—American workers on the bottom economic rungs. In the 1970s, most businesses employed everyone from the janitor and mailroom staff to the CEO as part of the team. Today, this idea of a "vertically integrated" company is positively quaint, as consultants and shareholders alike push companies large and smaller to outsource "noncore" duties—including cleaning, maintenance, accounting, and telecommunications services—to third-party vendors. This move reflects in part a need and desire to specialize and reduce costs, but it also results from the loopholes in the U.S. immigration system.

Today, big corporations—the Walmarts, Hiltons, and American Airlines—along with major universities, hospitals, and office buildings routinely contract out janitorial and other services to much smaller firms like Harvard Maintenance, ABM Industries, and other lesser-known companies.[33] These firms are responsible for paying wages, benefits (rarely provided), and checking immigration status. This outsourcing may or may not reduce direct labor costs, but it definitely protects brand-name businesses from the legal messiness of illegal hiring. While many of these smaller service companies adhere to U.S. immigration laws, others do not. When caught, they easily transform their names and registries. Whatever their scruples, they invariably take a cut of low-income worker wages.

Local laws too have had deleterious effects. Early in 2011, Georgia passed a strict new immigration law to "relieve" it of the burdens of illegal aliens. As the start date approached, immigrant farm workers fled Georgia's famous peach orchards and Vidalia onion fields. Searching for a solution, the governor asked farm owners to hire parolees.[34] The experiment ended almost as soon as it started, as nearly all quit within the first day, claiming the work was too hard. One participant observed, "Those guys out here weren't out there thirty minutes and they got the bucket and just threw them in the air… They just left, took off across the field walking." By mid-June, Georgia farmers were desperate for help; there were eleven thousand vacant field-hand positions, and the economy had already lost hundreds of millions of dollars.[35]

More comprehensive studies reaffirm this anecdotal evidence. A study by University of Alabama researcher Samuel Addy estimates the combined effects of lost sales and income taxes (somewhere between US$80 million and US$350 million) and the fall in aggregate demand from lost consumers (eighty-five thousand unauthorized immigrants, roughly 5 percent of the state's workforce) from Alabama's restrictive immigration laws could shrink the state's annual GDP by up to US$11 billion (6 percent).[36] Studies by the Center for American Progress and the University of Arizona have found that deporting unauthorized immigrant workers would have a similar effect in California and Arizona respectively.[37] A different study by the Americas Society / Council of the Americas suggests that restrictive laws hurt rather than help local employment in the long run.[38]

IMMIGRATION AND AMERICAN WORKERS

In 2008, Pennsylvanian Keith Eckel—a fourth-generation farmer—closed up shop. Recent immigration raids had scared off the hundred-plus workers he needed each August and September to hand-pick the millions of tomatoes on his seven hundred acre farm. Many of Keith's workers had been coming to his farm for twenty-five years but now feared traveling the usual harvest circuit, working their way up by week and month from Florida to Georgia, Virginia, Maryland, and finally reaching Pennsylvania. Though his regular workers (paid by the carton) averaged over US$16 an hour, Keith couldn't find locals able or willing to take the job and, seeing no hope that Washington would ease the visa process anytime soon, he shuttered his farm.[39] In California—America's biggest farming state—farm worker jobs remained unfilled despite being advertised across four states. As one worker put it, "If people know English, they go to work in packinghouses or sit in an office."[40]

Academics, policymakers, and politicians debate if immigration hurts native-born workers, and if so by how much. Here is what we know. Nearly all economists agree that immigration presents a net benefit for the U.S. economy and for U.S. wages.[41] Most agree that the costs and benefits are unevenly distributed—varying by race, gender, and education levels. Women, college educated, those with some college studies, and even those living in areas with high immigration (10 percent or more) benefit. Native-born men with a high school degree or less don't fare as well, with the best estimates putting the costs somewhere in the range of a couple of dollars a week (less than 1 percent of wages). Those hurt the most are previous immigrants—who directly compete with the new arrivals.[42]

The presence of a high number of immigrants doesn't seem to correlate with lower wages either. In Nevada, where the unauthorized population is thought to be 7.5 percent of all residents, the median wage for high school dropouts is just over ten dollars. In Ohio, where these immigrants are just 1 percent of the population, the median is less than eight dollars and fifty cents.[43] Unemployment levels also show little cause and effect. States with lots of immigrants, such as Texas, New York, Florida, or Illinois, have similar rates of unemployment as those with few immigrants—Kentucky, Mississippi, or Maine, for example.

While some may find the limited effects surprising, it reflects the complicated realities of immigration. Over the last thirty years the number of Americans without any college education has steadily declined—which means a smaller number is vulnerable to local low-wage competition.[44] In addition, the U.S. job market is not a zero-sum game. Immigrants and their families help spur growth and new jobs by buying groceries, going out to dinner, and shopping at the local mall. Also, long-time locals and new arrivals gravitate toward different jobs. U.S.-born workers are more likely to serve food in restaurants, check out shoppers as retail clerks, check in families at hotel front desks, hold manufacturing jobs, or manage construction or janitorial crews that have less-than-perfect English. In fact, study after study shows that foreign-born and native workers more often complement than substitute for one another.[45]

Academics also find that the pressure on low-skill wages stems not from immigration per se, but from the illegal nature of so many of today's arrivals, which allows unscrupulous employers to underpay, undercut, and underprotect employees. One such study suggests that if immigrants were legalized, wages for all workers—citizens and noncitizens alike—on the bottom educational rungs would increase rather than fall.[46] Finally, economists also agree that other forces—technological change, educational disparities, the decline in manufacturing, and changes in labor force participation—hit high school dropouts harder than immigration.[47]

The mismatch between U.S. laws and economic needs creates many of today's challenges. It is virtually impossible today for a Mexican with no close family connections or specialized skills to enter the United States legally. Yet if they come, migrants can easily find gainful employment.

Whether tomatoes, onions, strawberries, lettuce, oranges, or milk, America's fields and farms are suffering from the disconnect between needs and workers, even in a difficult economy. There is an element of truth to the claim that the whole agricultural industry has designed itself around an influx of cheap labor, delaying investments in expensive labor-saving technology that would increase productivity.[48] But, in the end, the wages for farm labor can increase only so much. More likely, with the margins in the grocery business already razor-thin, the United States would rely more on imports—in part from Mexican farms on the other side of the border.

Something similar can be said of service industries. Immigrants, many of them undocumented, are the ones willing to take jobs cleaning buildings large and small, often late at night after children have left their classrooms, hospital patients are asleep, and nine-to-five workers are long gone. One estimate shows that 250,000 undocumented immigrants are janitors, 350,000 are maids and housekeepers, and 300,000 are groundskeepers.[49] It is hard to imagine many Americans encouraging their increasingly college-bound children to move into these jobs. The current demand for foreign labor will continue undiminished.

What is true is that the U.S. immigration system today encourages many—migrants, employers, neighbors, churches, and communities—to break the law. This challenge cannot be fixed by more police raids, higher walls, or the National Guard at the border—all elements of the "enforcement first" approach. Instead, it requires a fundamental rewriting of the rules on the books.

Over the last three decades the U.S. government wrongfully presumed that it could open up goods and capital markets with its southern neighbor while closing off the movement of labor. Instead, trade and personal ties deepened in tandem, though the outmoded immigration laws drove up the costs for both societies and economies. Today's dysfunctional system leaves the United States and Mexico less able to manage the flows in ways that would be beneficial to both. To reduce the current common rule-breaking, the United States needs to provide a legal means for both workers and employers to respond to market supply and demand and to the transnational realities of today's families and communities.

IMMIGRATION'S EFFECTS ON THE UNITED STATES

Mexican migration has changed and is changing the United States profoundly—just as similar migration waves did before. Mexican culture has hit the mainstream. Salsa outsells ketchup.[50] More people in Los Angeles, Houston, Sacramento, and Miami receive their nightly news from Univision's Jorge Ramos and María Elena Salinas than from any other network anchors. No translation was needed when Arnold Schwarzenegger, as the Terminator, popularized "Hasta la vista." César Chávez's motto "Sí se puede" is now the rallying cry for Latino and non-Latino activists alike. And starting in 2001, the White House began celebrating Cinco de Mayo alongside St. Patrick's Day and the annual lighting of the White House menorah.

Mexican immigration has transformed U.S. cities big and small—most often for the better. Transplanted Mexicans have revived the downtowns of communities as diverse as East Chicago, Illinois; Imlay City, Michigan; Painesville, Ohio; and St. Paul, Minnesota—opening taquerías, grocery stores, taxi services, and clothing stores, and stabilizing neighborhoods (and the local tax base) by buying and building homes.[51] Though some towns fear the competition for already scarce jobs, others see the benefits to their communities from the influx of workers, consumers, and families.

One of the seemingly forgotten lessons of America's past is that its cities were built and powered by immigrants. Today, the source of the influence may have changed, but it hasn't lessened, as immigrants increasingly play a revitalizing role in these same centers.

The last few decades have not been kind to Midwest "rust belt" cities. The emptying of Detroit is the starkest case, but it is far from alone. The population of St. Louis has fallen to levels last seen during the 1870s. In Ohio, nine of the ten largest cities shrank in the 2000–2010 decade. As factories closed, dozens of red-brick-lined main streets—once bustling with shoppers, diners, and businesses—took on a desolate appearance. Commuters passed by empty storefronts and vacant blocks, deserted by six in the evening, on their way out of downtown and back to the suburbs and strip malls. The nightly emptiness encouraged bad behavior, punctuated with broken bottles, graffiti, and discarded needles. This unwelcoming dynamic left little for the ambitious young to do except move away. But some communities throughout the United States are indeed thriving. In many cases, immigration is the reason.

Proud home to the Frankfort High Hot Dogs, Frankfort, Indiana, was founded by German migrants nearly a century and a half ago. A stopping-off point for goods and people on the Nickel Plate, Pennsylvania, and Monon railroads, by the mid-twentieth century nearly half of the town depended on the railyard. As America changed, so did Frankfort. It became an agricultural and logistical center, benefiting from the miles of flat fertile land surrounding it, the intersection of State Routes 28 and 38, and the easy access to nearby Interstate 65, another central Indiana artery. Less than an hour from Indianapolis, this Clinton County town boasted over fifteen thousand residents in 1960. Supported by soybeans, candy, and auto parts manufacturing, industrial parks sprang up on its outskirts.

Bearing the hallmarks of so many small Midwestern cities, Frankfort suffered the same fate. As the postwar boom ended, so did Frankfort's dynamism. The town suffered as the railroad lines died and the farm debt crisis took its toll. By the mid-1980s, Frankfort's once-vibrant downtown was in decline, with storefronts mostly vacant, buildings in disrepair, the ornate white stone courthouse desperately needing a facelift. Locals feared the virtual death of their beloved home as the population began to shrink, with young people leaving for Indianapolis, Chicago, and beyond.

But the 1990s represented a renaissance of sorts. Already on the migration trail due to its farms, Frankfort's new meatpacking plant and other nearby food processing factories began attracting permanent Mexican migrants from the arid hills of Zacatecas and tropical coast of Veracruz.[52] There were jobs to be had detasseling corn, canning tomatoes and beans, and preparing goods for shipping. Over the decade, the Hispanic population increased sixfold, more than compensating for native-born emigration and bringing Frankfort's population to all-time highs.

The influx revitalized the city's center, as newcomers and old-timers both frequented the Tortilleria Del Valle on Walnut Avenue and Mama Ines's Mexican Bakery on East Wabash Street. Brightly painted and decorated Latino businesses now intermingled with the more sedate Anglo-owned establishments. Pews that had become half-empty were now often filled to capacity, particularly for Spanish-language services. Vacant desks and classrooms too came alive as new families settled. Demand for education extended to the higher reaches, encouraging Purdue University to expand its local extension school and add classes for Spanish speakers. The influx changed the visual landscape, as curved archways of Southwest-inspired homes sprang up among the sharper angles of traditional brick and Victorian frames. While Frankfort remains slightly poorer and cheaper than other Indiana towns, average incomes and housing prices increased significantly with the new arrivals, as did tax intakes.

The rapid demographic change didn't come without its tensions. Hispanics now represent a fourth of the population of sixteen thousand, but the mayor's office and city council remain lily-white, raising questions about the integration of Frankfort's civic life. The 1998 murder of a white resident by a Hispanic one in a bar brawl exacerbated tensions, leading to rumors of a local Ku Klux Klan revival. Immigration marches in 2006 ruffled feathers, as seen in the letters to the editor of the *Frankfort Times*. But overall, most long-time Frankforters have worked to understand their new employees, customers, business colleagues, and neighbors, welcoming the latest Hoosiers into America's globalizing heartland.

Mexican immigrants and Mexican Americans have changed more than just the feel of America's downtowns. Ten years younger than the overall population, they now power whole segments of the consumer economy, spending nearly $1 trillion a year. Companies large and small have set their sights eagerly on this new demographic. Most emblematic is Goya Foods. Started by a Spanish couple during the Great Depression, it imported olives, sardines, and a few other products that were reminders of home to a nostalgic local clientele. From its original lower Manhattan storefront, it set its sights on America's Spanish-speaking immigrants. Goya now dominates whole aisles of supermarkets across the country and sells to tens of thousands of smaller retailers. From beans and rice to peppers, spices, and mole sauces, it offers over 1600 different products and brings in over $1 billion in yearly revenue.[53] The company transformed its marketing from a local Hispanic niche to the American mainstream, now boasting of products suited "for every taste and every table."

Long-standing middle-America brands got into the game too, with Frito Lay creating spicier snacks, and Hanes pantyhose and Miller beer adjusting packaging and advertising, with profitable results. Sports teams and others in the entertainment business look for ways to build their Hispanic fan base Most notable is the National Basketball Association (NBA), which now hosts numerous "Noches Latinas" where one can go see San Antonio's "Los Spurs" play Miami's "El Heat" or Phoenix's "Los Suns." On these nights, the songs of Carlos Santana, Shakira, and Jennifer Lopez replace Bon Jovi during the timeouts. Perhaps most illustrative of this new market's potential was Toyota's 2006 Superbowl commercial. In this priciest of mainstream airtime, the advertisement featured a discernibly Hispanic father driving his son in a Toyota Camry hybrid, the conversation switching between English and Spanish as a parallel to the gas and electric of the car, and subtly positioning both—the Hispanic boy and the hybrid car—as the future of America.

UNFOUNDED FEARS

Samuel P. Huntington, the late Harvard professor and preeminent social scientist, crystallized the lurking fears that Mexican migration is different than past (mostly European) waves in his 2004 book *Who Are We? The Challenges to America's National Identity*. Huntington argued that Hispanic immigrants have not assimilated into mainstream U.S. culture and "threaten to divide the United States into two peoples, two cultures, and two languages." Assuming a monolithic national identity, he claimed Latinos reject Anglo-Protestant values, eschew English, and generally "lack initiative, self-reliance, and ambition." He was not alone in his thinking. Others too see something amiss with today's assimilation, worried that Mexicans—due to their proximity, language, and cultural traits—will never integrate, and might even try to break away, "reconquering" the southwest United States.[54]

The data doesn't bear out these fears. A 2003 poll by the *New York Times* found that nearly 70 percent of foreign-born Hispanics identified more with the United States than with their country of origin.[55] Even while immigration restrictions force many into the shadows, inhibiting assimilation instead of promoting it, Mexican integration follows the trends of other ethnicities.[56] Mexicans and Mexican Americans acquire English in similar ways and at similar speeds as previous immigrants. Second and third generations pick up English as fast as—and many faster than—their Italian, German, or Polish predecessors. Among second-generation Hispanic Americans, nine out of ten speak English very well.[57] By the third generation, the problem is not their English, but often their ability to communicate with their grandparents and relatives who stayed behind.

Not only do immigrants want their kids to learn English; they also want them to excel academically. More than three-quarters of Latino youth say that their parents believe going to college is the most important thing to do after high school. Nearly nine in ten Hispanics believe that a college education is important for getting ahead in life—a higher percentage than the general American public.[58]

Despite the documented desire to learn, many worry that Hispanics are failing to catch up, and are even falling behind educationally. Comparisons show that Hispanic high school and college graduation rates lag. A study by the American Enterprise Institute finds that 69 percent of Hispanics finish high school, compared to 93 percent of Asians, 84 percent of whites, and 68 percent of blacks.[59] The disparities are similar for college graduation rates.

But a closer look at the numbers bears out a different story, one of generational mobility. Studies show that the children of Mexican immigrants perform better than their parents, and their grandchildren even better, staying in school just over twelve years (in line with the national average).[60] A recent Pew survey finds that second-generation Latino youths complete high school and enroll in college at similar rates to whites in this cohort.[61] Others show the expanding difference in education between the kids of those that come to the United States and those that stay at home—further supporting the idea of advancement and assimilation in the United States.[62] Still, while Mexican Americans have shrunken the gap, they have yet to fully catch up with native whites.[63]

Maria felt the hope from her parents, and it helped push her all the way to Harvard. All four of the Pedroza children—Juan, Maria, Pedro, and

Gaby—thrived academically. Though her father and mother just made ends meet, deboning cows in Chicago's stockyards and tailoring clothes, with the help of scholarships all four attended St. Ignatius College Prep, a stately, ivy-covered campus in the heart of Chicago's downtown. Thriving under the Jesuit tutelage, Juan, the eldest, headed to DePauw University to pursue an undergraduate degree, where he would meet his (American) wife. He continued on to the University of Indiana in Bloomington to earn a master's in public analysis and economic development, and then to Stanford for a PhD in sociology. Maria and her younger brother Pedro pushed their doors open through a caddying program that took them from the South Side to the country clubs of Chicago's North Shore and posh western suburbs. Each summer they walked the links with a bag over each arm, rubbing shoulders with Chicago's wealthy and successful. Their senior years both won prestigious Chick Evans scholarships, ensuring they could continue their studies. Maria went off to Harvard, pursuing a degree in government. Two years later, Pedro headed to Cornell. The youngest sister Gaby—born a U.S. citizen—would go to the University of Illinois at Urbana-Champaign.

Yet without papers, Maria could not put her Harvard degree to good use. She ended up taking a job as an off-the-books nanny (and getting two master's degrees), until she was finally able to change her legal status through marriage. Pedro's academic career was interrupted his sophomore year by a random police stop; he was pulled off a bus just outside of Buffalo when headed back to school from vacation. For four years he lived his life in limbo, waiting to find out if and when he would be sent back to a country he barely remembers. In 2012, he benefited from the Obama administration's stay on deportations, receiving a temporary work permit.

For those who do not make it to college, another well-trodden path for Hispanic youth is in the U.S. armed services. Latinos make up 12 percent of all enlisted U.S. soldiers—roughly equal to their numbers within the overall population.[64] According to California-based army recruiter Sergeant Brian Ditzler, "More than any other group, [Latinos] have a deep sense of pride about serving for this country."[65] These soldiers and their families know sacrifice and loss just like other Americans. Of the 578 U.S. fatalities in Iraq from 2008 to 2012, over seventy had Hispanic surnames.[66]

Another common assimilation barometer is what people do and earn. Here too Hispanics are catching up with other groups. While Hispanic immigrants concentrate in construction, cleaning, and maintenance jobs, their descendants lean toward sales and office positions, mirroring closely the professional choices of U.S. citizens more generally.[67]

The picture at home for the majority of Mexican immigrants also fits well with U.S. cultural ideals. The Osvaldos and Herminias have become the new Ozzie and Harriets—with the majority of second-generation Mexican American kids growing up in a nuclear family (higher than native-born Americans).[68] Many of these kids (and their kids) are likely to intermarry, intimately integrating into America's racial and ethnic mix. Rising incomes are also translating into greater home ownership, closing in on national averages. Even on the strictest of Huntington's measures— acceptance of Protestantism—Mexicans outpace all but Korean immigrants in their conversion rates.[69]

In some areas, Hispanic immigrants are perhaps becoming too much like Americans. The longer Hispanic families live in the United States, the higher their rates of divorce. Native-born Hispanics now divorce their partners just as frequently as native-born whites (three times the rate of recent immigrants). U.S.-born Hispanic women are also more likely to have a child out of wedlock than those born in Latin America.[70]

Also, in contrast to the conventional wisdom, the evidence suggests that those newly arrived are the least likely to commit crimes, meaning immigrants may in fact make U.S. cities safer. As noted by *New York Times* columnist David Brooks (and backed up with research by Harvard professor Robert Sampson, among others), "as [U.S.] immigration has surged, violent crime has fallen 57 percent."[71]

These and other studies find that immigrants commit fewer crimes than American-born whites or African Americans, and not by small margins. First-generation Hispanic immigrants are 45 percent less likely than third-generation and above native-born Americans to commit violent crimes; second-generation Hispanic immigrants are 22 percent less likely to run afoul of the law.[72] Incarceration rates for young immigrant men are also lower: in 2000, they were five times less likely to be behind bars than their U.S.-born counterparts.[73]

Little Village, Chicago's largest Hispanic community, has all the trappings of a crime-ridden neighborhood—bad schools, high poverty, persistent unemployment—but without the crime. These hundred or so blocks have long been the home to immigrants, starting with Irish and Eastern Europeans at the turn of the twentieth century, then Polish after the Second

World War. The far west side neighborhood along the L's blue line hit hard times in the 1960s and 1970s, as steel mills closed and white flight to the suburbs left streets and shops empty. But during the 1980s Mexicans began arriving in force. With mariachis replacing polka bands, Twenty-Sixth Street—the main commercial drag—came back alive. The sidewalks bustle on a normal day, and are jam-packed on Saturdays and for special events, such as the Mexican Independence Day parade.

Though the facades are brighter, and the Virgin of Guadalupe is more ubiquitous today than St. Patrick or St. Casimir, the warmth radiating from within is the same, as these new-world immigrants endeavor to provide "old-world hospitality." Veteran landmarks—including the original Home Run Inn pizza—are now joined by the best Mexican food joints in the Windy City, such as Taqueria Los Gallos and El Gallo Tapatio. With nearly one thousand local businesses, Little Village's Twenty-Sixth Street corridor ranks second only to the much tonier Michigan Avenue in retail sales.[74]

Little Village is not an unencumbered paradise. Alleyways can fill with trash, and gangs such as the Latin Kings hover in the shadows. But despite being one of Chicago's poorest neighborhoods, it ranks in the top third city-wide in terms of safety—alongside the much more affluent Lakeview and Edgewater.[75]

More broadly, while earlier immigration waves from Europe were linked to increases in crime, the more recent Mexican-led migration has coincided with the reverse. What has been described as the "Latino paradox" by sociologists leaves some scratching their heads, but many attribute this to tight-knit families and communities.[76] Whatever the reasons, these immigrants appear to be much less violent than people born here.

There are, of course, differences from past immigration waves. In absolute terms, there are more Mexicans than previous immigrant groups to the United States. In relative terms, Mexican immigrants represent roughly a third of the total foreign-born population in the United States—similar to the Irish and Germans in the mid-nineteenth century.[77]

The length of the current immigrant wave is also unprecedented. A large wave of Irish immigrants came to the United States in a brief ten-year period between 1840 and 1850, the Germans between 1848 and 1860, and the Italians between 1900 and 1915.[78] Mexicans have been coming (and going) for a century or more, the most recent influx lasting some thirty years. First-generation Mexican migrants mingle with second-, third-, fourth-, even fifth-generation neighbors. Mexico's nearness just amplifies this mixing of new and old, fresh-off-the-boat and deeply rooted natives. Layer on the combination of Spanish-language television, cheap airline tickets, cell phones, and Skype, and migrants can now sustain ties not only to their country but to their small villages in ways unimaginable for earlier groups.

But contrary to the narrative on talk radio or even on CNN, many of Mexico's migrants to the United States hope not to stay. Take Rico Flores and his wife, Maria. In 2007, they finally fulfilled their quite common dream: saving enough to go home for good. After eighteen years working in Napa Valley—he in a vineyard, she in a nursery—they headed back to their hometown of Los Haro, Zacatecas. He now uses (and advises his neighbors on) the organic farming techniques he learned in California, increasing the marketability of the village's fruit in the specialty shops of Monterrey, Mexico, some six hours away. She keeps their large, two-story concrete house, tends the olive, peach, and plum trees out front, and runs an annual summer exchange for California-based Zacatecan kids. Part public service, part outlet for her unbounded energy, the three-week July camp matches the transplants with locals. A metaphoric nursery, she hopes to foster roots to the children's original hometowns. While happy to be back, Rico and Maria lament the always-closed doors and shuttered windows that line their street, testifying to the still unmet dreams of their neighbors still in the north.

Mexican immigration has again stirred America's fabled melting pot, adding new faces to the workplace, bringing a new language to many cities' streets, and new foods and traditions to the patchwork of American culture. It provided the workforce needed to support several years of economic growth (at a time of historically low unemployment), even as the United States dealt again with the difficulties of integrating a large group of nonnative workers into American society.

MIGRATION'S EFFECTS ON MEXICO

But for all the effects up north, the changes have been even more profound in Mexico. Migration has provided immediate cash to families back home, opened up Mexican society, and irrevocably tied it to the United States. To be sure, migration has also taken a toll—enticing away its young and able and tearing at the nation's social fabric by separating families. The challenge for Mexico today is to leverage the good and limit the bad from this

movement—in the end providing citizens with realistic options for supporting their families and pursuing their dreams wherever they so choose.

The most direct effect of immigration to the United States is the flow of
remittances home. About one in five Mexicans receives these flows from
abroad.[79] Though these transfers average just US$300 apiece, tens of mil-
lions of transactions add up to more than all foreign direct investment combined.[80] Remittances rank second only to oil dollars flowing to Mexico, averaging over US$20 billion per year.[81]

Much of this money goes to basic needs, such as food and housing, combined with just a touch of luxury: a dinner out, uniforms for the private school
in town, a store-bought crinoline-laden first-communion dress, or a new cell
phone to call the States. But some of this money provides the capital needed
to create and sustain local businesses: buying a taxi, stocking a local store, or
opening a repair shop. Many families also use remittances to cope with major
life changes: unemployment, medical emergencies, children, or old age. At
times remittances have funded local infrastructure, as migrants pool resources
(often matched by Mexico's local, state, and federal governments) to bring
roads, plumbing, schools, parks, and other public works to their hometowns.

Decades of migration have changed more than just household economics. The direct experiences of millions of Mexicans in the United States
gave many a taste for democracy and economic openness that they then
brought back to their own families and communities. Andrés Bermúdez
left Zacatecas state as an impoverished field hand in 1974. He and his preg-
nant wife sneaked across the border, hiding in the trunk of a car. After a
short stint in a suitcase factory, Bermúdez headed to the fields of northern
California. Always a tinkerer, his luck changed after he invented a device
for transplanting tomatoes. It earned him the nickname "the tomato king,"
as well as a small fortune. Two decades after he left Mexico, the crowned
migrant went back to his sleepy hometown of Jerez, determined to shake
up the old system. Running for mayor, he vowed on the campaign trail to
"get the rats out of city hall," bring responsive and accountable government
to the local people, and even to turn his central Mexican highland town
into a mini-America—well governed, prosperous, with real jobs, so that
the next generation could choose to stay. He defeated the town's old guard
on his second political run, and, though few of his promises came to fruition (and critics later charged him with fraud, corruption, and nepotism),
he went on to be one of Jerez's most popular mayors.[82]

Mexican immigrants' time in the United States has helped to debunk the facile stereotypes of the PRI days, including views of Mexico's northern neighbor. Nearly six in ten Mexicans see life as better in the United States; for those with friends and relatives up north the number is even higher. Today over half of Mexicans have a favorable opinion of the United States, near Spain and Britain.[83]

Yet Mexico's widespread and long-standing migration to the United States has had its drawbacks as well. Over six hundred thousand (or about a sixth) of all Mexican college degree recipients and roughly half of all PhD holders reside in the United States.[84] Here, U.S. gains are Mexico's losses, as these professionals make their careers, start their businesses, and contribute to communities far away from their native land. Economists call this phenomenon "brain drain"—an exodus of talent from the very countries that need it most.

Remittances too are not an unqualified benefit. The money sent back to families divides small towns between the haves and the have-nots. The influx of dollars to migrants' hometowns can drive up local prices, making it harder for those that remain to make ends meet. This pushes even more to migrate, perpetuating a cycle that ensures survival, but not development.

The streets of countless small Mexican towns tell the complicated story at home. For decades, the August rains deluged the small town of Jomulquillo, Zacatecas, physically dividing families and neighbors caught on the other side of the central gully for weeks at a time. Money from migrants—matched by the local, state, and federal governments—has sewn the community back together. The main intersection now sports a state-of-the-art bridge above a sturdy new retaining wall, which safely channels the yearly floods through and out of town.

Yet, visiting on a hot June day, ours is the only vehicle to cross this new overpass. Guided by Rodolfo García Zamora, an economics professor at the state university, we are halfway through a day-long tour of three Zacatecas towns, together the home base for thousands of U.S. migrants. The fifteen of us file off the bus and meet three locals—two who have made the trip north but are back, one who has stayed. Talking under the shade of a large tree, they recount their personal choices, the community's once-vibrant festivals, and the (so far unsuccessful) efforts to create local jobs through a sewing cooperative and vegetable farming. During our half hour together in the town center, just the local bus—empty of passengers—passes by. Jomulquillo used to boast some 750 residents, but now claims less than half that number.

Despite the solitary feel, the town is awash in construction. Bricks—not people—line the town's sidewalks. Directly in front of us is a completed two-story red house, adorned with ornate black grates and a line of carefully tended trees facing west. Yet even in the midday heat, the windows and doors remained shuttered, attesting to the owner's absence. Next door are remnants of Jomulquillo's past—a one-story unpainted structure, the fallen-in roof exposing decaying mud bricks. A house much like the town— empty but not gone.

REVERSING MIGRATION

The anti-Mexican sentiments of Arizona sheriff Joe Arpaio, Alabama judge Roy Moore, and Tea Partiers such as Congresswoman Michele Bachmann from Minnesota and former Senator Jim DeMint from South Carolina, overlook and misunderstand the history, causes, and consequences of U.S.-bound Mexican migration. Over the last two hundred years, migration has ebbed and flowed in response to economic needs, public policies, family bonds, and demographics on both sides of the border.

The tide that led to the roughly twelve million Mexicans living in the United States today is no different. It rose in response to peso crises and economic recoveries, population bubbles, immigration reforms, and community ties. It will recede as conditions change. The U.S. economic recession has already slowed migration north (though it has done little to send migrants home). And as Mexico's demographic bubble further deflates, so too undoubtedly will the force behind the migration wave of the last thirty years.

Indeed, all measurements indicate that Mexican immigration to the United States is already dropping dramatically. Apprehensions on the southern border have been falling due in large part to the fewer arrivals from Mexico.[85] The drop has been so great that in 2011 Douglas Massey, head of the Mexican Migration Project (a long-term survey of Mexican emigration at Princeton University), claimed that, for the first time in sixty years, Mexican migration to the United States had hit a net zero.[86] Soon after, a Pew Hispanic report published similar results; estimating that the number of Mexicans entering the United States roughly equaled those leaving (boosted by a sharp increase in deportations).[87]

In part, economic calculations—the interplay between more limited job prospects up north and improving ones in Mexico—are behind the decline. More young people are deciding to stay at home and in school, investing in their future. And the somewhat contradictory forces of growing U.S. enforcement and organized crime at the border are increasing the costs and potential for violence during a journey north. But perhaps the biggest shift is demographic.

In Mexico, changing family patterns mean that fewer teenagers are and will be coming of age—and needing jobs. Since 1970, when the birthrate was still near seven children per mother, the number of kids per Mexican family has been falling steadily. In 1995, it was three; by 2007, Mexican and U.S. fertility rates were, on average, just over two children—about the number needed to ensure a steady population going forward (called the "replacement rate" by demographers).[88] Mexico's declining birthrate can now be seen in the number of working-age adults joining Mexico's economy every year. In the 1990s—years of heavy immigration to the United States—Mexico's economically active population grew by one million every year. In the late 2000s, the growth rate fell by half to roughly five hundred thousand (and U.S.-bound migration declined as well, down 40 percent).[89] Looking forward, these numbers will continue to decline. After 2020, somewhere between one hundred thousand and two hundred thousand fewer Mexicans will be coming of age each year compared to 2010. This translates to at least a half million to a million fewer Mexicans looking for jobs in the 2020s. The thirty-year wave of supply-led migration between the United States and Mexico has now passed, and will likely never happen again.

On the U.S. side of the border, the demographic trends are different but just as definitive. As the eighty-million-strong baby-boomer generation looks to its retirement years (the first members turned sixty-five on January 1, 2011), the economic challenges for the United States are hard to overstate. With baby boomers making up a quarter of the U.S. population, never has the age pyramid been so top heavy. The sixty million Generation Xers that follow will have a difficult time single-handedly filling the soon-to-be open professional slots, leaving approximately five million open jobs by 2018, according to a study by Barry Bluestone and Mark Melnik of Northeastern University.[90] Upending the current thinking, the coming decades' quandary may be whether we have *enough* workers.

Some do recognize this growing need for migrants to boost the U.S. labor force—mostly at the high end of the scale. Thomas L. Friedman and others have called for the government to "staple a green card" to every PhD and engineering diploma.[91] Numerous studies show the benefits that well-trained immigrants and their children bring to the U.S. economy. They create jobs—founding a quarter of all the engineering and technology-related companies—and disproportionally drive growth through new inventions and patents.[92] Other nations also understand this and are competing to attract the global best and brightest—the founders of the next Google, Intel, or eBay.

Less heralded but perhaps as vital is the need for lower-skilled labor. In 1960, half of the native-born male population never completed high school. Today, less than 10 percent drop out before graduation. Yet jobs at the low-skill end—such as fast food, retail, and transportation—will only increase. Studies suggest that by 2016, over seventy million jobs will require a high school education or less, and will likely be increasingly filled by immigrants.[93]

In addition, as the retirement population in the United States booms, the numbers of U.S. immigrants moving to Mexico will likely follow. Already an important part of the one-million-strong American expat community in Mexico, these empty nesters have taken over places such as San Miguel de Allende, Guanajuato, or the shores of Lake Chapala in the state of Jalisco.[94] Pushed by shrinking savings, uncertain labor markets, and rising health care costs in the United States and pulled by the warmer climate, cheap real estate, even cheaper services, and adventure, millions more may move south. As many attest when explaining their decision to migrate, "you go to Florida to die, but you come to Mexico to live."[95] These "foreigners" generally do not speak the local language (many even after years abroad), live in enclaves, socialize among themselves, and maintain strong ties to their homeland. Yet Americans expect Mexico to welcome them into its heartland.

The decades-long human flow means that millions of Mexican and U.S. citizens now have parents, children, siblings, or other relatives on both sides of the border. The United States and Mexico are increasingly joined in a virtual family. The challenge today is to make these deepening human ties bring our governments closer together, rather than push them further apart. The parallel political and economic bonds, to which we now turn, make getting the relationship right all the more important.

MEXICO'S LONELY STRUGGLE FOR DEMOCRACY

On the eve of his 1981 State of the Union address, Mexican president López Portillo was in his element, commanding the full power of the PRI presidency at a time of great prosperity. As the autumn began, Mexico's treasury was still filled with oil money and foreign loans, and the state-dominated economy was growing at an 8 percent clip. Foreign bankers eagerly courted the government, lavishly lending to public works projects. All attention was turned toward López Portillo himself, as he coyly received the flattery of rival politicians anxious to be given his nod to become the PRI's candidate and assuredly the next president.

Several years earlier a poor Mexican fisherman named Rudesindo Cantarell had shown up at the local Pemex office to complain about an oil spill. A dark tar had ruined his nets while he was shrimping in the Bay of Campeche. As it turns out, he had inadvertently discovered Mexico's most productive oil field and the second largest in the world. By 1980, the Cantarell field was generating over one million barrels per day, pumping billions of dollars into government coffers and breathing new life into the PRI's political model. The government used these winnings to fund pork-barrel projects and expand social programs to students, professionals, workers, and farmers—essentially bribing politicians and the electorate alike.

Though seemingly its apex, this was, in fact, the system's swan song. It was the last time the PRI's political stranglehold, its party machine, and its imperial presidency would go unchallenged. Under López Portillo's successor, Miguel de la Madrid, Mexico's unwitting transformation would begin. Pushed by economic crisis, and pulled by an active political opposition and an increasingly demanding independent press and civil society, Mexico would finally open politically. Unlike the fall of the Russian or Eastern European Soviet regimes, there was no wall to destroy, no "Velvet Revolution," or Perestroika. Instead, Mexico's opening occurred slowly, at times imperceptibly, over two long decades. It would encompass not just the introduction of political competition, but also shifts in Mexico's economic, social, and cultural foundations. All these changes—some far reaching, some less so—would begin with the 1982 debt crisis.

CRACKS IN THE FACADE

In May 1982, Jesús Silva Herzog, Mexico's finance minister, was again lunching at the Federal Reserve with its chairman, Paul Volcker. In their numerous secret Friday meetings, the two men tried to find a palatable way to solve a glaring problem: Mexico was effectively bankrupt. With the markets sensing blood, capital was fleeing, the peso plummeting, and inflation and unemployment rising. Of more concern to the United States, this grim scenario threatened to spread. If Mexico fell, so too would many celebrated U.S. banking giants, endangering the global financial system. And Mexico's July presidential election was just around the corner. Washington disliked Mexico's nondemocratic system, but it feared instability more, and it was determined not to upset the status quo.

While both financiers suspected an economic collapse was inevitable, Volcker authorized a series of massive short-term loans to the Mexican government to help buy time—and the PRI its electoral victory. This ensured that the authoritarian system would remain intact, even if everything else fell apart. That it did, on Friday, August thirteenth, when Silva Herzog returned to Washington to announce that Mexico could not pay the interest on its US$80 billion foreign debt. To shore up the world's financial system—and the PRI's political capital—the U.S. government quickly compiled a rescue package and jump-started debt renegotiations. While ultimately successful, a full-blown debt crisis—one that would spread from Mexico throughout the developing world—had begun.

Despite the efforts of both the U.S. and Mexican governments, the crisis changed the political game for the PRI. The PRI had long ago structured itself along "corporatist" lines—creating official labor unions, peasant groups, business organizations, and professional associations to channel interests and demands through the party faithful. With the economic pie at home no longer expanding, the government could not as easily mollify these vested interests, chipping away the glue of patronage that held the system together. De la Madrid also used the economic crisis as an opportunity to ram through his preferred economic policies—upending the economic and political system to the consternation of many party elites (not to mention the masses).

As these first few cracks appeared, Mexico's political opposition was finally ready to take advantage. The long-standing and long-suffering opposition National Action Party, or PAN, had gotten past its 1976 midlife crisis—when internal divisions and strife kept it from even fielding a presidential candidate.[1] Now reunited and reenergized, it benefited politically from the PRI's cavalier and destructive economic ways, welcoming professionals, business leaders, and ordinary folks into its core group of activists. The independent left too was on the rise, and later was bolstered by discontented PRI leaders that broke with the party.

The first region to turn decisively away from the PRI was the north. Cities such as Ciudad Juárez, Chihuahua, and Monterrey had always been suspicious of the capital's authority, complaining about inward-looking economic policies and taxation systems that favored the center. The economic downturn was for many the last straw.

The political rumblings began shortly after the debt crisis started. In the local 1983 elections—to the shock of PRI and PAN operatives alike—voters swarmed to the opposition. In its best showing to date, the PAN swept Chihuahua's biggest cities and gained ground in other northern states such as San Luis Potosí, Durango, and Sonora.

This volatile situation came to a head in 1985, after three years of belt tightening, when an 8.1 Richter-scale earthquake hit Mexico City. Striking at just past 7 a.m., the first tremors lasted more than a minute, bucking the earth side to side and up and down, destroying hospitals, hotels, offices, apartment buildings, and schools. Whole blocks in the downtown neighborhoods of Roma, Tlatelolco, and the city's historic center disappeared into debris and dust. A second quake, measured at 6.5, hit the next day, compounding the damage and terrifying residents. All told, the tremors leveled nearly four hundred buildings (about half of them built by the government at one point or another) and killed ten thousand people.[2]

This natural disaster became a political one due to the limited and corrupt response of the ruling party. The all-encompassing PRI system, which discouraged citizens from organizing to solve their own problems, disappeared in the hours, days, and weeks following the quake. Few police, army, or officials came to help dig out survivors, hand out supplies, or shepherd the nearly two hundred thousand homeless to shelter. The little public aid doled out went not to the neediest citizens but to the PRI's loyal and powerful. The state-controlled newspapers even extolled de la Madrid's defiant rejection of U.S. humanitarian aid, illuminating the government's "let them eat cake" mentality toward the battered citizens of Mexico City.

With little government assistance forthcoming, Mexicans from across the city helped each other. Students mixed with bus drivers, day laborers with doctors, seamstresses with artists. Neighbors and total strangers joined together to form bucket brigades to remove rubble, evacuate the sick and wounded, rescue babies, disperse food, direct traffic, and console the less fortunate. Coalescing at first around housing projects and neighborhoods, some of these rescue and humanitarian actions evolved into organizations critical of the ruling party, and ready to join with other long-standing groups and activists and dip into politics.

These trends in the north and in the capital came together in the 1986 Chihuahua governor's race, redefining the political landscape. The PAN nominated Francisco Barrio Terrazas, a well-liked businessman who was mayor of Ciudad Juárez. Scion of a landed prerevolutionary Chihuahua family, the mustached Barrio Terrazas held the admiration of not just the state's economic establishment but also its more eclectic political opposition. He faced the PRI's bespectacled Fernando Baeza Meléndez, a thoughtful lawyer who had at one point been part of the PAN. This time, the PRI was more than ready for the PAN's surging popularity. Though polls showed the PAN would win the vote, the PRI made sure it won the count. In the weeks leading up to the election it scrubbed thousands of PAN sympathizers from voting lists and pressured local officials to create "extra" voting credentials. The day of the election the PRI stuffed ballot boxes, ejected poll monitors, and even sent out soldiers to intimidate the opposition. At the end of the day, the PRI declared victory.

Protests erupted throughout the state as Catholic bishops threatened to cancel mass, and business leaders and thousands upon thousands of ordinary Chihuahans stopped work, jammed traffic, and marched through Ciudad Juárez demanding the election's annulment. Straw-hatted *campesinos* walked tens of miles to march alongside well-dressed women, all waving the PAN's orange, blue, and white flags. The protestors occupied Juárez's international bridges, parking their pick-up trucks, setting up makeshift tents, and attracting the U.S. and international press to their cause.

The U.S. Congress waded into the fray, creating strange bedfellows in North Carolina Republican senator Jesse Helms and Massachusetts Democratic senator John Kerry, who both denounced electoral fraud and drug-laden corruption and pushed to decertify Mexico during the annual counternarcotics review. The PAN reached out to international organizations and even to the Organization of American States' Inter-American Human Rights Commission, claiming that its members' human rights had been violated by Mexico's electoral laws. Many of Mexico's most prominent intellectuals threw their weight behind the marches, with dozens signing their names to an open letter denouncing the fraud. But the PRI steamrolled over all these objections and crowned its candidate.

Though the ruling party emerged victorious, the blatant fraud seared opposition leaders from both the left and the right. Despite often ideological differences, protesters joined together to denounce the fraud and intimidation that undergirded the PRI's political monopoly.

Determined not to fade like the ink on voters' fingers, fledgling civil-society groups—including teachers, farmers, and the local chambers of commerce—coalesced into umbrella organizations, committed to advancing a single, measurable goal: clean elections.[3] Activists led street demonstrations, staged sit-ins at PRI-controlled factories, and organized collective hunger strikes.[4] Learning from these early trials, many prepared for the big showdown—the 1988 presidential election.

Pulling Back the PRI's Curtain

With the PRI's paternal mantle in tatters in the earthquake's aftermath, the economy barely recovering, and the pretense of fair elections under pressure, the 1988 presidential election loomed. Limited to just one six-year term, tradition granted the sitting Mexican president the right to choose the PRI nominee, who for decades invariably won by wide margins. Under a veil of party unity and deference, candidates and their supporters fiercely competed for the president's favor, balancing the need to raise their profile with the need not to outshine—and hence threaten—the sitting king. The president, in turn, hoped for a successor who would burnish his legacy, all the while working to put off the selection as long as possible to maintain his own unquestioned authority.

In 1987 the internal jostling was particularly intense. Throughout the PRI's history the presidency had shifted between party factions, enticing those not in control to wait loyally for their chance rather than strike out on their own. As the technocratic de la Madrid neared his term's end, those from other wings of the party felt it was now their turn in Los Pinos, Mexico's White House. Most vocal was a disgruntled leftist faction led by PRI royalty, calling itself the Democratic Current. Wrapping itself in the blanket of social justice, it railed against de la Madrid's economic policies and demanded an open nomination process in order to rebuild the PRI's loyal base. But the traditional closed-door process prevailed. De la Madrid crowned Carlos Salinas de Gortari, a controversial technocrat nicknamed the "atomic ant"—both for his boundless energy and his diminutive stature. Rebuffed, the Democratic Current broke away.

Grassroots groups and the independent left joined with these rebellious priistas to challenge the political status quo. As their candidate Cuauhtémoc Cárdenas traversed the country in his bid for Mexico's highest office, hundreds of thousands came out to see the son of revered 1930s PRI president Lázaro Cárdenas and hear his promises of a different and better future. Though hardly charismatic, the understated Cárdenas quickly gained public support, outshining Salinas. The PAN's candidate, the well-regarded businessman Manuel Clouthier, cut into PRI support as well, especially in the north. There was pressure on both sides as election night approached. With fewer of its proverbial carrots (handouts and patronage jobs), Mexico's governing party turned to its ready sticks—intimidation and fraud.

Salinas was not in the room when the federal government honchos decided to literally pull the plug. The early election night reports from Mexico City looked bad, as precinct after precinct went to Cárdenas, not the PRI. The utterly impossible seemed increasingly probable, that the dissident turncoat would win the popular vote. Just before eight o'clock in the evening, the powerful Ministry of the Interior cut opposition access to the vote tallying computer. The next day Salinas delivered his victory speech. When the final count was announced a full week later, Salinas had officially won the election with 50.4 percent of the votes.

Opposition supporters took to the streets, claiming fraud. Just days later, a quarter-million faithful filled the capital's vast main square, the Zócalo, to hear their candidate speak.[5] A carnival air, with children riding on their parents' shoulders and infants sleeping in grandmothers' *rebozo* shawls, mixed with an indignant and more menacing undertone, punctuated by intermittent shouts of "The people voted, Cárdenas won!" and "Death to the PRI!" As chants of "Justicia! Justicia!" and a sea of hands holding up two fingers for victory filled the raucous square, effigies of the PRI's standard-bearer were set on fire. Yet even as he spoke from the raised wooden stage to this willing army of followers, Cárdenas hesitated to enter into open warfare with his former colleagues. He instead chose to calm the crowd, talking only of legal redress.[6]

The PRI party machine had no such qualms. Thugs broke up rallies, police harassed Cárdenas's supporters, and the media threw its weight behind the ruling power. The PAN too turned away from demanding a transparent count, instead negotiating a backroom deal with the PRI for more congressional seats and reforms that would strengthen its future electoral chances.[7] By the late summer, the revolutionary window closed, leaving Salinas firmly in control.

With the 1988 election, the United States missed an opportunity to alter its traditionally passive approach toward its neighbor's internal politics. Mexico's economic and natural disasters had already weakened the PRI's grip. Moreover U.S. officials definitively knew they were not working with the good guys. The 1985 murder of Drug Enforcement Administration (DEA) agent Enrique "Kiki" Camarena laid bare the ugly corruption and violence permeating Mexico's government. As the details of the agent's kidnapping, torture, and death emerged, all knew Mexican security forces had done him in. Many believed the orders came from President de la Madrid's inner circle.

Nevertheless, U.S. reaction to Mexico's budding democratic movement was studied silence. No support emanated for the marchers, the opposition parties, or the nongovernmental organizations demanding a clean and transparent election. Washington moved ahead and recognized Salinas as president. Ronald Reagan, along with Spain's Felipe González, were the first international leaders to offer congratulations. Despite the glimmers of political change within Mexico, the White House firmly chose sullied stability over democracy, reaffirming for all Mexicans the disconnect between U.S. rhetoric and reality when it came to democracy.

The opposition parties eventually forgave the United States for its acquiescence, but it meant another decade of PRI control. This affected the path of Mexico's economic opening—monopolies were allowed to remain firmly in place even as the economy opened and the state receded. The change in leadership did nothing to stem migration north, as many left to escape the PRI's politics and its repeated economic crises. And it affected Mexico's security by delaying the arduous work required to establish a fair, democratic rule of law.

But luckily for Mexico, the 1988 election was not the end of the story. This saga stripped away much of the PRI's electoral legitimacy and spurred reforms that, in unintended ways, did in fact open up new political space. Nodding to voter dissatisfaction, Salinas decided to recognize the PAN's triumph in the 1989 Baja California gubernatorial race, marking the first time the PRI had accepted such a high level opposition victory. This ended, once and for all, the PRI's absolute political monopoly. In a move to consolidate his power, Salinas created the National Solidarity Program, or Pronasol, a new social initiative controlled directly by his office. Presented as an innovative program for local development projects, it allowed the president to bypass the PRI's traditional power structures while pumping cash into opposition-leaning neighborhoods and cultivating the personal loyalty of its recipients.[8] Though the initiative boosted PRI votes in the midterm and 1994 presidential elections, it also upset the PRI's official labor unions, peasant organizations, and other vested interests accustomed to managing these types of patronage resources themselves. Many fought back, successfully retaining control of congressional seats and party leadership slots and regaining control of bureaucratic money pots (though these diminished substantially during the 1990s as privatized companies moved out of state-controlled hands and the Salinas government worked to shrink the public sector more generally).[9] The attempted shake-up did, however, weaken the foundations of the PRI's traditional political coalition, opening the door for future change.

In the wake of their defeats, both the PAN and the newly formed left-leaning Democratic Revolutionary Party, or PRD, continued to pry the democratic door open. Throughout the 1990s they filled the streets with demonstrators and the courts with lawyers, denouncing the regime's electoral shenanigans. Behind the scenes, the PAN and somewhat less successfully the PRD built up and professionalized their party structures, hiring full-time staff and creating internal norms, procedures, and even training programs for activists and would-be candidates.[10] They also set about governing in the growing number of local and state governments under their control.

In 1994, riding high on NAFTA's passage and a booming economy, even the assassination of its chosen candidate, Luis Donaldo Colosio, couldn't stop the PRI's electoral momentum. Colosio's campaign manager and haphazard successor, Ernesto Zedillo Ponce de León, had a much easier path than Salinas, by all accounts freely winning the presidential election.[11] Yet this uptick in the PRI's fortunes was short lived. Under President Zedillo the PRI's political monopoly would permanently end.

THE OPPOSITION'S ROAD TO VICTORY

Juan Quirino, a founder of the Barzón, a debtor-led social movement, watched the plastic melt unevenly onto the cobblestone sidewalks of Mexico's historic city center. Acrid smoke filled the air as his fellow protesters burned thousands of credit cards in front of the Mexican Banking Association's headquarters. Just the week before he had been part of a caravan of tractors headed to the House of Representatives to plead their case, snarling traffic throughout the city. Behind these dramatic scenes Barzón lawyers diligently filed lawsuit after lawsuit on behalf of small and midsize store owners, farmers, microentrepreneurs, taxi drivers, bank stock holders, credit card debtors—those hit by the 1994 peso devaluation and subsequent economic crisis, which led to plummeting GDP, soaring inflation, and the loss of millions of jobs. Debt taken on in good times—to buy a house, purchase supplies, or expand a business—skyrocketed as the peso went into free fall. The banks so far had taken a hard line, piling fees on top of the now over 100 percent interest rates. The Barzonistas didn't march for debt forgiveness, but for a fair shake. As these working and middle class activists struggled to hold onto their livelihoods, to their very homes, they noticed that the bankers kept driving their Mercedes. Then President Ernesto Zedillo announced a US$67 billion bailout—not for Mexico's hardworking citizens, but for the Hermès-tie-wearing financial crowd.

By the late 1990s, Mexico's growing economic center felt deeply betrayed by the PRI. The unspoken trade-off of political acquiescence for economic gain ended with the 1995 Mexican peso crisis. Two unforeseen shocks—one in the south, the other in the north—also helped overturn the decades-long status quo. On New Year's Day 1994 (the same day NAFTA came into effect), a group of three thousand men and women, dressed in all black, wearing ski masks, and carrying AK-47s, descended on the town square of San Cristóbal de las Casas. They declared themselves the Zapatista National Liberation Army, and demanded the government stop stealing their natural resources and oppressing the local people. Two weeks later—facing the imminent arrival of fifteen thousand troops—the Zapatistas retreated into the remote Chiapas jungle. But they continued their cause through skirmishes and a savvy media campaign. Their spokesperson (though not technically leader) was Subcomandante Marcos, a light-skinned alleged former philosophy professor with a sense of humor and an eloquent way of discussing the injustices faced by Mexico's indigenous and poor. The Zapatista movement drew international press attention, celebrity visits, and inspired widespread domestic sympathy through its calls to protect indigenous rights and to end corruption. Just over two months later, the government faced a second crisis: the assassination of the PRI's presidential candidate and heir apparent, Luis Donaldo Colosio, at a political rally in Tijuana.

At the same time, changes within the government provided new space to voice discontent. In 1993 Salinas had thrown the opposition a few political reform bones, including official (though largely ignored) campaign finance restrictions and recognition for independent election observers. But with these two blows, and fearing for his own reputation and the potentially enormous costs of political turmoil for NAFTA, Salinas felt compelled to sit down with the opposition parties to hammer out more far-reaching changes. He acquiesced to leave the Federal Electoral Institute (IFE) in the hands of citizen councillors, to open Mexican elections to greater scrutiny by domestic and international observers alike, and to criminalize electoral fraud.

President Zedillo, never a party insider, had no stomach for the rougher side of the PRI's politics. Opposition parties, independent scholars, activist judges, and electoral councillors, all keen to change the system, jumped on his openness to political reform. The 1996 electoral reform was a true game-changer. It fully freed the IFE from vestiges of PRI control, pulling it out from under the watchful eye and often heavy hand of the Ministry of the Interior. The now truly citizen-led electoral agency took on full responsibility for counting votes and confirming elections—cutting out the politicians and their previous vote-tallying tricks. The law went after the always lopsided financial balance. It opened up government coffers for more than just the PRI by mandating generous public financing for all parties. It also expanded the reach and independence of the electoral court, removing it from the executive branch's control and putting teeth into this once paper tiger.

The first big test of these new institutions was the 1997 midterm election. Opposition candidates won two of the six governorships up for grabs—their best showing yet. Cuauhtémoc Cárdenas, the 1988 presidential candidate, won in the first-ever election for Mexico City mayor—second only to the presidency in terms of political prominence. The biggest coup, however, occurred in Congress, as the combined right and left oppositions toppled the PRI's long-standing majority in the House of Representatives, meaning that for the first time the ruling party would have to deal with a fractious legislature to pass ordinary legislation. These substantial changes in the electoral map hinted at underlying shifts that became clear in the 2000 presidential election: the center had decisively abandoned the old regime.

Scholars debate whether opposition party organization, voter dissatisfaction, civil society activism, or access to resources mattered more in Mexico's slow democratization.[12] Whatever the mix, the 2000 election marked the presidential downfall of the PRI. On the election's eve, opposition politicians governed over half of Mexico's population at the local level (and controlled roughly one-third of state and federal positions). Insinuations of instability or even chaos under the opposition—used effectively by the PRI in earlier national elections—no longer resonated. Neither did the lackluster campaign of the PRI's candidate, Francisco Labastida. Despite the economy's revival and the incumbent's popularity, his campaign slogan of "Change with Direction" rang hollow.

Instead, the PAN presidential candidate Vicente Fox, a six-foot-five, cowboy-boot-wearing former Coca-Cola executive from the northern state of Guanajuato, won. Mexican political analysts were stunned; local and international followers alike hailed the arrival of democracy. In the postgame analysis, Mexico's rising middle class—led by city-dwelling high school and university graduates—had voted for change, finally tipping Mexico's political balance.[13]

Close watchers on the campaign trail saw the shift happening. Rallies for Fox brought out young students, middle class shopkeepers, small farmers, housewives, as well as the curious, creating an ethereal sea to which the open-collared, blue-shirted jovial candidate waved and flashed his two-fingered Y—symbolizing "Ya!" or "Enough!" Crowds howled in appreciation, whistling and chanting "Kiss! Kiss!" as the towering presidential hopeful doubled over to hug grandmotherly supporters.[14] Armed with blue and white PAN flags and foam fingers emblazoned with his rallying cry, the mosh pits of supporters treated the often sweat-drenched Fox more like a rock star than a politician, snapping pictures and trying to touch the candidate as he passed.

The contrast with PRI rallies was palpable. The slighter and graying Francisco Labastida relied on the party machine, rather than any macho charisma, to turn out supporters. Mexicans still dutifully showed up—often brought in battered buses from across the state by PRI activists—but shared none of the spontaneity or raw energy of the crowds following the PAN's "Marlboro man." Farmers and factory workers, promised a day's wage and a soft drink to attend (and sometimes threatened with dismissal if they didn't), could be heard questioning the PRI candidate, shouting "Don't break your promise!" above the din of perfunctory applause.[15] In Oaxaca, Labastida's pledge to put computers in schools that couldn't feed their students was met with sharp rebukes from critics, scoffing that the "students' first email would read 'we're hungry.'"[16] In the televised debate Labastida fared no better, complaining about Fox's campaign taunts and rough-hewn language, and unconvincingly describing himself as the candidate for change as leader of a "new PRI," even as he surrounded himself with the old-school party veterans, the so-called dinosaurs.

On election night, Fox crushed his PRI competitor by 2.5 million votes (and left the PRD's Cárdenas a distant third). Just after 11 p.m., President Zedillo, standing in front of a portrait of much-loved nineteenth-century president Benito Juárez, formally recognized this peaceful revolution. The PAN faithful, and not a few PRD supporters, flocked to the Angel of Independence monument on Reforma Avenue, a traditional focus for both protest and celebration in Mexico City. Just after 1 a.m., a smiling Fox mounted the steps below the gilded statue to greet his supporters. The confetti-covered crowd—backed by mariachi bands—broke into a rendition of "Las Mañanitas," Mexico's traditional birthday serenade. With the multitude, Fox celebrated his victory and his fifty-eighth birthday.

A Wasted U.S. Opportunity

The year 2000 offered a chance to redefine U.S.-Mexico political relations. NAFTA had already deepened economic ties and investment, while two decades of constant immigration had brought people and communities together. The arrival of homegrown democracy created an opening for a new official relationship between the two nations.

At first, it looked as if this would indeed happen. Presidents Fox and George W. Bush—both ranch-loving former border governors—got along well. After his inauguration, Bush quickly headed south to Mexico to visit his "amigo" at his Guanajuato San Cristóbal ranch. Walking past rows of broccoli, the two presidents—cabinet ministers, aides, and other officials in tow—held wide-ranging conversations about economic prosperity, border security, and immigration reform.

The U.S. president then invited Fox for his first state dinner, much to the Canadians' consternation. President Fox came in his tuxedo and cowboy boots, with his former press secretary and now bride beside him as official First Lady. The celebratory fireworks at the meal's end mirrored the excitement in both capitals. In less formal wear, staffers from both countries discussed immigration, trade, and visions of a mutual future. Mexican foreign minister Jorge Castañeda talked confidently about getting "the whole enchilada"—a comprehensive immigration reform—for his country in the first year of both presidents' administrations. It seemed as if the sedate policies of the past would be pushed aside by a bold new bilateral agenda.

Yet as had happened so frequently in the past, misunderstandings and hurt feelings derailed these initial advances. With the first hint of domestic pressure (much of it from within his own Republican party), President Bush began backpedaling on immigration. The September 11 attacks doomed the chances for reform, as immigration policy became a main tool for combating terrorism. Disparate responses from within the Fox administration, as well as from within the Mexican media and society, ruffled U.S. feathers.[17] Talk of mutual prosperity fell victim to a U.S. obsession with border security.[18] The growing tension between the two neighbors reached its peak in 2002 when Mexico, as a voting member of the UN Security Council, announced that it would not support a U.S. resolution to invade Iraq. The two presidents went from farm chums to hostile foreigners, pointedly ignoring one another at subsequent multilateral summits.

Plagued by misperceptions and domestic political pressures on both sides, neither country seemed able or willing to move beyond the old tropes, instead reasserting the diplomatic distance between the two nations even though economic, personal, and now political gaps had faded. As the United States turned to nation building and democracy promotion in Afghanistan and Iraq, it missed an opportunity to support another emerging democracy—this one much closer to home. It left Mexico seemingly alone to face the daunting challenges of building democratic institutions and a stable rule of law after decades of authoritarian rule.

FROM DEMOCRATIZING TO GOVERNING

Fox's presidency was one of positive changes, but also missed opportunities at home. The PRI's ouster from Los Pinos ended many of Mexico's old fiefdoms and undemocratic ways of doing business. More proactively, Fox began systematically unraveling the government's more repressive elements. He halved the funding for CISEN—Mexico's CIA—which had been used by the PRI to spy on opposition candidates such as himself, and he reformed (and weakened) the Ministry of the Interior, for decades the bastion of the PRI's hardball tactics and repressive hand.

Fox took to heart the aspirations (and demands) of his middle class voters. He managed to push through financial reforms that led, for the first time, to widespread mortgage and consumer lending, allowing home ownership to reach new heights. This was followed by the first-ever Civil Service Law, making hiring less opaque and more rigorous, at least for a segment of government workers. Fox also tried to tackle increasing insecurity, disbanding the notoriously corrupt judicial police and creating a new FBI-style agency. He created a new health-care system for Mexico's uninsured—roughly half the population.

Perhaps his biggest win was a freedom of information law, opening the dark corners of government to public scrutiny. Here Fox was pushed along by Mexico's budding civic organizations. Expectations were high, as Fox had barnstormed the country talking about transparency and openness throughout his campaign. While Fox and his new wife redecorated the marbled halls of the presidential compound, a group of journalists, editors, scholars, lawyers, and human rights activists met in the city of Oaxaca. Surrounded by lush gardens and blooming jacaranda trees, nearly one hundred representatives from across Mexico filled the halls of Anáhuac University, resolving to hold the government to its promise.

Returning to Mexico City, Grupo Oaxaca's technical committee began meeting in the home of a former PRI communications secretary and long-time *El Universal* editor Luis Javier Solana. For hours, the academics and news editors sat in the wood-paneled study and paced the dark blue and red oriental rugs, debating the broadest philosophical goals and smallest technical points as they struggled to draft their ideal bill. They gathered at breakfast and worked until well past Mexico's late lunch, with only brief breaks in the secluded backyard. These long days turned into weeks, then months. But by October the effort was complete; a detailed piece of legislation supporting broad access to information was ready to submit to Congress.

Grupo Oaxaca then began to feel its way through the newly minted democratic political system. Mexico's leading newspapers launched a full court press, publishing articles, op-eds, and interviews in support of the reform.[19] *Reforma* even started a new "Joe Citizen" column, which offered readers concrete examples of how an access law would directly affect— and improve—their daily lives. One column told the story of a taxi driver ignored after reporting the theft of his cab, and showed how the law would force the government to respond to his unanswered pleas.[20]

Members of the group also converged on the halls of Congress. With the country's leading editors and journalists in tow—Roberto Rock of *El Universal*, Jenaro Villamil from *La Jornada*, and Miguel Bernardo Treviño of *Reforma*—the doors of congressional PAN leader Felipe Calderón and PRI head Beatriz Paredes opened. The PRD too gave its early support for these citizen crusaders.

As public and political pressure mounted, the Fox administration urged Congress to pass transparency legislation, offering up its own, much weaker, bill. Grupo Oaxaca dove into the negotiations, edging its way into the closed-door committees and drafting and redrafting sessions. After weeks of debate, negotiation, and last-minute grandstanding, the final bill passed unanimously at the end of April 2002. In it, Grupo Oaxaca got nearly everything it wanted.

Mexico's transparency law became an international gold standard for access to information—rivaled by few in its scope and openness.[21] Through the new and independent Federal Institute for Access to Public Information (IFAI), it helped to open up the black box of Mexico's government, requiring every public agency and program to create "transparency portals" that post information for all to see, including budgets, staffs, salaries, new contracts, and concessions.[22] This means your average Josefina can find out who is building the new road that passes by her house, how much they are being paid, and how the construction plans might affect her property. Or your typical José can learn how many people work for the local police department, and how much they earn. The agency also created an online system so citizens can solicit further information from their government. Nearly seven hundred thousand such requests have been made and granted so far.[23]

Yet the openness varies across agencies and topics. The Ministry of the Economy is perhaps most open to interchange, while the Treasury, Attorney General's office, and federal police are more likely to dodge requests. And even though the law explicitly prohibits withholding any information—no matter how sensitive—regarding human rights violations, one of the most egregious violations came from the National Human Rights Commission itself. The agency demanded more than US$50,000 (averaging eight dollars per sheet) to fulfill a request for copies of six filed complaints.[24]

Nevertheless, these steps away from the previous bureaucratic opacity are monumental. Scoring one of independent civil society's greatest victories, the concerted campaign demonstrated to citizens and politicians alike the potential power of Mexican society.

Despite these real gains, Fox's scorecard remained sadly lopsided. In part he was held back by the weak formal powers of the Mexican presidency. The president can serve only one term, has limited line item veto power, and little influence over federal transfers to the states.[25] He was hindered by the deep divides among the three parties in Congress, and the difficulties of creating legislative coalitions necessary to pass laws big or small. But he also did not seize the momentum for change. This left untaken many of the steps necessary to strengthen Mexico's democracy: courts remained unreformed, police undertrained, economic competition limited, entrepreneurs stifled, education unchanged, and electoral laws untouched. Instead, Fox left these to his successor, who would also struggle within the confines of Mexico's political system.

A New President, the Same Challenges

Felipe Calderón was not Fox's preferred candidate. But, in a strong sign of the changes in Mexico, he did not have much choice. A party insider, Calderón deftly outmaneuvered Fox's interior minister Santiago Creel to win over the small cadre of PAN loyalists able to vote in the party's closed primaries. Securing the nomination, he then turned to the greater electoral threat—the PRD candidate, former Mexico City mayor and presidential heir apparent, Andrés Manuel López Obrador (dubbed AMLO by the media). A popular and populist leader, AMLO led in the polls in the months heading into July's election. Fox's earlier attempts to disqualify him through the blatantly political use of legal technicalities involving a land dispute during his tenure as mayor only made him more popular. The perceived injustice and persecution rallied AMLO's supporters—a broad-based mix of leftist intellectuals, older, middle-income voters, members of the Catholic Church, and the poor.[26]

As AMLO rose in the polls, so, too, did the silver-haired politician's rhetoric: he promised to create massive public works and to renegotiate NAFTA, and ranted against a mysterious ruling cabal conspiring against him. Though no match for this orator, the younger, more straight-laced Calderón countered with a tight, media-driven campaign, mixing promises of clean government, jobs, and better safety with attack ads painting his opponent as a menace and danger.

In the end it worked, as Calderón squeaked out a win validated by the country's autonomous electoral institute and tribunal—besting his leftist competitor by less than a percentage point and fewer than 250,000 votes (out of some 41 million). AMLO, scarred by the fraud-riddled 1988 presidential election and his own unfair loss in the 1994 Tabasco governor race, refused to accept the results. Mexico was thrown into turmoil as PRD activists camped across Reforma Avenue's six wide lanes for nearly two weeks, effectively shutting down the capital. Eight weeks later, in early September, the electoral authorities confirmed Calderón's triumph. Rather than accept the result— à la Al Gore in 2000 or even Cuauhtémoc Cárdenas back in 1988—AMLO just got angrier.

Tumultuous crowds and street demonstrations followed the spurned candidate's every move as he barnstormed across the country, and as he staged his own swearing-in ceremony in Mexico City's Zócalo.[27] He and members of his party tried to stop the official inauguration, cutting short the traditional hand-over in the halls of Congress. Calling himself the "legitimate president" of Mexico, he never recognized Calderón's victory.

Despite this rather inauspicious beginning, Calderón had many things going for him. A different man than Fox, he loved the rough and tumble of politics, lighting up rather than shying away from the congressional melee. Congress, too, had evolved in the decade of divided government; its political parties increasingly recognized the need to compromise to get anything done, and they often did. In his first years Calderón pushed through reforms to the public pension system, the tax code, and to Pemex, the state-owned oil monopoly (not to mention passing the annual federal budget). While his critics claim the legislation was watered down, the president repeatedly cobbled together successful coalitions from across the political spectrum to pass new laws.

His most potentially far-reaching win was the 2008 judicial reform, which, once implemented (by 2016), will fundamentally transform Mexico's justice system. Almost no one in Mexico claims that the former (and still active) system works. The numbers are more than disturbing. Studies show that at least eight out of ten crimes are never even reported.[28] Victims distrust the authorities or feel it would be a waste of time to report a crime. More perniciously, gatekeepers in the public prosecutor's office at times discourage filing charges in an effort to lower official crime-rate statistics.[29] Of the small portion reported, less than 20 percent are investigated. In the end, just one or two of every hundred crimes result in convictions. Even then, doubts repeatedly emerge as to whether the defendants—most of whom are quickly convicted—are actually criminals.

The challenges to getting a fair trial are laid out in cinematic clarity by the Emmy award-winning documentary *Presunto Culpable*, or *Presumed Guilty*. It tells the true, heart-wrenching story of Antonio "Toño" Zúñiga, a street vendor from Iztapalapa, a working-class neighborhood on the edge of Mexico City.[30] The film follows Toño's appeal process and his struggle to overturn a murder conviction. Even with several eyewitnesses testifying that Toño was miles away manning his market stall at the time of the killing, and the prosecution's main witness and lead detective discredited during their testimony, the judge refused to overturn the initial guilty verdict. When asked why she wanted to convict Toño if all the evidence pointed to his innocence, the lead prosecutor laughed and said "because that's my job."

Thanks to the cameras, a higher appeals court finally took the case and Toño was set free. But the shocking treatment and miscarriage of justice built into the system—and suffered by the thousands and thousands unfilmed—is palpable. The written process, which produces reams and reams of paper, makes public scrutiny almost impossible. When a prosecutor does take on a case, defendants face an uphill battle for freedom, as guilt is, for all intents and purposes, assumed. From the smallest to the most heinous crimes, confessions are the main source of evidence. No Miranda rights exist, and allegations (as well as substantial evidence) of torture are rampant. Juries do not exist, defense attorneys are weak, and judges rarely show up, much less search for the truth—the only constant is the typing away of the court stenographer, taking down pages of information on which the lives of individuals and families hang in the balance. Toño's tale hints too at a larger sad reality—those actually prosecuted and convicted come from Mexico's poorest. About half of those in Mexico City's prisons are there for petty theft of less than US$20.[31] For innocents thrown into the system—if one cannot buy his or her way out fast—the results can be horrific.

Still, reforming the beleaguered system was far from easy. As in Fox's successes, citizens again played a crucial role. It was Ernesto Canales's pro bono work that led him down the path to citizen advocate. Over lunch at Monterrey's El Granero, he described to me how he came face to face with the injustices of Mexico's legal system through his work at Renace, a nonprofit bringing together some of Mexico's well-known lawyers to offer legal representation to Mexico's less fortunate. One memorable case involved defending a man convicted of murdering a much younger one in a fight. If the judge had ever met the defendant, he would have seen the ridiculousness of the charges the poor pensioner was unable to stand, much less fight, having lost his legs years before.

After eight years working in the trenches, Ernesto and his colleagues began pushing for more systematic change. They started at home, calling on Nuevo León's governor (and, conveniently, Ernesto's cousin). While sympathetic, Governor Fernando Canales gently turned them away, saying that to move the political system they had to get the bureaucracy on board. And so Renace began holding seminar after seminar, open and closed events, and talking to judges, lawyers, professors, and business owners, then mayors, legislators, and party activists about the injustices of Mexico's court system, backing up their pleas with cases, statistics, and comparisons. Though some doors remained closed, they persevered. By 2004, Nuevo León's politicians were not only listening but finally acting through legislation, transforming the way the courts worked for local crimes. This groundbreaking change was soon followed by similar makeovers in the states of Mexico, Chihuahua, and Oaxaca.

But these state-level wins were just the start. Ernesto and his colleagues wanted more—a national overhaul. They joined with other like-minded lawyers, academics, and activists to form the Network for Oral Trials, which would grow to over a hundred organizations in the push for change, including one of Mexico's chambers of commerce, many well-known research universities, and media outlets such as *Reforma*. The group received support from international foundations as well as the U.S. government to do studies, surveys, and analyses that would, in the end, overcome the inertia and outright opposition from some quarters.[32]

Fox had tried and failed to change the judicial system under his watch, but his efforts put the courts' shortcomings fully on the agenda. Combined with Calderón's immediate concerns about the weak tools police and prosecutors had to go after organized crime, an opportunity opened up for rethinking Mexico's entire justice system. Like Grupo Oaxaca, the Network for Oral Trials brought together a handful of the best academic thinkers from Mexico's universities to draft their ideal reform. The larger group then began the political push. Courting the political parties, they first got the congressional opposition—the PRI and PRD—on board. The head of the House Justice Committee, César Camacho, became the bill's political champion. Wanting a deal—and not to be caught out politically—the PAN joined in. After months of haggling over different texts and amendments, between both the political parties and the House and Senate, the final reform took shape and passed with the full backing of the PRI and the PAN.[33]

The 2008 constitutional judicial reform does away with the worst of the old system—starting with the de facto presumption of guilt. It introduces oral trials, bolsters due process, better protects the rights of defendants and victims, and gives law enforcement new and stronger tools to combat criminal networks.[34] The reform, along with ongoing efforts to professionalize Mexico's federal police, represents the best of the Calderón government's achievements. Yet both depend on being continued, deepened, and, in the case of justice reform, which is not due for completion until 2016, enacted. The big question remains whether all of this will indeed happen.

Notwithstanding these advances, many also judge Calderón's six-year term as one of missed opportunities. Security overwhelmed the domestic agenda, pushing many crucial issues to the backbench. Advancements in infrastructure crept along at a glacial pace, even before the 2008 global financial crisis put a freeze on lending. Mexico's low tax rate, its concentrated industries, and its still at times opaque politics were just kicked down the political road for the next administration.

MEXICO'S DEMOCRATIC BALANCE

By the second decade of the twenty-first century, Mexico's electoral democracy was firmly established. On nearly every comparative international measure of democracy, Mexico ranks in the upper tiers. The POLITY index, which looks at the institutions of the central government and political groups, places Mexico solidly in the "democracy" category. The Bertelsmann Transformation Index (BTI), which includes economic indicators in its measure, ranks Mexico in the top third of 128 nations.[35] The Economist, whose measure incorporates civil liberties, placed Mexico among "flawed democracies," its second-highest ranking, alongside France and Italy. Freedom House has also historically ranked Mexico's political rights quite high as well, though in 2011 it slipped to the top of its "partly free" category, not so much due to government actions but its inactions and the violent rise of organized crime.

Three sizable parties and a few smaller ones compete regularly in largely free and fair elections from the presidency on down. The Federal Electoral Institute's standing and autonomy, if slightly battered, survived the contentious 2006 electoral storm. Relations between the executive and legislative branches have developed into the slow, plodding, and incremental approach so well known in other democracies—including the United States. While at times constraining changes that could boost Mexico's productivity, transparency, and even safety, it reaffirms that in a country once renowned for its imperial president, checks and balances now work. Divided government is the order of the day, with the president and the Congress battling it out over issues as large as defining the role of the military in the war on drugs and as mundane as allotting the appropriate number of parking spaces for members of Congress and their staff.[36] These restraints run vertically as well—up, down, and between the federal, state, and local governments—providing a voice for local politicians virtually ignored during the PRI's heyday.

Courts too have come into their own, at least at the highest levels. Where once the judiciary was at the beck and call of the PRI machine, after a mid-1990s overhaul the Supreme Court became an independent and final arbiter—weighing in on topics as diverse as the constitutionality of new legislation, the rules governing elections, and the jurisdiction of civilian courts over the military.[37] Now a real check on and balance to executive and legislative power, it provides a judicial alternative to the more traditional (and less democratic) conflict resolution through backroom political negotiations.

Other transformations, in particular the expansion of an independent press, provide ballasts for Mexico's democracy. During the PRI years the major media outlets were largely propaganda arms for the ruling party. In return for access, advertising, and cold hard cash, journalists and news outlets toed the party line. The culture of collusion was so great that the standard media business model depended not on circulation but on government largesse. In the late 1980s, one tabloid based in Mexico City had a circulation of some five thousand, a staff of 250, and quarterly profits of nearly US$1 million.[38] Journalists practically jumped over one another to provide favorable coverage, using fawning language to "analyze" the latest government program or presidential groundbreaking ceremony. Saving everyone time and pretense, the government often wrote many of the stories itself, with reporters just adding their bylines. Television was even worse; Televisa's owner (only half facetiously) was dubbed the "Minister of Culture."

Just in case the incentives weren't enough, the PRI held a monopoly on newsprint—and was able to literally stop the presses if displeased. And if a reporter or paper got too out of line, the government was not above outright coercion. The swift dismissal of *Excélsior*'s editor-in-chief Julio Scherer García, when he dared to criticize President Luis Echeverría's foreign policy and stance toward trade unions in the mid-1970s, provided a stern warning to those toying with taking a more independent line.

Nevertheless, the subservient status quo began to change just a few years later. Ousted from his national platform and deprived of government funding, Scherer started the maverick weekly magazine *Proceso*. Other nonconformists led the daily newspaper *Unomásuno* and, a few years later, *El Financiero* took an independent and often critical line during the debt crisis. As the PRI government veered right, these renegades were joined on the left by *La Jornada*. Celebrating its first anniversary just as the 1985 earthquake devastated the capital, it filled its pages with the true stories of trauma and loss, and of the government's shortcomings. It told the fate of eight thousand female garment workers in the sweat shops of Calzada San Antonio Abad, trapped under the rubble while government equipment saved only the sewing machines. It ran missing persons lists, worked to reunite families, and listed soup kitchens and shelters. In 1988, it became the voice of the opposition—the only news outlet to cover the presidential campaign of Cuauhtémoc Cárdenas.

In the 1990s the cracks between the government and the fourth estate opened even wider. While regional papers such as *El Norte* in Monterrey and *Siglo 21* in Guadalajara had already brashly rejected the standard deal, the challenge came to Mexico's capital in 1993. *El Norte's* publisher Alejandro Junco, known as both an iconoclastic and tenaciously principled journalist, bet US$50 million of his family's money on the launch of *Reforma*.[39] Hiring young writers rather than professional journalists, paying higher salaries, and forbidding government handouts, the new daily newspaper challenged the old ways from the beginning. Alongside hard-hitting front pages, he added fashion, food, and real-estate sections—unheard of in the capital's media fishbowl. The PRI fought back via the newspaper distributor's union, refusing the newcomer access to thousands of newsstands citywide. In response, *Reforma* set up its own network—at first turning to its own reporters, columnists, and assorted volunteers, then slowly building an army of sellers that now walk Mexico's intersections and street corners and deliver papers to supermarkets, stores, and some eighty-five thousand homes. *Reforma* quickly became a trusted source for Mexico's chattering classes. As the decade wore on (and declining government largesse pressured newspapers to look for readers) the more traditional print media began following *Reforma's* lead.

Television coverage got a boost too, as the upstart TV Azteca nudged in on Televisa's long-time monopoly. Created in 1993, the brasher, more sensational, and more politically open network doggedly gained a following, catching its storied rival flatfooted by daring to interview the opposition. When Televisa deigned to show the opposition candidates on air during the 1994 presidential campaign, it was only in a negative light—replaying students throwing rotten eggs at PAN hopeful Diego Fernández de Cevallos, or selectively and deleteriously editing Cuauhtémoc Cárdenas's campaign stump. TV Azteca, on the other hand, aired full segments of Fernández de Cevallos's and Cárdenas's speeches, and panned to the enthusiastic crowds that came to their rallies.

Events swept away many of the remaining limits. The Zapatista uprising and the assassinations of presidential candidate Donaldo Colosio and later Salinas's ex-brother-in-law and PRI secretary general, José Francisco Ruiz Massieu, confused and frightened not just the Mexican public but also reporters and government officials themselves. The usually smooth political machine was caught off guard, unable to pull together a cohesive narrative, leaving reporters to develop their own voices. The 1995 economic crisis further broke the trust (and, importantly, the payments) between the state and reporters. Journalists stopped ignoring the vast discrepancies between official information and the reality they were experiencing in the streets. The public, too, turned away from those still reflexively reciting the government line, rewarding instead more independent publications. As public advertising and subsidies shrunk, some thirty papers closed up shop. By the late 1990s, the government and readers alike were abandoning the old-style media. To survive, even the most traditional began professionalizing and modernizing their ways.

Today the government no longer controls the media—if anything the tables have been turned. Televisa and TV Azteca dominate the airwaves, and favorable coverage has become a precious commodity for ambitious politicians. Politicians are (rightfully) fearful of ending up on the wrong side of an editorial piece, as the media duopoly has not held back when displeased with a policy direction. An egregious example of politicians running for cover unfolded in the months before the 2006 election, when members of the Mexican Senate quietly passed the Federal Television and Radio Law. Known derisively as the Televisa law, it virtually assured the continuing duopoly of Televisa and TV Azteca, automatically renewing their licenses, giving them preferential access to new bandwidth, and limiting the president's and regulator's ability to foster competition.[40] A year later the Supreme Court struck down most of the provisions.

While some bemoan the commercialization of the Mexican media, it is an improvement over the past. For the high-minded, Mexico now has the problem apparent in many countries with open and competitive presses: gossipy glossies such as *TV y Novelas* (Mexico's version of *People* magazine) routinely outsell more serious newsweeklies.[41] Still, there does seem to be some room for public-interest work. And on television, programs that delve deep are broadcast on smaller stations and more substantive and investigative pieces are featured alongside lifestyle and true-crime stories.

As the press broke free, so too did Mexico's citizens throw off the shackles of the old system. Like their media brethren, civil society organizations had long been coopted or coerced through either legal carrots or, at times, extrajudicial sticks. Whether through control of labor unions, farmer associations, popular organizations, chambers of commerce, or neighborhood watches, the PRI had infiltrated Mexico's associational life. And while not always mandating that citizens join official organizations, the ruling party actively—and fairly effectively—discouraged efforts to organize outside these confines.

Initial steps to throw off the PRI's heavy yoke began in the 1970s. The first independent organizations were focused on human rights, led by distraught mothers, leftist priests, and fearless lawyers denouncing the torture and disappearance of hundreds of political dissidents.[42] In the 1980s, these groups turned to defend the masses of Central American civil-war refugees coming across Mexico's southern border. Banding together in a loose network, they were supported by international compatriots such as Amnesty International, Human Rights Watch (then America's Watch), and later other U.S. foundations. Their combined pressure, along with the murder of a prominent activist, forced President Salinas in 1990 to create a National Human Rights Commission.[43]

In the early 1990s a small group of leading intellectuals, activists, and NGOs coalesced into what became Alianza Cívica, or the Civic Alliance, to demand and force freer and fairer elections. In the months leading up to the 1994 presidential elections, it knit together hundreds of other organizations to back the cause. Standing against the PRI machine, the Civic Alliance organized twelve thousand volunteers to monitor polling stations and document abuses, fraud, and lazy mistakes, such as allowing voters to show their ballots to one another.[44] They did a series of quick counts, making outright fraud at the ballot box much more difficult. The group gained international notice and funding from the National Endowment for Democracy, the National Democratic Institute, and the United Nations Development Programme. By the mid-1990s, they had become the most credible election-monitoring group in Mexico. Staying above the partisan fray, they also became one of the first citizen-based organizations not only to raise its voice but also to provide a real check on government power.

Democracy's victory in 2000 caused something of an identity crisis for Mexico's emerging civil society. Some of the most prominent leaders followed Fox into government, leaving their organizations rudderless. Others, after so many years out in the cold, found it hard to shift gears and adapt to the new landscape, working with, rather than against, the government. Restrictive rules and an uncooperative tax code further hamstrung the sector. The laws limited administrative expenses to just 5 percent of total costs, making it hard to pay the salaries necessary to attract talented people. Mexican citizens could not make tax-deductible contributions, leaving most organizations dependent on international foundations. All together, these left the sector comparatively weak, with fewer organizations than many of Mexico's neighbors and peers.

Nevertheless, the nonprofit sector started to find its democratic footing. Internally, many worked successfully to change the legal framework, making it possible for Mexicans to write off donations to an ever-widening variety of causes. Organizations also began to professionalize, adopting best administrative practices and focusing more time on conducting first-rate studies and drafting technical documents—the nuts and bolts of change in a democratic process. Exemplars such as Grupo Oaxaca or the Network for Oral Trials showed how dedicated people and organizations could make a difference, and others arose to take on issues such as education reform, environmental protection, and the role and rights of women. Many of these groups can now claim significant influence on the direction and depth of Mexico's democracy today.

DEMOCRATIC LIMITS

Despite a competitive electoral field, working checks and balances, an independent press, and blossoming citizen groups, concerns about the quality of Mexico's democracy are only rising. Political watchers fear the authoritarian legacies that continue will not only limit further democratic gains but will also threaten Mexico's newfound openness and responsiveness. Mexico's new generation of leaders still battles an old guard—be they monopolists, political party "dinosaurs," or drug traffickers—for Mexico's "hearts and minds." In this fight, they wield weak and often incomplete tools.

Elected officials often remain unaccountable to voters, and more than a few use their office to enrich themselves and their families. An outrageous case is that of José Antonio Ríos Granados, former mayor of the city of Tultitlán de Mariano Escobedo, just outside of Mexico City.[45] Long ago known for its lakes and fields, today it is filled with industrial parks and warehouses, serviced by crisscrossing railroads bringing both people and goods in and out. Big names such as international chemical giant BASF, national juice maker Jarritos, and Volvo Buses make their wares and have their distribution hubs here. In 2001, with a population of five hundred thousand, the town was practically bursting at the seams, and in desperate need of new schools, roads, sewers, and basic infrastructure. Yet Ríos Granados found it possible to pay himself US$19,000 a month—some US$4000 more than then United Kingdom prime minister Tony Blair earned. Ríos Granados also found time to indulge in his hobbies, most notably movie making. He produced and starred with a buxom blonde (rumored also to be his girlfriend) in the utterly forgettable shoot-'em-up drama *Orquídea Sangrienta* (Bloody Orchid). The municipality was nice enough to chip in Mex$150,000— roughly US$15,000—to help defray production costs.[46]

Some of these obvious abuses are now harder to pass off. The old amorphous budgeting category of "nonspecified expenses" is no longer allowed; instead governments have to be much clearer about how and where money is spent. But the transgressions have not ended. For instance, to ensure favorable coverage by the local news, most governors now have outsized press kitties paid for by public funds—reaching millions of pesos a month in some cases. For the two primary television networks, Televisa and TV Azteca, democracy has been quite profitable.

The "sunshine" from the transparency law has filtered down only fitfully to the state. For instance, a recent study found only 30 percent of Mexico City's public agencies to be in compliance with the baseline openness mandated by the law and regulated by the capital's freedom of information agency.[47] Requests are at times turned down by bureaucrats who claim the information "doesn't exist" or that the filing contains "procedural errors"—meaning that the solicitor didn't ask the right office within an agency, or use the correct bureaucratic jargon.[48] Devolving at times into a cat and mouse game, it can defeat all but the most intrepid citizens or reporters. Even if caught, officials are rarely prosecuted for their misdeeds. With little public accounting, many politicians feel free to spend as they wish.

Mexico's electoral rules also work to limit accountability. Taking the idea of term limits to the extreme, Mexico does not permit reelection, period. From the president all the way down—governors, senators, mayors, local town council seats—no Mexican politician can remain for more than a single term in the same office. Initially written by officials wary of creating political fiefdoms, these rules concentrate power in the hands of party leaders.

Politicians have little incentive to follow through on campaign promises or appease local voters, eyeing always the next position (with a different constituency). Citizens cannot directly "punish" bad leaders or reward good ones because whatever their merits, they will move on at the end of their first and only term.

Perhaps as problematic as the blatant abuses is the lack of continuity these stringent limits create. Officials with the best of intentions have little time to make their mark, and few political incentives to think in the long term. For instance, local mayors in Mexico serve for three-year terms. During the first year they are settling in, appointing their staff, learning the ropes. In the second year, if citizens are lucky, they work hard to deal with local issues. By the third year, they are looking toward their future—which cannot be as mayor. Locals cannot reward them for good service or undivided attention, and so many times they get neither. Combined with increasing electoral competition, the rules encourage local politicians—particularly mayors and governors—to spend, spend, spend, boosting their popularity in the short term, but leaving a fiscal mess for their successor.

To be sure, the extremes are now just that: extreme. The story of a cocky, newly elected Veracruz representative who, while visiting a hardscrabble village in his district, uttered, "Take a good, long look at my face...because this is the last time you will see it in this [expletive] pueblo," is a particular affront now largely relegated to the past.[49] Votes matter, as most of Mexico is up for grabs. Some 90 percent of local governments and over two-thirds of state-level administrations have changed party hands at least once since democratization. And even in some of the most recalcitrant states, voters have overcome impressive odds to punish bad leadership.

The central state of Oaxaca is one such case. The 2004 election of PRI Governor Ulises Ruiz Ortiz was mired in controversy—ranging from vote rigging to murder. Assuming office, Ruiz ruled for six years with an iron fist, harassing independent news outlets, indigenous groups, and civil society organizations. These skirmishes reached a tipping point during a dispute with the local teachers' unions. Rather than negotiate, he sent in the police, spraying protesters with tear gas and rubber bullets. When they dared to defy orders to disband, real bullets flew.

The standoff ended after hundreds of arrests and at least seventeen deaths. The teachers dispersed. But the battle was not over. In the lead-up to the 2010 state elections, Ruiz's chosen successor enjoyed all the benefits—among them an uneven playing field—Ruiz once had. Accusations of extra ballots, imaginary voters, and illicit campaign funds flew. But despite the considerable odds, opposition candidate Gabino Cué Monteagudo won handily, as did his legislative slate. In a massive turnout, ordinary voters overcame the electoral shenanigans and ended eighty years of local strongman politics, opening up the possibility of a different future for their poverty-stricken state.

In this more competitive environment, parties have realized that they need to run popular candidates—not just party hacks—in order to win elections. The most vivid lesson occurred in the 2006 presidential race, when the powerful but unpopular PRI leader Roberto Madrazo finished an embarrassing third in the contest. Having learned its lesson, the PRI changed its tune in later gubernatorial elections. In 2009 in Nuevo León, PRI leaders turned to public name recognition and citizen support to resolve their differences. Reflecting this new strategy, the clear winner of internal polls, Rodrigo Medina de la Cruz, became their candidate for governor and then went on to win the office. In fact, in competitive districts, primaries have flourished since the late 1990s. In this way voters can and do hold parties— if not individuals—accountable.

Also at the local level, there is increasing evidence of what political scientists call "retrospective voting"—with voters judging the performance of the sitting governor when they head to the ballot box to elect a new one. In 2009, the PRI's candidate lost his sizable lead and later the Sonora gubernatorial race after a tragic fire in a local day-care took the lives of forty-nine toddlers and revealed systematic public mismanagement and graft under the existing PRI administration. That same year, voters dissatisfied with the status quo threw the PAN out of the governor's office in San Luis Potosí. Still, direct accountability is limited.

In the economic realm, disparities continue to reign. Mexico's monopolies and oligopolies extend well beyond the telecoms and media industries to sectors as diverse as bread, tortillas, cement, soft drinks, sugar, and glass production (not to mention state-owned electricity, gas, and oil). In the United States, this concentration of sector after sector would quickly raise legal hackles, as well as the interest of antitrust lawyers. In Mexico, these industry heavies operate and indeed thrive relatively unperturbed. Along with increasing costs for Mexico's consumers, this concentration also leads to outsized political power. Regulatory agencies have been slow to get off

the ground and often are ineffective in carrying out their most basic responsibilities—the result, at least in part, of the effective pushback of vested
economic interests. The 2006 Televisa law, which would have protected the
current network duopoly, is just the most blatant example of the political
heft forged by economic concentration. One broader sign of the clout of economic elites is the fact that Mexicans and Mexican companies, on average,
pay some of the lowest taxes around—ranking last within the Organisation
for Economic Cooperation and Development and among the lowest in the
Western Hemisphere.[50]

Perhaps the greatest challenge to Mexico's democracy today is its weak
rule of law. Mexico suffers still from the twin evils of corruption and impunity. These benefit not only hardened criminals, but also Mexico's connected
families and prominent politicians—as might often overcomes right.

The Path to Deeper Democracy

The challenge for any democracy—but particularly a new one—is to create and perfect the intertwined guardians of openness and accountability:
a strong independent court system and law enforcement, a merit-based and
decently paid civil service, a media sector able and willing to investigate bad
behavior, and citizen-led groups demanding the best—and pushing back on
the worst—of their government. This is a tall order in any society, and especially one with decades of corrupt informal rule as the modus operandi.

Mexico also faces the challenges of moving beyond the euphoria of
change to the long slog of consolidation. There is a real question today as
to whether Mexico will continue its path forward—uprooting its remaining antidemocratic vestiges—or whether vested interests will overwhelm its
still nascent institutions.

This unsteady democratic balance is even more apparent at the local level.
It is in Mexico's small towns and state capitals that the democratic rubber
meets the proverbial road. It is here that initial changes to courts took shape
and competitive elections first gained ground. But local politics has also
become the authoritarian's last stand. In nine states—including Tamaulipas,
Veracruz, and Coahuila—and hundreds of municipalities, the PRI's hold
has not lessened. If anything, the old style and structures are even more
firmly rooted, fed in part by the uptick in money coming from the central
government.[51]

Mexico has made enormous political strides in the last two decades. An energetic if imperfect democracy, it now boasts a competitive party system and generally free and fair elections. Pushing Mexico's presidents and parties forward democratically are an organizing civil society, an independent media, and an increasingly demanding voter base, made up of a growing middle class. Yet America's neighbor today stands at a political crossroads, struggling to follow a path of continued openness and enhanced participation.

Many today worry about a return to the past, with less than democratic forces regaining the upper hand within Mexico's evolving political system. Indeed the corruption, opaqueness, and violence today do challenge the democratic system and rule of law. But Mexico's institutions are stronger than many give credit. And most understand that security and stability will come only through greater openness and accountability rather than a return to the past. Mexico's market-based democracy, though here to stay, still needs support to control the bloodshed, weed out the corruption, and open the political system more broadly. This movement toward greater consolidation is vital not just for Mexico but also for the United States, given the growing importance of our neighbor's economy for our own.

CROSS-BORDER DREAMS: MEXICO'S GROWING MIDDLE CLASS

The American dream affirms that through individual enterprise anyone can achieve a life of middle class prosperity. On U.S. shores, rags can transform into riches, overcoming any barrier—race, class, or the past. This alluring vision brought millions of poor immigrants through Ellis Island during the last century, and today brings millions more across the southern border. These immigrants hope that their hard work will provide a better life—a middle class life—for themselves and for their children. But the great story of recent years, in which Mexico has a prominent part, is the rise of the global middle class. This dream is becoming a reality not just for those who leave, but for many who stay.

Marco Aceo grew up in the crumbling splendor of Mexico City's center, playing on the cobblestone streets and ornate stoops of the seventeenth-century buildings just off the main Zócalo. Originally from a small Michoacán town, his parents came to Mexico City in the 1950s searching for a better life as factory workers. But like so many others, they found a precarious existence in the slums of the capital. The youngest of seven,

Marco's youth centered around the local church—where he and his family prayed on Sundays, celebrated on holidays, and received their one square meal most weekdays.

Unlike his brothers and sisters, Marco made it past primary school. With his high school diploma in hand, he landed his first job—washing diplomats' cars behind the imposing concrete block of the U.S. Embassy. I met him fifteen years later, when he was a fleet chauffeur for the embassy, driving a comfortably appointed gold minivan for a manageable eight-hour shift each day. With a monthly salary of Mex$16,000 (or roughly US$1200) and full benefits, plus his wife's earnings selling tiles in a local store, Marco and his family are firmly in the rising middle class. With help from the government mortgage-subsidy program, he and his wife bought a small house for themselves and their two children on the outskirts of Mexico City. In the all-new housing development, the food is ample, hot water is always available, and their basic comforts assured. Both of their children will make it through high school, and Marco dreams about college—enabling his children to someday use the distinguished title of *licenciado*.

For too many Americans, the grinding poverty they witness while traveling from the airport to the air-conditioned hotels of Cancún, or during their visits to border town cantinas, embodies Mexico. The contrast with the United States is, of course, stark. Several million Mexicans do still live in extreme poverty, getting by on less than two dollars a day. Mexico's per capita income is one-third that of the United States.[1]

Yet compared with the rest of the world, Mexico now ranks in the top third in terms of per capita wealth. And what remains unseen by most visitors to tourist destinations is the true blossoming of its middle class.

Economists, commentators, and policymakers debate the best way to define this middle sector. Some take an expansive view—for instance including everyone who makes it across the World Bank's poverty line (two dollars a day)—though to us in the United States or those in other advanced Western economies many of these people would almost certainly be considered abjectly poor.[2] Others, such as the Organisation for Economic Co-operation and Development (OECD), determine poverty rates based on median household income.

Independent scholars have created their own metrics for measuring the global and Mexican middle classes, taking into consideration both international comparisons as well as local purchasing power.[3] And the Mexican government's National Council of Evaluation of Social Development Policy (CONEVAL) also does its own measures, incorporating access to health care and education into some of its calculations, and distinguishing between urban and rural costs. These different definitions lead to disparate absolute numbers and percentages. But even CONEVAL, the most restrictive, puts a small majority of Mexicans today in the middle and (much smaller) upper classes. By their count, out of a total population of 110 million, some fifty million Mexicans are poor.[4] But that also means that nearly sixty million are not, a fundamental shift from the past.

From Crisis to NAFTA

During the first fifty years of the PRI, Mexico's middle class grew to around a third of the population, benefiting from a revolutionary commitment to accessible education and to the expansion of public-sector jobs. The 1982 economic crisis ended this progress, sending millions back into poverty. The economic reforms and privatizations of the late 1980s and early 1990s further hit the government-nurtured middle sector by trimming public jobs and largesse. But these economic changes also paved the way for the emergence of a new, broader-based middle class.

Once firmly in office in 1988, President Carlos Salinas turned to his main ambition: remaking Mexico's economy. First, Salinas pushed through constitutional reforms that increased competition in some areas and renegotiated Mexico's heavy debt burden. Next, he launched into a flurry of privatizations. He started with Mexico's telephone system, then steel companies, banks, flour mills, television stations, airlines, toll roads—over nine hundred public companies in all. While chipping away at the state's economic responsibility auction by auction, Salinas worked to put in place an even grander design—permanently opening up Mexico's economy to world markets.

This transformation fit with Salinas's neoliberal sensibilities. But it also resulted from the stark truth facing Mexico—it needed cash. Even after renegotiating its debt, there were no public funds and little private savings available to boost Mexico's economy.

Salinas first looked east and met with European leaders at the 1990 World Economic Forum Davos summit, hoping to entice them into trading and investing in Mexico. Each snubbed his advances. They were more interested in the nations emerging from behind the now crumbled Berlin Wall and in their own negotiations in the lead-up to the 1992 Treaty of Maastricht establishing the European Union. Even Salinas's free-market compatriot Margaret Thatcher was indifferent to Mexico's requests.

Still needing a deal, Salinas and his cabinet started thinking closer to home. The ties between the Mexican and U.S. economies had already begun deepening during Miguel de la Madrid's presidency as a result of his reforms and opening of the economy in the wake of the 1982 debt crisis. During the late 1980s, trade between Mexico and the United States more than doubled.[5] A formal agreement would ensure that Mexico's current access to U.S. markets would not change with the vagaries of politics, encouraging more trade and investment. Salinas's economic team first approached Carla Hills, U.S. trade representative for President George Bush Sr., and then expanded its outreach to include a Texas triumvirate: James Baker, Bush's powerful secretary of state; Robert Mosbacher, secretary of commerce; and Lloyd Bentsen, the Democratic chair of the Senate Finance Committee. While the United States was not yet ready to stand up for democracy next door, it was willing to promote economic globalization. This began a process that would lead to the largest and, at the time, most ambitious trade agreement in the world, the North American Free Trade Agreement (NAFTA).

From the initial conversations, NAFTA's over two thousand pages took two years to nail down and another difficult year to be ratified in the United States, Mexico, and Canada. It took on tariffs and nontariff trade barriers, beefed up contract and intellectual property protections, and ensured a fair hearing for investors through international arbitration. In the end, NAFTA fundamentally changed trade, foreign and domestic investment, supply chains, and labor demand across the three countries.[6]

By itself the passage of NAFTA was a feat. In the early 1980s, a group of prominent Mexican and U.S. business leaders had tried to place free trade on the agenda, only to be shot down by both governments.[7] Early in his tenure, Salinas himself had dismissed the elder President Bush's initial overtures to begin free trade negotiations, stating that the economic differences between the countries made a balanced deal impossible.[8] Shortly after NAFTA was signed, free trade agreements were met with considerable skepticism in the United States, and fast-track negotiating authority (which binds Congress to vote up or down on the final agreement, without amendments) was pulled—dooming the hemisphere-wide Free Trade Agreement of the Americas.

But in the early 1990s a confluence of people and events made an accord possible. Salinas, Bush, and Brian Mulroney in Canada favored the agreement. With the end of the Cold War, more space opened up for economics in U.S. foreign policy. The stalling of the Uruguay round of the World Trade Organization (threatening the failure of a global trade deal), combined with the formation of the European Union and worries about rising Asian competition, led many in Washington to see regional trading blocs as the best—and for others the only—path forward. This led to a sudden interest in the United States' neglected neighbors—first Canada, and then Mexico.

Despite the good timing, the sales job was monumental.[9] In Mexico, the PRI worked with the private sector to move the agreement forward. Under the auspices of the Association for Exporting Companies (COECE), Mexican business was in the side room throughout much of the negotiation process, consulting and pushing the Mexican government for important concessions, but also keeping its own members in line once tough decisions were made, and spending over $1 million on its own to lobby for NAFTA.[10] The PRI also put the full power of Mexico's docile media behind the agreement, planting numerous sympathetic interviews and stories every week.[11]

Over the course of the campaign the Mexican government spent nearly US$30 million in the United States, where the outcome was less certain. It hired well-known lobbyists Burson-Marsteller to lead the public relations charge, lined up three dozen former U.S. government officials to speak on its behalf, and shepherded some fifty congressional staffers around Mexico on official tours. COECE stepped up to the plate as well, coordinating with its U.S. counterparts; nearly one thousand corporations and trade associations joined together in a coalition to sway legislators.[12] More subtly, the government orchestrated a blockbuster traveling art show, entitled *Mexico: Splendors of Thirty Centuries*. Hyperbole even for the PRI, the exhibit was designed to create the image of a potential partner with a long history, a refined culture, and a modern state and economy right next door.

NAFTA was one of President Bill Clinton's toughest initiatives in his first year in office. Many traditional Democrats—especially labor unions and environmental activists—vehemently opposed the agreement, and the vote threatened to divide the Democratic Party. Yet Clinton had warmed to the unprecedented vision of tying the United States more closely than ever to its neighbors, and he was determined to pass the treaty. To rally support,

Clinton painted a rosy vision of North America's future. NAFTA would increase Mexico's GDP, reduce U.S.-bound immigration by creating jobs for Mexicans at home, and help bring "democracy and freedom" to America's neighbor, all while creating jobs and wealth in the United States. Somewhat understating the challenges and limitations of the agreement, Clinton worked to create a myth of free trade's benevolence and omnipotence. He also engaged in serious horse-trading. Granting special exemptions for high-fructose corn syrup (mollifying the sugar lobby), providing funds for border development (gaining crucial bipartisan border-state votes), and even promising a family photo with the First Lady boosted the final vote count.[13] After weeks of pleading and cajoling, the White House corralled over one hundred Democrats to vote with even more Republicans in the House to push the bill through 234–200. Sixty-one senators soon followed suit, finally passing NAFTA in November of 1993.

On the southern side of the border, many Mexicans did not love NAFTA either. Some directly opposed President Salinas's economic project. Others doubted his expansive promises: that NAFTA would breathe new life into the Mexican economy, end the ever-looming threat of economic crisis, and lead Mexico fully into the developed world. A coalition of independent workers, farmers, and opposition parties coalesced to challenge the agreement. But with the PRI still firmly in control, NAFTA's passage relied solely on back-room negotiations with labor's chief boss, a few party honchos, and business leaders. And through the PRI-controlled press the government had done its usual good job of shaping the nature of the debate, building on Mexicans' cautious optimism that things were finally changing, and suggesting that NAFTA would be the linchpin. With the power brokers on board and the Mexican people willing to give the government the benefit of the doubt, the Senate ratified NAFTA after just twelve hours of discussion, and with just two non-PRI senators dissenting.

NAFTA's Scorecard

Despite its now sullied reputation, NAFTA was a net win for both countries (as well as for Canada). Attributing economic successes or failures directly to NAFTA is difficult given all the other economic changes of the last fifteen years—yet general trends are clear. In the years after NAFTA's signing, the economies of all three countries grew faster than the OECD average.

Trade between the partners, too, increased much faster than overall world levels. Mexico's exports to the United States grew fivefold and U.S. exports to Mexico quadrupled, bringing the annual trade total to approximately US$460 billion in 2011.[14] While the United States was already Mexico's most important export market, it is now even more so, and Mexico has become the second most important destination for U.S. exports in the world (following Canada).

NAFTA obviously meant different things for each country. The sheer magnitude of the U.S. economy meant NAFTA's effects on this side of the border could seem modest. NAFTA trade represents 28 percent of total U.S. trade, and just 7 percent of the United States' fifteen-trillion-dollar economy. Nevertheless, it has had significant effects for particular industries—furthering the transformation of the auto industry and boosting U.S. exports of computers, fabrics, and parts for appliances. NAFTA was one of many factors spurring a 30 percent rise in U.S. manufacturing revenues during the 1990s to over $1 trillion each quarter.[15]

The effects on Mexico—with its smaller and still-developing economy— were much greater. Perhaps most important, NAFTA cemented the economic reforms of the previous decade and made sure there was no turning back. It boosted foreign direct investment, as Mexico became a darling of emerging markets, receiving over US$150 billion in investment from its NAFTA partners during the first fifteen years. Much of this flowed into export-oriented manufacturing—new technologies, equipment, and factories. These funds and the accompanying know-how helped transform Mexico's economy. Where oil once dominated, manufactured goods grew to nearly 90 percent of all exports. Mexico is also now Latin America's largest exporter, far surpassing any other single country.

Surprising supporters and critics alike, NAFTA had little overall effect on the number of jobs in the United States. Overall, most economists estimate that the treaty resulted in at most a small net gain in jobs—anywhere from a wash to just under one million (depending on who is counting and how the counting is done).[16] Certain plants closed up north and others opened up south of the border, leading to painful layoffs for some American workers. But the dreaded wholesale outsourcing—the "giant sucking sound" of jobs going to Mexico that Ross Perot had predicted in 1992—never occurred. Close analyses, such as those highlighted by the nonpartisan Congressional Research Service, show that the changes in the U.S. job market have had more to do with technology and innovation than with free trade. Monetary and fiscal policies matter even more for job creation.[17]

Perhaps more unexpected than the limited effects in the United States, Mexico's job growth did not pick up drastically either. There was an initial burst in manufacturing jobs, pushing the total number to 1.3 million in 2000. Most of the positions were located in Mexico's north, in new maquila factories. Yet economic opening and billions in foreign investment did not affect employment more broadly. The "backward linkages" that development economists praise were few and far between, as the new brand-name factories rarely turned to local businesses and suppliers for their needs. Corresponding services—research, design, and development—were slow to take off as well. Even as these factories moved beyond simple labor-intensive production to more complex goods such as automobiles and computers, the effects on the larger Mexican economy were minimal. Jaime Serra Puche, an economist and the Mexican trade secretary who negotiated NAFTA, notes that the export multiplier effect, which measures how exports expand the overall economy, is much lower in Mexico than in countries such as Brazil, and is about half what it is in the United States. He attributes this to Mexico's uncompetitive monopolies and oligopolies, which stifle growth through high prices and unfair business practices, and to the lack of financing for new ventures.[18] This meant lackluster growth, despite the huge inflows of cash and outflows of goods. In 2001, China's accession into the WTO undercut Mexico's previous comparative advantage vis-à-vis labor outsourcing, reducing job gains from trade even further.

The new manufacturing positions largely just offset losses elsewhere—particularly in the countryside. Since NAFTA's start, the number of people living off the land has declined by some two million. To be sure, some of this change resulted from the transformation and modernization of Mexico's economy. As countries climb the per capita income ranks, rural agriculture jobs disappear in favor of more urban manufacturing and service employment. Still, some of the biggest aggregate losers from NAFTA were Mexico's small farmers, and rural poverty increased in the years following the passage of the free trade agreement.[19] As these markets opened up to (often subsidized) international competition, Mexico's government did little to help small-scale growers. A study by John Scott of the Centro de Investigación y Docencia Económicas (CIDE) shows that the government's flagship agricultural program, Procampo, spends the vast majority of its funds on large agricultural producers.[20] Shamefully, a substantial amount also goes to government officials, politicians' families, and even relatives of narcotraffickers.[21]

Where Mexicans really benefited from NAFTA (and the investment and competition it encouraged) was as consumers. Mexican stores began to carry Wisconsin butter, Quebec maple syrup, Massachusetts cranberry juice, and Washington apples. Clothing, electronics, and cars became widely available—providing new options and lower prices at the same time. The way people bought things changed too. Retail giants such as Walmart entered the market—allowing Mexicans for the first time to browse patio furniture, produce, tortillas, and televisions all on the same visit.

Many worried about the effects of imports on domestic agricultural production, and the expansion of chain stores for local merchants. The arrival of international retailers undoubtedly drove some small shopkeepers and farmers out of business, but it also reduced the costs of fruits, vegetables, and other basics. Since 1994, the price of household goods in Mexico has decreased by half, according to Tufts University's Global Development and Environment Institute.[22] The widespread availability of more products of better quality and at lower prices transformed the lives of tens of millions of Mexicans for the better.

NAFTA made a difference for U.S. consumers as well. Nebraska shoppers could now easily buy fresh strawberries, tomatoes, and grapes—not only in June but also in January. Falling prices for avocados, mangoes, and papayas turned once-exotic fruits into normal purchases. With a routine trip to the local supermarket, one could now cook an entire Mexican meal in Cleveland, Ohio—from the corn tortillas to the tomatillo sauce. The bargains weren't limited to the grocery stores. Lower-priced Mexican-made flat-screen televisions, computer monitors, and other electronics filled first the shelves of the local Best Buy, and then the living rooms of many Americans.

Critics of the pact point to ongoing illegal migration, environmental problems, and growing income disparities both within and between the countries. These are important issues, but they are ones NAFTA was never designed to address. NAFTA was neither the utter disaster that its critics depicted nor the panacea envisioned by its champions. What NAFTA did do was propel the integration of the members' economies, bringing concrete net benefits to all its participants. It also was a turning point in U.S.-Mexico relations, permanently interlacing the two nations as never before.

THE 1995 PESO CRISIS

As NAFTA officially started on January 1, 1994, a pervasive optimism swept Mexico. In the capital's financial hub, bankers and businessmen in silk ties filled the tables at La Galvia, a well-heeled Mexican restaurant, and Remi, a Manhattan transplant half a block away. The hourly flights between Mexico City and the industrial hub of Monterrey were quickly filled with lawyers, accountants, headhunters, corporate executives, and ubiquitous bankers, all making the most of Mexico's economic surge.

Mexico's expanding middle class joined in the enthusiasm. Newly privatized banks, which had never before been interested in those who actually needed to borrow money, began offering business loans and credit cards to Mexico's professionals. The value of home mortgages, amounting to less than US$450 million a year in the late 1980s, skyrocketed to over US$9 billion annually by 1992—despite interest rates of around 15 percent.[23] Car dealerships stepped into the financing game as well, leading to a boom in sales. Even the working class got into the fray, with a few pioneering stores setting up weekly payment plans for the washing machine, television, or blender you took home today. Millions of Mexicans began to believe President Salinas's promises that Mexico was irrevocably rising to join the developed world.

Yet NAFTA had done little to change many of Mexico's underlying economic problems, starting with its overvalued exchange rate and huge current-account deficits. Mexico was bringing in many more goods than it was sending out—to the tune of over 11 percent of its GDP in the early 1990s.[24] Some were capital goods that would boost Mexico's economy. Pedro Aspe, Mexico's finance minister, spoke with mock exasperation about the nearly half-billion dollars that the 1991 decision by Daimler-Benz to build a new Mercedes plant in Mexico would add to Mexico's current-account deficit. But not all of the imports were long-term investments that would boost jobs and future economic growth. Dolce and Gabbana, Hermès, and Zegna opened flagship stores along Mexico City's Masaryk Avenue, catering to consumers hungry for international luxuries. On less glitzy streets the sales were still as brisk, as Mexicans hauled home imported furniture, refrigerators, dishwashers, and all kinds of sports equipment from baseball gloves to soccer balls in record numbers.[25] The increasingly overvalued peso made these imported goods seem cheap compared to their domestically made counterparts, undercutting local industries and jobs.

Added to this, the crony capitalism that imbued the privatization process created a weak banking sector, unable to withstand an economic shock. And the government launched its traditional spending splurge to boost the economy and support the PRI heir designate—first Donaldo Colosio, and then, after his assassination, Ernesto Zedillo.

With its economic borders now permanently open, Mexico was more exposed to the opinions—and investment decisions—of businesses and fund managers around the world. In the euphoria leading up to NAFTA, foreign investors had piled into the Mexican stock and bond markets. But in 1994 these same portfolio managers' calculations began to change. Internal Mexican turmoil scared some. The U.S. economic recovery—and subsequent rise in treasury rates—made Mexico's sovereign debt less attractive to investors balancing risk and return. To keep the money flowing Salinas and Aspe sweetened the pot by offering dollar-denominated short-term bonds—dubbed *tesobonos*. These treasury bonds took away the currency risk for foreign investors by promising to repay all principal and interest in U.S. dollars—placing all the risk of fluctuating currency rates squarely on the Mexican government. Investor interest in the short-term instruments rallied, and firms gobbled up nearly thirty billion dollars' worth—equal to 7 percent of GDP. But when confidence in Mexico again faltered, the dollar-denominated bill arrived—nearly bankrupting the country.

Just shy of NAFTA's first anniversary, the peso crisis hit. As investors stampeded for the exits, the peso's value quickly dropped by half. GDP plummeted 7 percent; inflation rose by 50 percent. Interest rates topped 100 percent, pummeling those financing trendsetters who had taken advantage of Mexico's first mortgages, car loans, and credit cards. Millions lost their jobs.

As Mexico fell deeply into economic crisis, the United States took quick action. After three weeks of failed negotiations on Capitol Hill, the White House tapped into the Treasury's little-used economic stabilization fund and leaned on its European colleagues and the IMF, coming up with $40 billion in loans and guarantees. Mexico just narrowly escaped yet another international debt default. But this time it paid back all the loans—early and with interest.

NAFTA made climbing out of this deep economic hole easier. It stopped Mexico from raising tariffs or slamming the door shut on investment. Instead, the government was forced to eat its proverbial spinach—lowering government expenditure, tightening the amount of money in circulation, and letting the currency fall. This led to a deep—but fortunately short—recession.

Just a year later the Mexican economy revived, growing over 5 percent. NAFTA, combined with a lower peso, helped in the recovery, boosting exports north.[26] Unemployment fell and average incomes rebounded, leading many into—or back into—the ranks of the professional classes. In 1999 per capita income pushed beyond US$8000 for the first time.[27] With Mexico recovering, so too did fast-paced growth in U.S. exports to Mexico—up nearly 50 percent from pre-NAFTA levels.[28] Mexico would again face tough economic times, but to date the 1995 crisis has been the last self-inflicted crash. And the incipient transformation spurred by the economic reforms of the 1980s and early 1990s would continue, moving Mexico from a predominantly poor country to the middle class nation it is today.

Mexico's Middle Class

The magnitude of Mexico's economic shift is hard to overstate. In the mid-1990s, seven out of ten Mexicans were considered poor by the Mexican government's measures. Today, it is closer to two in five. As mentioned before, some fifty million Mexicans—far too many—still live in poverty. But the majority of Mexicans profited from the changes, no longer filling the ranks of the poor.

Day to day, these individuals and families in Mexico's growing middle class have homes full of modern appliances—refrigerators, televisions, washing machines, and cell phones.[29] Nearly half own a car and nearly a third a computer. But this transformation isn't just about more dollars—or pesos—in Mexican pockets. It is as much a state of mind as an income bracket. It entails a revolution in the way millions of Mexicans live their lives.

The new middle class is a decidedly urban phenomenon. The movement away from Mexico's farms and rural areas to a growing number of cities began in the postwar boom and accelerated with the 1980s debt crisis and ensuing economic reforms. According to the World Bank, a full three-quarters of Mexicans are now city folk—donning their sombreros in celebration, not profession. The burgeoning middle classes are much less directly dependent on the government than were their compatriots of the past, as most now work in the private sector. Filling the ranks of Mexico's now-dominant service sector as well as its high-value, capital-intensive manufacturing industries, they include accountants, lawyers, engineers, entrepreneurs, specialized factory workers, taxi drivers, and mid-level managers, among other professions.

The workplace has changed not just in terms of where and what, but also who works. In the last three decades more and more women have entered the paying workforce.[30] Forty-five percent of women now work outside their homes—more than double the rate of just a few decades ago. While still low compared to world standards, dual-income households are an increasing norm rather than an exception. Women-led households too are on the rise—representing roughly one in four homes.[31]

Family life, hopes, and aspirations have changed too. While in the 1970s the average Mexican family numbered almost nine, today most women have just two children—equal to the United States.[32] Fewer children mean outsized attention from parents. Education is paramount—as a means for advancement and fulfillment. The search for excellence (and an escape from the weak public school system) has led to an explosion of private schools over the last ten years. There are approximately forty-five thousand private schools today, roughly a third of all educational institutions in Mexico.[33] The new schools appear not just in the traditionally well-off areas but in working and lower middle class neighborhoods such as the borough of Iztapalapa in Mexico City and Lomas de Polanco in Guadalajara.

Middle class dreams don't stop with a high school diploma. Antonio Villa's family is a case in point. The fifty-seven-year-old chauffeur finished only eighth grade himself, but he determinedly worked for a different path for his two children. For the last several years, he has routinely spent half of his US$15,000 annual salary on their tuition and books. Marco Antonio, his eldest, has now graduated and works at a local bank. His younger sister, Erika, is studying law.[34] With higher education a harbinger of middle class-dom, the college-bound population has doubled in the last fifteen years to nearly a third of young Mexicans.[35]

And those in the rising middle have become avid consumers, enjoying their newfound ability to move beyond the basics and working hard to keep up with the Pérez's next door. They go on vacation—to the beaches of Puerto Vallarta or Mazatlán or to Orlando's Disneyworld—juggling school breaks and busy work schedules.[36] Everyone seems to have a cell phone, on which they can talk about the latest cable TV show, make dinner reservations, or plan to see a film—on one of the nearly five million available movie screens (a fivefold increase since pre-NAFTA days).[37] All these purchases have created a fragile but virtuous economic circle of consumption-led growth—generating new jobs in tourism, retail, and goods and services that further fuel the middle ranks.

Politically, Mexico's middle class is both increasingly important and independent. Unveiling its power in 2000, the middle turned away from the PRI, helping usher in electoral democracy with the election of Vicente Fox. In 2006 it gave President Felipe Calderón his razor-thin vote advantage, taking him to Los Pinos. A crucial voting bloc in the years to come, the middle class is also a group up for grabs—with its members shedding party ties to join the rising ranks of Mexico's independents.[38]

ECONOMIC ACHIEVEMENTS

This emergence of the middle class—overlooked in Mexico and virtually unknown north of the border—resulted from many factors. It depended crucially on the government getting its economic act together. For years economic mismanagement spurred boom-and-bust cycles, each time wiping out citizens' savings. But since the 1995 economic crisis, the government has managed its finances quite admirably. The federal government both cut its budget deficits and paid down its debt. The fiercely independent central bank stabilized a floating exchange rate and kept inflation in check.

Newfound stability, along with a recovering and open economy, encouraged private sector investment. International corporations such as Citigroup, LG Electronics, Home Depot, and Whirlpool set up shop. Local companies got into the game as well, as capital markets opened up to Mexico's best-known corporate names, funding ambitious expansion plans for Femsa, Mexico's largest beverage company; Bimbo, first Mexico's and now the world's largest bakery; and steelmaker Grupo IMSA. The investment led to new products, new companies, and new jobs, powering the growth of Mexico's middle. More flowed in from remittances, as the ever-growing wave of U.S.-based Mexican sons, daughters, husbands, and wives sent back hard-earned wages to those left behind. These trickles of a hundred, two hundred, or three hundred dollars a month created a billions-strong current, flowing to poor households and communities and lifting more and more families into the middle ranks. Per capita income rose steadily and substantially from US$7100 in 1996 to over US$15,000 in 2011.[39] Inequality lessened slightly as well—spreading more of these gains among the larger population.[40]

Perhaps as important as rising incomes for the middle class was the emergence of credit. Reaching beyond the upper crust, it transformed daily life and future possibilities for millions of Mexican households. One of the financing pioneers was Elektra. Founded in 1950 by one of the families behind Salinas y Rocha, a chain of discount furniture and mattress stores, Elektra initially made and later sold radios, TVs, and household appliances. It catered from the start to hardworking day laborers, maids, taxi drivers, and street vendors rather than to Mexico's moneyed. But by the early 1980s it managed fewer than one hundred outlets and was on the brink of bankruptcy, hit hard by the debt crisis and the weak economy of the "lost decade."

In 1987, a thirty-one-year-old Ricardo Salinas Pliego took the helm of his family's company, transforming the distressed business into the thriving five-thousand-strong mega chain of stores that it is today. His first step was to modernize the business's inner workings. After a day-long visit with Sam Walton, the legendary founder of Walmart, Salinas invested massively in computerizing his stores. He also began an aggressive expansion plan—betting on the buying power of Mexico's lower classes.

Salinas's main innovation was not just locating more of his now-efficient shiny yellow emporiums in less affluent neighborhoods. It was offering extensive credit to his clients. While few of them could fork over the Mex$7500 needed to buy the Whirlpool—or Elektra brand—washing machine outright, they could pay Mex$250 a week for the foreseeable future for the ease of mechanically cleaning their clothes. And Elektra's management didn't care if the customers' salary was official (or taxed). They just needed to know where the customers lived and a bit about their life and family, and to have their understanding that an Elektra employee—specifically, one of their army of bright-yellow-jacketed collectors on a motorcycle—would be coming to their home if they began missing payments. The company's increasingly sophisticated computer-based analysis—along with sky-high interest rates folded into the weekly peso payments—cushioned against defaults.

So too did the pent-up desires of its humble customer base. Finally granted access to a world of goods before seen only in *telenovelas* and in the houses of their employers, consumers came in droves.[41] Ricardo Salinas's bet on Mexico's rising middle class made him a billionaire several times over and the second-wealthiest man in Mexico today.

Credit was available for bigger-ticket items as well, especially housing. For decades, few Mexican couples starting out could even dream of owning a home. Accumulating the cash to buy a house outright was a years-long—and for many insurmountable—struggle. Even those with a plot of land had a tough time. Mexico's cement companies did a brisk retail business, as families bought one bag at a time. The sight of rebar sticking out of dwellings in middle and working class neighborhoods was common. In spite of the obstacles, owners dreamed that someday they would build a second floor.

In the early 1990s, access to financing began to change the nature of this glacial building process, but it came to a halt after the peso crisis and ensuing financial mayhem. Things picked up again in the early years of the Fox administration, as the government kick-started home construction by changing bankruptcy laws to make it easier to use houses as collateral, by providing partial financing and federal guarantees to banks and mortgage lenders, and by developing Mexico's first credit score tool and mortgage backed securities. Combined with the increasing purchasing power of Mexico's middle, a true mortgage market evolved.

With financing finally available, private construction companies exploded onto the scene. One of the most successful has been Homex Development Corp (Homex). An equal opportunity builder, Homex's wares range from entry-level homes for just over US$14,000 to more well-appointed abodes costing roughly US$140,000. A typical model boasts a kitchen, dining room, living room, two or three bedrooms, and two baths for a total of about eight hundred square feet of living space. Homex mostly serves lower middle and middle class families—thirty-somethings and their small children—who are thrilled to enter the peace and quiet of the often gated communities. Their brightly painted houses stand shoulder to shoulder in neatly spaced rows, adorned with water tanks and colorful roofs. The wide, well-paved grid-like roads and uniform small front yards stand in stark contrast to life in the labyrinthine streets of many of Mexico's city centers.

From its original roots in the northern city of Culiacán, Homex now operates in thirty-four Mexican cities, spread across twenty one states, and has exported its housing model to Brazil and India.[42] At home, like its competitors, it benefits from the financing offered through Infonavit and Fovissste, two government-backed mortgage lenders that finance over half a million mortgages a year.

In just ten years, almost seven million new homes have been built—a quarter of Mexico's overall housing stock—chipping away at the huge deficit created by years of stagnation.[43] Housing remained an economic bright spot even during the 2009 recession, buoyed by backlogged demand—estimated at nearly nine million homes—and continued government financing.[44] On the edges of large and small cities alike, hundreds of new houses now stretch away from the main roads into the distance. Though the homes are modest by U.S. standards, the chance at ownership is transforming everyday life for many Mexicans and their families.

Also expanding, though at a much slower rate, is bank financing. Whether for business loans or consumer credit, Mexican banks are beginning to move beyond their traditional conservative base. Ricardo Salinas was again a pioneer, starting Banco Azteca in 2002. Today it has fourteen hundred branches and over fifteen million clients.[45] Walmart also got into the game, putting bank tellers inside their stores and converting cash registers into virtual bank branches.[46] Changes to Mexico's banking rules in 2008 allowed customers to make deposits and withdrawals, and to pay bills at everyday stores: the local pharmacy, convenience store, gas station, or mom-and-pop shop.[47] Some sixteen thousand locales are already participating, far surpassing the entire banking sector's traditional branches.[48]

A World Bank study shows that when these local banks open, small businesses in the surrounding neighborhood survive longer and wages increase. Access to financing—even in small doses—makes a huge difference in the lives of these middle and lower middle class families. Other studies show that credit not only creates jobs for would-be entrepreneurs, it also brings indirect benefits for overall job numbers, salary amounts, and even children's education.[49]

In the last fifteen years, Mexico's middle has blossomed. An open and diversifying economy, expanding home ownership and credit, new schools, new products, and new opportunities have all worked in its favor. Yet despite its successes, the economic center remains quite fragile. Serious obstacles threaten its growth and stability. The next challenge is to find ways to consolidate and broaden this middle class, to build picket fences from Nuevo Laredo to San Cristóbal.

ECONOMIC HURDLES

These years have also shown that economic liberalization alone can't be the engine for growth. When other countries—particularly China—followed suit, Mexico's initial NAFTA-based advantage ended. In response, the country must address the other factors holding it back. Chief among them are its long-standing monopolies and oligopolies.

Despite economic opening, one or a few companies still dominate major sectors of the economy. The result, according to OECD estimates, is that the average Mexican family pays 40 percent more than they should for everyday basics.[50] Perpetuating these economic fiefdoms increases inequality and limits productivity, innovation, and ultimately growth.

Part of the problem is weak regulation. During the 1990s Mexico privatized with a vengeance, but the regulatory agencies that oversaw these new private sectors were much slower to develop. Savvy new owners found ways to easily gut not only onerous restrictions, but also at times even standard oversight.

One of the more egregious cases is telecommunications. Twenty years after privatization, Carlos Slim's Telmex controls 80 percent of the fixed-line phone market and its sister company, Telcel, controls 70 percent of the mobile market.[51] While prices have come down, they still remain well above international levels. And Mexico ranks far behind not only all other OECD countries, but also its developing-country peers—Brazil, South Korea, and China—in terms of telephone access. Meanwhile, Slim has become the richest man in the world.

The Mexican government at times has tried to rein in Slim's market power. The Federal Competition Commission (CFC), Mexico's antitrust watchdog, has repeatedly found against Telmex, and later Telcel, for having and abusing its "substantial market power."[52] But the company's litigation strategy has been as effective as its marketing plans. For years, during protracted battles led by an army of lawyers, Telmex continued with business as usual—solidifying its market control and making billions in profits. Too frequently, the courts have decided against the government, claiming insufficient proof of the company's monopolistic tendencies, despite Telmex's obvious market dominance and ample evidence of high consumer costs, limited choices, underinvestment, and even downright dirty dealings with would-be competitors.[53] One of Telmex's only losses came at the hands of the U.S. government in the World Trade Organization's court, which found the company guilty of overcharging U.S. companies and consumers by some US$1 billion.[54]

The specific telecommunications regulatory agency, Cofetel, is even weaker. Housed within the Ministry of Communications and Transport (SCT), it has less leeway and often less inclination to take on its biggest client. It has backed down in battles over consumer's rates, interconnection fees, and equal access for other providers.[55]

Legislation passed in 2006 does give Mexico's regulators more teeth, including the power to investigate anticompetitive companies, to block mergers, and to impose heftier fines. In 2011, Calderón signed a bill—approved unanimously by both houses—to fine monopolies 10 percent of their revenues and jail their CEOs for up to ten years. The law also awarded more powers to the CFC, such as allowing the regulators to conduct unannounced raids on companies under investigation. Even the courts have jumped into the fray, taking on cases against the most visible offenders, and at times striking down legislation favoring Mexico's economic giants. In 2011, the Supreme Court decided that regulatory edicts, even if contested, would go immediately into effect (rather than waiting until after the companies exhausted all legal means and appeals), strengthening the government's hand. Nevertheless, regulation in many areas still remains a David and Goliath struggle, with Mexico's economy hanging in the balance.

Physical infrastructure holds Mexico back as well. Since the 1980s, the government has been slow to invest. Angangueo, Michoacán, famed winter home of North America's monarch butterflies, is a case in point. One of Mexico's most prized tourist destinations, visitors come from all over Mexico and around the globe to this UNESCO world heritage site to see one of the world's natural wonders. In late December 2002, my husband and I, with two visiting friends, joined the flock. Our journey began smoothly enough. With so many gone for the Christmas holidays, we sped out of the capital, heading west on Route 15 through the industrial center of Toluca and toward Ciudad Hidalgo. But once we crossed the border from the state of Mexico into Michoacán and turned off the highway, the potholes multiplied. By the time we passed through the town of Ocampo, the road, though technically paved, was so broken up that the asphalt seemed more a hindrance than a help, the jagged edges scraping the sides of our tires. A few locals—mostly young kids—came out with shovels and dirt, energetically filling in the holes and smoothing the piles as our beat-up 1994 Texas-plated Honda Civic passed, reaching out their hands as we crawled by, asking for a donation for their efforts.

Once we reached Angangueo, we abandoned our car along the main drag, and hired one of the numerous locals to take us up the road to the butterfly's sanctuary in his Dodge Ram truck. The four-mile, forty-five-minute trip was a real-life rollercoaster, only without seatbelts, much less roll bars. Large pick-ups careen up and down the one-lane dirt road, banking hard lefts and rights to narrowly miss huge potholes and washouts along the way. Our driver carried not just one but a couple of spare tires and the cabin din attested to the short lifespan of mufflers on this terrain. A blessing in disguise, the racket meant he could hear the other muffler-less trucks coming in the other direction, averting any head-on collisions. Though just over one hundred miles from Mexico City, the one-way trip took nearly four hours.

In fact, less than 40 percent of Mexico's roads are paved—unchanged over the last decade.[56] Other infrastructure is as bad. Mexico has over ten thousand miles of railroad track (most built before the 1910 Mexican Revolution)—roughly 60 percent less per square mile than the United States, and a third less than a country such as Argentina.[57] According to the World Bank, the government spends just half of what is needed for basic transportation maintenance, never mind the needed additions.

The deficit carries over to basic services as well. Thirteen percent of rural Mexicans don't have access to treated water, and 32 percent lack adequate sanitation services.[58] Even in tonier neighborhoods of Mexico City one hears the repeated refrain of "Agua Electropura," as salesmen on bikes pedal the streets, selling their five-gallon jugs to residents afraid of drinking tap water. Mexico's state-owned power companies are notoriously inefficient, ranking near the bottom of the Latin American pack.[59] With the government investing barely enough to keep the aging infrastructure going, Mexicans suffer through routine blackouts, particularly during the summer rainy season.

The private sector hasn't picked up the slack. Since Telmex's privatization, Mexico has fallen behind its neighbors and peers in terms of telecommunications infrastructure and investment.[60] Internet access is worse: fewer than 20 percent of Mexicans have it in their homes, putting them dead last among the thirty-four mostly large and industrialized OECD countries.[61] Interest in and auctions for road, airport, and port concessions have been exceedingly slow, limiting private sector investment in infrastructure to less than 1 percent of GDP over the last decade. This places Mexico last among the large Latin American economies (in terms of infrastructure investment as a portion of GDP)—and far behind its OECD counterparts.[62]

Early in his term, President Calderón announced a major national infrastructure plan, but it was a profound disappointment—suffering first from a lack of politically and technically savvy personnel able to take charge and push through the projects, and then later from the effects of the global economic crisis. Less than half of the projects got off the drawing board, and Mexico slipped in the World Economic Forum's infrastructure rankings in the process. The limitations caused by roads, railroads, ports, water systems, electricity grids, telecommunications, and the like increase the cost of transportation, hamper efficiency and productivity throughout the economy, and hinder the creation of the backward linkages needed to spur economic growth.

Mexico's infrastructure challenges are matched by societal ones. In the United States, we fully believe in—and have at least a few good examples of—rags-to-riches stories. Andrew Carnegie, John Rockefeller, Oprah Winfrey, and President Barack Obama all started from humble beginnings. The idea that hard work and dedication can and will be recognized is the basis of our venerated meritocracy. We idealize the center; those from both high and low ends of the economic scale call themselves middle class. And our faith in social mobility remains quite high, despite definitive signs that America's wealthy have pulled away from the pack.

Challenging Mexico's middle class future is the lack of social mobility. The ability to move from the bottom to the middle—much less to the top—is limited. For those born in the bottom 20 percent, half will stay there.[63] Those that do escape generally make it just one rung up—still in the lower and lower middle class. This inertia occurs at the top end as well—the wealthy generally stay so from generation to generation, no matter their inherent talents or determination.[64] Los Angeles mayor Antonio Villaraigosa succinctly summed up the challenge at a dinner in Mexico City hosted by magnate Carlos Slim. When asked about the differences between our two countries, he said, "Simple. If my family had stayed in Mexico, I would be serving the food tonight. Instead, we left for the United States and today you are holding this dinner in my honor."[65]

One of the gravest obstacles to social mobility is the schools. In the last few decades Mexico has made great strides toward getting kids into the classroom. In 1990, most kids just made it through primary school. Today, the majority remains through high school and most of those students enroll in college.[66] But while educational spending is relatively high (at 6 percent of GDP), it is questionable whether Mexicans are getting their money's worth. Mexico is falling behind, scraping the bottom when stacked up against its OECD counterparts and far outpaced on international tests by other emerging economies, as seen by its repeatedly dismal performance on international standardized tests.[67] One big problem is Mexico's teachers' union. With over a million members, it is much better at protecting teacher perks than at educating students. Rather than seeking out and hiring those with the necessary skills and energy, teaching positions are often inherited or auctioned off to the highest bidder.[68] The union has repeatedly resisted efforts to require training, to link teacher pay to standardized test results, or even to keep a roster of which teachers are assigned to each school.

Weak public schools and undertrained and unaccountable teachers hurt the poorest most—those who are unable to afford other alternatives. To be fair, small steps have been made. President Calderón and the notorious head of the teachers' union, Elba Esther Gordillo, did agree on some performance standards. But fundamental reform is not on the table, despite the importance of building human capital for Mexico's future.

Even the salutary increase in university degrees—up more than 30 per cent since 2001—has yet to boost the economy.[69] Employers complain about the mismatch between their needs and the skills of graduates—too many political science majors and not enough engineers. Other opportunities often entice skilled graduates to leave. One-sixth of Mexico's college graduates live and work in the United States. Roughly half of Mexican PhDs are up north.[70]

Another problem for social mobility is that though access to loans has expanded, it started from an extremely low base. While in the United States many worry about overly easy credit, Mexico has the opposite problem: its middle class and private sector still remain undercapitalized. Mortgages, car loans, and credit cards have entered the popular lexicon—a total transformation from just a few decades past. But Mexico trails not just other emerging economic powerhouses such as China, Brazil, and Singapore, but also less formidable competitors such as Nicaragua, Tunisia, Liberia, and Egypt in terms of relative credit available in the economy.[71] Too few can find the extra cash needed to build a house, or to start or expand a business.

Even the ability to open a bank account is nowhere near universal. Over half of Mexico's municipalities have no traditional banks. And it isn't as if these institutions are just on the other side of the county line. For any of the forty thousand residents of Tecpatán, Chiapas, visiting the nearest bank requires a jarring eight-hour bus ride.[72] This reality forces millions of citizens to stuff their savings under the proverbial mattress—limiting individuals' ability to save, businesses' ability to grow, and money's potential to multiply throughout the larger economy.

These factors play into a larger challenge Mexico faces: inequality. Here many point to the harsh austerity measures, mass privatizations, and neoliberal economic policies that benefit the few and not the many.[73] The worry here—supported by studies by the World Bank and others—is that such an uneven playing field not only leaves many in poverty and without economic opportunities, but also holds back the whole nation.[74]

Looking at economic data from the 1980s and into the 1990s, the trends are worrisome. The most used technical measure of inequality is the Gini coefficient, which places income inequality on a scale of zero (where everyone earns the same amount) to one (where one person controls all the wealth). A study by Colegio de Mexico economist Gerardo Esquivel calculates that Mexico's Gini increased steadily from 0.49 in 1984 to 0.54 in 1996, coinciding with Mexico's economic opening (as well as two profound economic crises).[75] This change reflects a 40 percent fall in social spending during this time period, which diminished the (already meager) social safety net for Mexico's poor. It also resulted from plummeting wages for blue-collar workers throughout the so-called lost decade of the 1980s, and through the mid-1990s.[76]

But by the turn of the twenty-first century, these trends started to shift. According to both OECD data and the Mexican government's annual household survey figures, inequality has consistently declined over the past fifteen years, reaching, in 2006, the same level as before the 1980s crisis.[77] Poverty is also down slightly, with five million fewer people living on four dollars a day or less in 2010 than in 2005.[78]

A number of factors are behind this trend.[79] First, Mexico's macroeconomic stability (even with slow growth) has been particularly beneficial for the poor—the group that studies show is hit the hardest by economic crises.[80] Real wages also improved, due to a mix of broader education and increased worker productivity. Finally, social spending targeting the poor rose. Programs such as *Oportunidades* (started under President Zedillo as *Progresa*) provide some six million low-income families with monthly stipends to keep their kids healthy and in school.[81]

Inequality still clouds Mexico's future and too many still live on too little. Mexico is the second most unequal country in the OECD (besting only Chile). It has yet to tackle its quite regressive tax system (it has some of the lowest tax collection rates in the hemisphere, and relies strongly on regressive value-added taxes). Still, overall, the numbers are moving in the right direction.

THE BINATIONAL ROAD FORWARD

Mexico has come a long way in the last three decades, shifting from a closed to an open economy, from booms and busts to macroeconomic stability, and from a poor to a middle class nation. But it has yet to unlock its true growth potential, or to match the economic gains and growth rates seen in many of its emerging market peers—China, South Korea, Brazil, and Peru.

One might sum up U.S. interest as friendly concern for a neighbor, and it is indeed that. But the U.S. economic future is also increasingly tied to Mexico. A real economic partnership between the two neighbors can be more than just an engine for Mexico's economic middle; it can help protect and expand America's middle class.

The United States' economic reliance on Mexico is no less real just because it is overlooked. Already twenty-two of the fifty U.S. states claim Mexico as their first or second destination for exports. Leading the pack are the border states. Each month Texan companies send over US$7 billion and their Californian counterparts almost US$2 billion in goods to their neighbor.[82] But this bonanza isn't limited just to the border. The economies of states such as South Dakota, Nebraska, and New Hampshire now depend on exports to Mexico as well. U.S. companies in industries as diverse as electronic equipment, household appliances, paper products, red meat, pears, and grapes rely today on Mexican industry and consumers for their livelihoods. Because of these ties, economic expansion to the south will boost growth to the north. The opposite is also true; future downturns in Puebla will mean layoffs in Peoria.

This dependence through economic integration with Mexico is only deepening as companies worldwide transform the way they make things.

American businesses such as Ford, General Electric, Honeywell, Intel, and Hewlett-Packard have rebounded by "near-shoring" or opening factories in nearby Mexico. Less recognized, this has saved many U.S. jobs in the process.[83] Studies estimate that roughly 40 percent of Mexican-made products' value is actually "made in the U.S.A."—ten times that of Chinese-made goods.[84] In this age of inexorable globalization, U.S. economic cooperation with Mexico holds out the hope—and indeed the promise—of stopping the wholesale decampment of manufacturing firms to trans-Pacific locales.

Misunderstood by U.S. politicians and pundits alike, NAFTA, and Mexican outsourcing more generally, can be a good thing for U.S. workers and the U.S. middle class. With a different mindset and approach, U.S.-Mexico economic ties can help boost America's chances in the global economic race. Using raw data collected confidentially from thousands of large U.S. multinational manufacturing firms, two Harvard Business School professors, along with a colleague from the University of Michigan, upend the conventional wisdom, finding that as companies ramp up investment and employment abroad they also invest and hire more people at home.[85] Companies become more productive—and more competitive—and with their better products, lower prices, and higher sales, they create new jobs all around.[86] The study shows that, on average, when a firm hires ten employees abroad, it will actually hire, not lay off, at least two employees at home. This means that efforts to stop "off-shoring" might actually have the reverse and perverse effect of undermining U.S. jobs.

Just look at Caterpillar's history. Founded between the world wars through the merger of two rival tractor companies, it branched into road construction and other equipment in the 1930s. During World War II the company doubled its workforce, working around the clock to meet U.S. military needs for engines, machines, and tractors. But it was after the war that Caterpillar as a worldwide brand took off, opening its first foreign subsidiaries to supply the European rebuilding effort. With huge profits from the Marshall Plan, it developed new products and spread to new countries, coming to dominate the world's earth-moving machinery market.

Despite its renowned history and enviable reach, it began to falter in the 1980s, suffering from labor disputes and losing market share to Japanese and European equipment manufacturers in Asia and Latin America. Throughout the 1990s profits plummeted and its stock price plunged.

Financial analysts questioned not just the dominance of the iconic yellow and black brand, but its very survival.

Yet fast forward to 2006, and Caterpillar's feted CEO was telling a different story. Profits again soared and the stock price more than tripled. Caterpillar regained its title of number one heavy machinery provider in the world. With 70 percent of its sales outside the United States, the company is now one of the country's largest exporters. Even after the 2008 worldwide financial crisis, Caterpillar continued to edge out competitors and increase profits.

Mexico helped pave the way for Caterpillar's return to dominance. Though many see the company as antiunion—and its investments in Mexico as further evidence of the management's callousness toward U.S. workers—Caterpillar's factories next door have saved and even added American jobs in the process.[87] For instance, in 2005 the castings plant for Caterpillar's smaller engines moved from Mapleton, Illinois, to Saltillo, Mexico. But these castings are then shipped to a brand-new factory in San Antonio to be machined, and then out through the port of Houston to global markets.

Caterpillar's near-shoring to Mexico boosted international competitiveness, and the uptick in sales created thousands of new U.S. jobs. Even as the Saltillo factory took 560 Mapleton jobs, Caterpillar added another 1500 positions just in Illinois. In fact, since NAFTA's signing, Caterpillar has increased its U.S.-based posts by nearly a third.[88] Unlike Caterpillar's operations in China, Brazil, and Russia, Mexico's plants allow a good part of the production process to remain in the United States.

This same logic applies to the big three U.S. car companies. An accepted wisdom is that the auto industry has been one of the hardest hit by NAFTA. News articles, policy reports, and congressional testimonies bemoan not just plant closings in Dayton, Ohio, or Fremont, California, but factory openings in Chihuahua or Toluca, Mexico.[89] Mexico's gains are portrayed as America's (and American workers') losses. These zero-sum conclusions miss the real, more complicated story, and in particular overlook the benefits of integration with America's neighbor.

The U.S. auto industry has indeed been transformed. The traditional model of in-house production developed by Henry Ford over a century ago hasn't existed for decades. For good or bad, Ford, General Motors, and Chrysler no longer, in truth, "make cars." Instead, vast networks of hundreds of suppliers are the real engine behind these iconic brands. Some are small operations, like Global Industrial Equipment or Shane Steel Processing, which specialize in manufacturing particular bolts, bearings, or brackets. These bottom-tier operations are often so specialized that they do only one thing—for instance headlights or taillights, but not both. They sell to the next tier up—companies like Dana or AC Delco, which take these small parts and create components such as drive shafts, gearboxes, or fans. The next rung up, companies like Johnson Controls, Global Electronics, Bosch, and TRW, bring together these prefabricated components to create modules such as sound systems, brake systems, seats, instrument panels, or fuel injectors. These more recognizable pieces are then delivered to a Ford or General Motors assembly plant for the final act. Lesser-known suppliers do everything from basic manufacturing to, increasingly, research and design, providing 80 percent of the value—and of the jobs—in the auto industry.

Changes in how also changed where cars are made. Over a fourth of U.S. car parts are made abroad—the largest percentage coming from Mexico.[90] But the tiered supplier system also means that movement is rarely just one way. In fact, the Chevy Malibu sold in Omaha, Nebraska, may have crossed the border not once but multiple times, as parts combine into components, components into systems or modules, and finally modules into cars. Every Ford Fiesta sold in Guanajuato, Mexico, is no different—having also already seen both sides of the border before hitting the showroom down south.

NAFTA did not cause these profound transformations in the worldwide auto industry. But it did help ensure that, given the enhanced competition brought by globalization, U.S.-brand cars remain competitive at home and abroad. Yes, some plants have moved on. But others have remained, and even expanded—able to do so precisely because of production in nearby Mexico (and Canada).

These same globalizing forces have encouraged some Mexican companies to come north. Founded in 1929, Mexican company San Luis Rassini makes the springs that cushion the ride for passengers in General Motor's Silverados, Tahoes, and Suburbans, in Ford's F-Series and Ram pickups, and in Toyota's Tacomas.[91] As its success grew, so did its geographic dispersion; San Luis Rassini now owns plants in Plymouth, Michigan, and Montpelier, Ohio. Another Mexican transplant is engine block and transmission parts producer Nemak, whose plants in Dickson, Tennessee; Sylacauga, Alabama; Glasgow, Kentucky; and Sheboygan, Wisconsin employ over two thousand American workers.[92]

These links stretch far beyond cars. Grupo Bimbo started with the family cake shop, El Molino, of a Spanish immigrant, Lorenzo Servitje. At first, Bimbo's little white bear emblazoned just ten trucks that made daily Mexico City rounds, delivering presliced loaves to small local stores across the city. But the company quickly expanded, to more products and more locations throughout Mexico, and then began feeling its way into the United States— initially through the Hispanic market. From border towns to major hubs such as Los Angeles, Dallas, Miami, Chicago, and Houston, Bimbo's cakes, breads, and tortillas began filling local shelves.

Post-NAFTA, Bimbo went on a buying spree, quadrupling its sales in the following fifteen years. Bimbo literally became as American as apple pie, buying Entenmann's, Mrs. Baird's, Oroweat, Thomas' English muffins, and Sara Lee.[93] Now the largest baker in the United States, it manages tens of factories, thousands of routes, and even more employees.[94]

What are emerging in cars, computers, televisions, and appliances, as well as in clothing, footwear, medical equipment, tools, and toys, are tightly integrated regional supply chains. The border today is a choreographed dance of parts and processes, moving back and forth to create a final competitive product for our own markets and for the world. This dance, it turns out, can be good for U.S. workers and the U.S. economy.

By labeling all foreign factories as bad for the United States and its workers, public opinion neglects the promise of Mexican markets as well. Cars made in Ford or General Motors Mexico plants are often sold to Mexico's avid consumers and to others throughout Latin America. U.S. manufacturers with operations in Mexico, such as General Electric and Westinghouse, now sell more locally than they ship north. These international sales create jobs. Some, maybe most, are not in the United States. But others—designers, engineers, marketers, financial analysts, managers, and factory workers—are. Mexican consumers increasingly power the U.S. export economy, underpinning millions of American jobs.

TODAY'S SPEED BUMPS

The importance of Mexico for America's economic health is most visible at the border. Nearly one million people cross the U.S.-Mexico border on a daily basis—to shop, visit family, or commute to work.[95] More than US$1 billion worth of goods pass through the forty-two border crossings by truck every day—US$52 million an hour.[96] Yet while the back and forth have skyrocketed, the paths across haven't kept pace. In some places the so-called ports of entry are literally falling apart. At the San Ysidro port of entry between San Diego and Tijuana—the world's busiest crossing—a checkpoint roof collapsed in 2011, leaving huge chunks of concrete across thirteen lanes of traffic and injuring several travelers in the process.[97] The result of the decrepit border infrastructure: delays for travelers, costs for companies, and losses for both the U.S. and Mexican economies.

For a supplier sending products from Illinois to Monterrey, Mexico, it takes a couple of days to drive the fourteen hundred miles from Chicago to the border—from the "windy city" through St. Louis, Missouri, past Little Rock, Arkansas, and then through Texas. Then the fun starts. Driving down Texas I-35 to the Juárez-Lincoln International Bridge that links the two Laredos over the Rio Grande, the traffic routinely backs up for five miles. Billed as "The gateway to Mexico," it more often resembles a giant parking lot, with fume-spewing eighteen-wheelers idling for hours during peak times. Since few U.S. trucks can enter Mexico, the initial drivers drop their goods in one of Laredo's thousand warehouses, ready for inspection by the Mexicans. Once examined, the Mexican brokerage company usually must spend the morning getting the remaining paperwork in order. At this point they hand over their cargo to short-haul vehicles—called "drayage" trucks—joining the undoubtedly long line. Warehousing, inspection, classification, verification, unloading, and reloading can take anywhere from one to three days. Once across, the short-haul truck hands off the trailer yet again, this time to a Mexican trucking company, which hitches up to go the final distance. The final 150 miles go quickly, reaching the city of Monterrey in a few hours. The trip involves ten separate steps, at least three different drivers, and between US$300 and US$650 in fees.[98]

The trip northward is not much better. Upon reaching the border, a drayage truck must again take over. After making it through Mexican inspections, the trucks line up again to wait, at times for several hours. When they reach the border, the unlucky will be subject to a secondary U.S. inspection, which can take the better part of an afternoon. Once finally dropped off at a local warehouse, the goods await another long-haul tractor-trailer to take them to their final destination, having lost most likely a full day in border transit.[99]

It takes nearly the same amount of time to drive from Chicago to Monterrey as it does to move just a few miles across the border, due to the overwhelmed infrastructure and inane bureaucracy. These woes aren't limited to the Laredos. Built in the 1970s, the Mariposa border crossing between Nogales, Arizona, and Nogales, Sonora, was designed to handle some four hundred rigs a day. During harvest season, some sixteen hundred trucks squeeze through the dated infrastructure. Going north, at peak times trucks can idle in line for eight hours. On the worst days they slowly inch forward through the night, the costs mounting as their strawberries, tomatoes, cucumbers, and bell peppers ripen far away from supermarket shelves.

These delays hurt both economies. Goods sit. Produce rots. Flowers wilt. Cattle stand weary in the midday sun. These delays hit "just in time" delivery, the basis of most manufacturing today, the hardest. From cars to appliances to high-tech gadgets, companies all work to boost profits by cutting idle inventory. In today's world, "just in time" doesn't require absolute proximity—many auto part suppliers are some five hundred miles away (equivalent to a day's drive) from their buyers.[100] But it does require precision timing—which can be hopelessly thrown off by uncertain border waits and customs snafus. In the end, companies and manufacturers decide to move elsewhere, searching for more assured and predictable terrain. A California study estimated that border waits between Tijuana and San Diego alone cost the United States and Mexico $6 billion in lost output and over fifty thousand jobs a year.[101] A broader study by the U.S. Commerce Department estimates that every minute delay on the border costs the United States over US$100 million and more than five hundred jobs. With aggregate waits averaging over an hour, this adds up to billions of dollars and tens of thousands of jobs lost each year—a hefty price tag for U.S. businesses, workers, and families, and one that we can directly reduce through targeted investment.[102] If not dealt with, these losses will only grow.

Conversely, the benefits of trade flows are readily apparent in places such as McAllen, Texas, in the heart of Rio Grande Valley. Over the last twenty years, a wave of investment changed thousands of acres of farmland into shopping centers, apartment complexes, and new industrial parks. Over five hundred companies, including several Fortune 500 members, have set up shop. As cities are dying across the Rust Belt, Forbes declared McAllen as the city with the second-highest job-growth rate and one of the best places to do business in the country.[103] Locals are not resting on these laurels. In 2009, the city opened the first new U.S.-Mexico border crossing in more than ten years, and officials lobby tirelessly to bring I-69 through The

Valley—to finally lose the ignominious distinction as the largest urban area in the United States without an interstate highway. Many talk ambitiously of consolidating the cluster of cities on both sides of the border into a single metropolitan sprawl known as Borderplex.[104]

Laredo, El Paso, Brownsville, and Otay Mesa outside of San Diego are all working to expand, improve, or completely rebuild their ports of entry, with an eye to improving their local bottom lines. Even Arizona, a state known for its inflammatory immigration positions, celebrated the opening of its new crossing in San Luis, some twenty miles south of Yuma, in November 2010. Governor Jan Brewer talked up the investment and jobs the new port would bring to "invigorate the region's economy."[105]

Yet overall, the broader U.S. approach has been timid. The U.S. department of transportation estimates a gap of over $10 billion in highways and infrastructure leading up to the border. The border also remains hopelessly understaffed. Fewer than sixty thousand customs officers oversee the flows of hundreds of millions of people and hundreds of billions of dollars in goods.[106] In Texas alone, independent studies estimate that five thousand more officers are needed just to keep up with today's trade.[107]

Most of the U.S. spending has gone to border control—usually between crossings—rather than to the official ports of entry. This focus is somewhat counterintuitive, since the vast majority of contraband, illegal drugs, weapons, and, increasingly, unauthorized people come through established crossings.[108] In fact, investing in border infrastructure would help the United States achieve two goals at the same time: allowing in the good trade, and keeping out the bad.

Together, federal, state, and local governments are trying to pick up the pace. Working with the private sector, plans are in the making for new rail lines, airport links, and border crossings in general—with over a dozen proposals on the table. For instance, the Kansas City Southern Railway Company is spearheading an East Loop Bypass Project to construct fifty-one miles of track around the Laredos.[109] The San Ysidro crossing between San Diego and Tijuana and the Mariposa crossing at Nogales are also now under construction, and new crossings are in the making at El Paso and Otay Mesa.[110] This should help ease some of the problems and help spur the local and national economies.

There are other small steps being taken in the right direction. In 2011, the Obama administration announced a pilot trucking program that will finally fulfill the U.S. side of the NAFTA bargain, allowing registered and screened Mexican trucks to continue to their final destination. The U.S. government also started another pilot program, the Secure Electronic Network for Travelers Rapid Inspection (SENTRI), which enables customs screening at the factory of trusted suppliers, allowing them to bypass border lines, benefiting overworked customs agents and "just in time" delivery alike.[111] But so far these are just small demonstration programs, and the urgent need for more ambitious efforts remains ignored.

* * *

Economic history shows us that trade has been a positive engine for wealth creation. From the vast Roman and British empires to the successes of the smaller Nordic trading states and the merchant republic of Lebanon, international exchange has underpinned economic growth and higher standards of living for centuries. Empirical evidence supports the relationship between economic openness and development—more open economies do better in terms of life expectancy, education, and income.[112] Closed economies, on the other hand, fare poorly. Historically, many just fade away—Pomerania, overcome by the more open Prussia (now Germany), or Burgundy, subsumed by France. Today's protective standouts include Myanmar, North Korea, and Cuba—countries few Americans would willingly trade in their passport to join. Worse, economic protection and political oppression often go hand in hand.

America's past lessons point away from closing U.S. borders as a way to defend American workers and well-being. The now infamous Smoot-Hawley Tariff Act of 1930, which raised tariffs on some twenty thousand imported products, did not benefit U.S. companies or workers. In fact, many economists and historians blame it (and the retaliatory tariff increases from other nations) for deepening the Great Depression. Yet finding a path that broadly spreads the benefits of trade and opening is still difficult, and one with which the United States now struggles. Former U.S. treasury secretary Larry Summers summed up the quandary well: "The twin arguments that globalization is inevitable and protectionism is counterproductive for almost everyone have the great virtue of being correct, but they do not provide much consolation for the losers."[113]

The United States became the world leader it is today on its economic prowess. While it continues as the world's most important economy, it too must adapt to the current economic realities. How best to navigate inexorable globalization—and to make sure the benefits are spread broadly—is the U.S. challenge today.

An important part of a more inclusive solution to this dilemma lies in closer economic connections with America's neighbors, and in particular with Mexico. After three decades of change, Mexico now boasts a strong, stable, and open economy, and, more than many nations, largely complements rather than competes with the United States in global markets. Rather than rejecting closer ties, we should be embracing the back and forth across the border, as it has the potential to create a rising economic tide, lifting all boats.

MEXICO'S RISING INSECURITY: A REAL ILLNESS WITH THE WRONG PRESCRIPTION

Cesáreo Carvajal, secretary of public security for the central Mexican state of San Luis Potosí, greeted us at the airport, a wiry forty-something in a brownish suit. He was flanked by Severino Cartagena, director of the San Luis Potosí Police Academy, and several other well-dressed men. Arriving midmorning from Mexico City, our five-person U.S. delegation came for a tour of the school and the regional security command center. Once finished with introductions, we piled into an armored white Suburban and took off, followed by others in a "chase car."

Cesáreo drove, quite quickly, as we began a day-long tour of the state's security operations. Our first stop was the expanded Police Academy, where the newly created federal investigative police force trains. Impressive young men and women filled the classrooms in identical collared shirts and jeans, standing at attention as we entered and met their Mexican, Colombian, and American teachers.

Later, back in the car on our way to state police headquarters, Cesáreo began recounting the hard facts of his two years as head of security for this

Mexican state. His first week began as expected. Sent from Mexico City—where he had been an elite member of the federal police force—he spent the first days settling into his hotel room at the Camino Real, hanging his many plaques of commendation from Mexican and U.S. law enforcement around his new office, and receiving his first local visitors. A pair soon came, each with a small suitcase stuffed with cash, to greet the new security boss and to propose a mutually advantageous relationship. Cesáreo responded by throwing them in jail.

Within weeks, the first assassination attempt occurred. Just as he arrived at the hotel after a long day of work, a bazooka ripped through a nearby tree and into a parked tractor-trailer full of Corona beer. Glass flew everywhere, but left Cesáreo unscathed. They tried again several months later, once more unsuccessfully. Meanwhile, he launched operation after operation against the Zetas—the dominant cartel throughout the city and state. Not trusting the local police, he brought in the military and federal forces to raid local safe houses, shut down extortion rings, and break up prison networks. In the following months they arrested over ten thousand people and seized hundreds of weapons and tons of drugs. After two long years, huge technology and equipment investments, and many deaths, Cesáreo confidently stated that San Luis Potosí was back from the brink of anarchy.

Still, after a day of impressive demonstrations and discussions, as he took us back to the airport for our return flight to Mexico City, he announced his exit. When the new governor assumed office in six weeks, he said, he would be gone, returning to the federal police force—perhaps sent to another hotspot. The thought that lingered for everyone was what choice the next head of security would make when, as expected, two men show up to greet him, each carrying a small suitcase.

Along with the economy, Mexicans' biggest worry today is security. Midday gunfights, brazen assassinations, and gruesome beheadings capture U.S. and Mexican headlines each day. The government estimates that over sixty thousand people were killed in drug-related violence between 2006–2012 (some outside sources claim tens of thousands more), rivaling the better-known war zones of Iraq and Afghanistan.[1]

According to the government, most—perhaps 90 percent—are criminals killing criminals. Others, including Human Rights Watch, cast doubt on these estimates, pointing to the increasing number of noncombatants caught in the crosshairs.[2] An estimated three thousand police officers have been killed since 2007, and a number of politicians have also been assassinated, including twenty mayors in 2010 and 2011, the PRI's gubernatorial candidate in Tamaulipas, and a former governor of Colima state.[3] Mexico, too, is one of the most dangerous countries in the world for journalists, with nearly seventy killed between 2000 and 2010.

Violence of course is nothing new in Mexico, and, in fact, the recent spike comes after a twenty-year decline.[4] And though the current butchery is spreading geographically, it is still concentrated in less than 10 percent of all municipalities.[5] In 2010 nearly a fifth of all drug-related killings occurred in just one border town, Ciudad Juárez.[6] Statistically, homicide rates are no higher, and in some cases are lower than in many other Latin American nations, including Brazil, Colombia, and Venezuela. But whatever the appropriate comparisons, the rapid escalation and graphic public nature of the violence have dramatically affected the country.

This upsurge is rooted in the drug trade. The illicit business has always entailed some level of violence, as contract disputes, as well as "mergers and acquisitions," are resolved through bloodshed. But the recent spike reflects other factors—changes in the worldwide drug market, Mexico's democratic opening, and the Mexican government's more recent efforts to go after the drug cartels. The United States—through its insatiable demand for drugs and half-hearted efforts to stop the flow of guns and money south—contributes in no small part to the carnage.

Though spurred by drugs, the violence has now taken on a life of its own as criminals seek new opportunities and move into new businesses, preying more and more upon ordinary Mexicans in the process. With such complicated origins, the potential solutions are not simple. To create lasting security, Mexico will have to find a way to build and support a broad-based democratic rule of law, anchored by professional police and strong courts. While some efforts have begun, these changes must happen more quickly, drawing on Mexico's citizens and its northern neighbor alike if the government hopes to stem the current bloody tide.

THE ORIGINS OF VIOLENCE

Mexico has long been a source of illegal substances and goods for U.S. consumers. Opium was Mexico's first major illicit crop, with production ramping up at the start of the twentieth century. Prohibition in the United States added alcohol to the list of profitable illegal substances, and Mexico became a haven for drinkers and rum-runners alike. Marijuana sales, long a staple for Mexico's smugglers, soared in the 1960s with the rise of the U.S. counterculture. A decade later hippies gave way to yuppies, and Colombian cocaine became the U.S. drug of choice. Synthetic drugs rose in prominence at the turn of the twenty-first century as use of amphetamine-type stimulants— commonly known as "crystal meth" or "ice"—became more prevalent than cocaine.[7] While Mexico has been on the ground floor of all these trends, supplying the evolving tastes of its larger neighbor, in recent years its role has changed.

Thirty years ago, Colombians dominated the region's drug business, producing and controlling the wholesale distribution of cocaine and other drugs throughout much of the United States. Mexican traffickers played a minor part in this larger production and distribution chain, providing an alternative transit route to the popular Caribbean-Miami path.

During the 1980s and 1990s, this situation began to change. The United States poured billions into securing the southeastern seaboard through the Caribbean. It also began working more closely with Colombia—going after well-known drug kingpins and dismantling the large cartels on their home turf. And so the trade and transit shifted to Mexico. As Mexicans learned the ropes, they increasingly cut themselves a better deal with their Colombian counterparts—taking over more of the logistics and demanding a greater percentage of the profits. By the late 1980s Mexicans began referring colloquially to the emergence of their own drug cartels. Over the next twenty years these criminal organizations would be defined by geography (the Sinaloa cartel, the Juárez cartel, the Gulf cartel, the Familia Michoacana) and by leaders (the Arellano-Félix Organization, the Beltrán-Leyvas, the Zetas), as policymakers, police, journalists, and others tried to document their whereabouts, alliances, splits, and relative power.[8]

Cashing in on their comparative geographic advantage, today the Mexican cartels dominate the business, working with local and international producers to supply, transport, and distribute nine out of every ten kilos of cocaine, as well as the vast majority of marijuana, heroin, and methamphetamines headed to the United States. U.S. Department of Justice reports estimate that Mexican criminal organizations now operate in over one thousand U.S. cities.[9] Evidence also suggests they control much of the increasing trade to Europe, Russia, and Latin America. One of the outcomes of the forty-year "war on drugs"—at the cost of billions of U.S. taxpayer dollars—has been to push its epicenter to our border.

The increasing flows of money into Mexico prompted these illicit businesses to improve their techniques—creating more sophisticated schemes to process, clean, and disburse billions of dirty dollars. Estimates are hard to come by, but many say Colombians were clearing some US$2.5 billion a year during the 1980s when they dominated the cocaine trade.[10] Today conservative studies put the Mexican trade at more than twice that amount, and official U.S. government sources estimate returns as many times more.[11] Evidence from some of the few successful money laundering cases hint at the sheer size. Federal investigators believe that over the course of a few years, Mexico's criminal organizations laundered billions of dollars through bulk cash and wire transfers via Wachovia Bank (now part of Wells Fargo) alone.[12] These court cases also demonstrate the cartels' heightened sophistication. Mostly gone are gentlemen bringing suitcases of cash to the teller window, and instead cartels use a complex mix of multiple accounts, false identities, and rapid wire transfers to obscure the origin of their money.

To protect their routes, products, and returns, Mexican drug cartels invested heavily in enforcement, beefing up security wings and acquiring more and higher-powered arms. The "hardening" of the U.S. border over the last two decades just accentuated this trend, weeding out the mom-and-pop providers in favor of more sophisticated and violent operations. Police and military seizures now typically include AK-47–style and AR-15 assault weapons, as well as Cold War–era grenades.[13] The most notorious case of escalating militarization involves the Zetas, whose founders defected from the Mexican army's special operations unit to become the enforcement arm of the Gulf cartel. They later split from their original sponsors, becoming one of the most aggressive and violent criminal organizations in Mexico.

Yet the transformation of the global drug market, and Mexico's role within it, is just the first part of the story. Another reason for the heightened violence reflects a darker side of Mexico's democratization. Political opening disrupted the long-standing, unwritten arrangements between drug traffickers and the old authoritarian government—in which PRI officials ensured few legal or law enforcement hassles in exchange for a cut of the profits. The election of opposition officials upended this status quo, requiring drug lords to renegotiate deals and encouraging rival traffickers to jump into the fray.

Ties between PRI officials and traffickers began during Prohibition. Flamboyant individuals such as Enrique Fernández Puerta, the "Al Capone of Ciudad Juárez," could be seen brazenly cavorting around town during the roaring twenties, flanked by an official police escort.[14] When his days of glamorous consumption ended with a bullet, the complex web of political and underworld connections continued under new management.

By the end of the Second World War, drug traffickers and PRI party officials cemented these links, developing fairly established patron-client relationships (not all that different from those in other areas of the economy). Local, state, and at times national political and security officials would guarantee safe transit for traffickers, keep law enforcement and courts from meddling in their affairs, and ensure that the next government (always led by the PRI) would not change the terms of the deal. The drug traffickers, in turn, paid the PRI for use of particular trade routes, or *plazas*. By the 1980s, internal passageways cost hundreds of thousands of dollars, and the going rate for border cities such as Ciudad Juárez and Tijuana topped US$3 million a year.[15] Traffickers kept the killing to a minimum—purposefully leaving politicians out of it. These unwritten rules defined the playing field, and they remained remarkably stable even as drug production and transit increased in the 1970s and 1980s.

The changing nature of Mexico's internal politics eroded the old modus operandi. President Salinas's decision to recognize the election of more opposition mayors and governors disrupted the old understandings between drug traffickers and the PRI hierarchy. Now local drug traffickers had to approach each new government to establish (or reestablish) the rules of the game. Other traffickers—previously kept out of the process—saw an opportunity to step in and try to negotiate lucrative deals with new police and politicians.

Uncertainty in the market meant more bloodshed. In fact, as opposition leaders won office in the 1990s, violence often followed. Baja California saw a spike in violence after the ascension of the PAN's Ernesto Ruffo Appel to the governor's seat in 1989, the first to break the PRI's state office glass ceiling. In Chihuahua (another early convert) murder rates escalated some 60 percent in the few years following the 1992 election.[16] The 2000 election of Vicente Fox to the presidency truly broke the old system, and with it the remaining informal "regulation" of the drug trafficking market.

Democratization had a further deleterious effect (at least in the short term) for security. With the election of Vicente Fox, Mexico experienced what nearly all democracies face at some point—gridlock. Particularly at the start, Mexico's three political parties were unaccustomed to negotiating with the executive branch or to working together in Congress to pass legislation. This hobbled the government's ability to react swiftly and effectively to organized crime, corruption, and violence. Necessary reforms to strengthen and improve the justice system and law enforcement stalled for years, even as crime expanded unabated.

With democracy, Mexico's federalism finally became a reality, and this too affected security. With the end of the dominant one-party regime, Mexico's states gained autonomy—as did their police forces, court systems, and bureaucracies. These layers rarely coordinated and often worked at cross purposes, at times coming to blows (and nearly to bullets). Not unheard of were standoffs of the sort that occurred in 2009 in the town of Escobedo, part of the industrial city of Monterrey. Late on a summer day at the busy intersection of Manuel L. Barragán and Sendero Divisorio, a scuffle broke out between the local and federal police. Initial taunts and pushes escalated quickly to drawn guns, with Mexico's finest pointing their AR-15 rifles at each other.[17] Military and federal police deployed to drug-infested towns routinely disarm the local cops, reflecting a deep lack of confidence in their supposed brethren. The disconnect and downright distrust between levels of administration has also strengthened the cartels vis-à-vis the government. With their rising importance in the hemisphere's drug pipeline, their increasing resources, and their militarized operations, the power dynamic began to shift in the criminals' favor.

Felipe Calderón's presidency is another, if shorter-term, explanation for why Mexico's drug trade became more violent. Upon entering office in December 2006, Calderón proclaimed a war on drug trafficking, sending the Mexican military to take back the streets. Many attest that his decision was based on deep-seated convictions, only enhanced by the death threats he received during his campaign for Mexico's highest office. Others suggest that his "tough on crime" approach was more a means to move beyond the contested 2006 election and shore up his new government. But whatever the reason, his decision added ammunition to an already raging battle. His government quickly set records in terms of interdictions, arrests, and extraditions, capturing or killing two-thirds of the thugs on Mexico's Most Wanted list.

These successes upset business as usual. As leaders were arrested, old bonds of loyalty were broken, spurring in-fighting between those left behind, and increasingly fragmenting markets. It also meant that power often shifted from the more seasoned businessmen (and a few women) to the second and third generations of cartel members—many from the enforcement arms and much more prone to violence. This pressure, combined with the hardening of the border, led transnational criminal organizations into other businesses—kidnapping, human smuggling, extortion, retail drug sales, and robbery. This brought them closer to the Mexican population, who became both customers and targets.

U.S. worries have grown in tandem with the rising violence. Congressional hearing after congressional hearing debate whether Mexico is becoming a "failed state." High-ranking federal officials compare Mexico to Colombia at its worst, labeling its narco-traffickers "insurgents" and "terrorists." Texas representative and active member of the Homeland Security committee Michael McCaul led a movement to classify Mexican drug cartels "in the same manner as al-Qaida, the Taliban, or Hezbollah."[18] Local and state politicians, desperate for funds (and votes), lambast Washington's blithe ignorance of the border's "war zones." One of the most vehement has been Arizona Governor Jan Brewer, who demanded the federal government send the National Guard to deal with the "terror and mayhem."[19] The usually more Mexico-friendly Texas Governor Rick Perry hasn't been too far behind, por-traying El Paso as a city besieged by bullets and bombs.

U.S. worries about spillover violence are so far mostly that—worries. As murders topped five a day in Ciudad Juárez, its sister border city, El Paso, had just sixteen homicides during 2011, making it the safest city of its size in the United States. Other cities near the border—San Antonio, Austin, San Diego—are also known for their peace and quiet, not just compared to their Mexican counterparts but also relative to similar cities in the United States. In fact, murder and robbery rates in cities within fifty miles of the border are consistently lower than state and national averages. Available data on often unreported crimes, such as kidnappings, suggest that in the U.S. border cit-ies these too are falling.[20]

This doesn't mean there aren't other "spillover effects." The most wor-risome is corruption, as the money seeping across the border does not distinguish between blue and green passports. Cases against active U.S. border agents grew almost fourfold from 2006 to 2011.[21] In the U.S. border areas, local papers are increasingly littered with tales of law enforcement on the take: Sheriff Conrado Cantú of Starr County, Texas, pleading guilty to charges that he accepted bribes from drug traffickers, and Mayor Eddie Espinoza of Columbus, New Mexico, caught smuggling guns.[22] These transgressions reflect the perennial temptation created by large sums of money, but also, somewhat counterintuitively, the rapid expansion of boots on the border. Over the last decade the Border Patrol more than doubled to twenty thousand strong. These new recruits diluted the once-tight ranks, engulfing the experience, knowledge, and ethos of the veteran corps. The rapid expansion seems to have made America's largest police force more vulnerable to corruption, as more than a few applicants have been found to have ties to organized crime. Of the 10 percent of applicants taking lie-detector tests, more than half fail, raising serious concerns about the integrity of recent border patrol hires.[23]

The Ups and Downs of
U.S.-Mexico Security Cooperation

As both countries struggle with the repercussions of these long- and short-term trends, the history of U.S.-Mexico security cooperation complicates matters. In part, the rocky relationship stems from a history of failed efforts and limited progress. Mexico's first official post–World War II antinarcotics venture, dubbed the "great campaign," was anything but. For nearly twenty years it boiled down to occasional raids on poppy and marijuana farms, with Mexican soldiers spending long, backbreaking days pulling up and destroying crops. Due to a lack of manpower, equipment, and often interest, these efforts barely made a dent in the illegal flows north. Here and there Mexican law enforcement collaborated with U.S. operatives, but these unsystematic and unofficial relationships did little to change the overall picture—one of a seemingly ever-increasing drug supply for U.S. markets. Behind numerous summits and press conferences, all touting ongoing and expanding cooperation, lay inertia, frustration, and even hostility.

This haphazard approach ended in 1969, when exasperated Nixon administration officials launched Operation Intercept. For twenty days in early fall, U.S. Customs officials followed the letter of the law, painstakingly checking each and every person, car, and truck coming into the United States from Mexico—effectively shutting the border to narcotics and everything else. Few drugs were found, but traffic backed up for miles on major highways and thoroughfares.[24] As crossing times extended for hours, even days, toxic leaded gas fumes dizzied even the most hardened truck driver; Mexican tomatoes and peppers spoiled, and commuters lost jobs. Hotels and racetracks to the south sat empty while store shelves to the north remained full, each waiting for customers caught on the other side. The Mexican government howled in protest, but in the end the economic blackmail worked and Washington got what it wanted—visible security cooperation.[25]

Now finally allowed to do their own surveillance, American agents made their way south. They started meeting regularly with Mexican justice officials to share observations and at times information. Ending years of carefully cultivated independence, Mexico accepted nearly one hundred U.S. helicopters and planes, as well as automatic weapons and pilot training for counternarcotics missions, becoming one of the largest recipients of U.S. drug-control funds.[26]

In 1975, Mexico inaugurated Operation Condor, a massive drug eradication and interdiction program. The government sent hundreds of police and thousands more soldiers into the battle. The thirty DEA agents stationed in Mexico worked hand in hand with police to plot strategies, study reconnaissance photos, and choose targets.[27]

The gains initially seemed quite real. During the first three years the cops and soldiers destroyed nearly fifty thousand marijuana fields and twice as many opium plots. Mexico's share of the U.S. heroin market plummeted by more than half (the campaign also coincided with one of the worst droughts in the history of Sinaloa, an opium center). Marijuana production declined so precipitously that some in Mexico talked of its total eradication. DC policymakers were elated by the market shifts and the changing U.S.-Mexico security relationship. One U.S. narcotics official remembered it as a time of enthusiasm, commitment, and cooperation, effusing that "never have we had the working relationship with Mexican officials that we've had since the launching of this year's campaign."[28]

But the longer-term results were not just less effective, but also counterproductive. Operation Condor changed the dynamics of the Mexican trade—felling the small-scale producers and distributors while leaving the major drug traffickers untouched. These more powerful organizations came to dominate the trade, strengthening their hand vis-à-vis producers and the government alike. By the mid-1980s, Mexico's drug production picked back up again, with opium exports more than doubling.

U.S. officials grew increasingly frustrated. While DEA agents initially were allowed to tag along to watch the pesticide dumps, as the campaign progressed, they were left on the ground. No longer able to see what was happening for themselves, stories came back from informants of brilliant green marijuana plantations, acres upon acres of luminous leaves framed by miles of unirrigated brown. Others told of pilots dumping their poisons in the empty desert before returning to declare their mission completed, and of Mexican officers escorting rather than arresting their declared targets. To the United States, this was a blatant disregard for, and defiance of, supposed bilateral security efforts. The disappearance, torture, and murder of DEA agent Enrique "Kiki" Camarena in 1985 doomed the already fragile bonds of trust and cooperation between the two governments, exposing the power of Mexico's drug traffickers and the corruption of the state's security core.

Born in Mexicali, Mexico, Camarena became a naturalized U.S. citizen after moving to Calexico, California, when he was nine years old. A star high school athlete, he spent time as a marine and police officer before joining the DEA.[29] By all accounts he was a passionate, tenacious, and charismatic agent, making a name for himself in Guadalajara, a vital if at the time overlooked hub of the hemisphere's expanding and accelerating drug trade. On a sunny February afternoon, Camarena headed out to meet his wife for lunch, to talk about their upcoming transfer back stateside. The story told by Mexico's police—but never confirmed by eye witnesses—was that several armed men jumped him and dragged him off. He was never seen alive again. Mexican authorities offered a series of suspects to U.S. investigators, many not even linked by circumstantial much less concrete evidence (but conveniently dead, and so unable to offer their story). U.S. officials blamed drug kingpin Rafael Caro Quintero, though many questioned whether he was working alone.[30] And some even believed the intrigue extended into President de la Madrid's closest circle.[31]

With his death Camarena became a public hero—lionized by the DEA and common citizens alike. Red ribbons appeared on the lapels of Americans pledging to lead drug-free lives (only several years later the red bow would be more closely identified with HIV/AIDS), and Camarena Clubs popped up across the country, earning the attention and praise of First Lady Nancy Reagan. Congress quickly made the last week of October official "red ribbon week," encouraging communities to join together against illegal drugs.[32] The campaign, started in Camarena's memory, still brings thousands of schools and millions of students together each year.

Drug-related violence in the United States, along with the rise of cocaine's poor cousin, crack, changed the domestic political playing field. Though he had never been all that interested in the topic, President Reagan designated counternarcotics as a national security issue in the lead up to the 1986 midterm elections.[33] Not to be left out, Congress legislated an annual certification process to rate U.S. partners in the drug war (and punish those not making the grade), and ratcheted up the DEA's budget. Chastened, Mexico mouthed the appropriate responses of mutual concern and effort, but the security relationship remained difficult.

The years following Agent Camarena's death were ones of cautious circling. Cooperative steps forward were met with just as many setbacks. Rapprochement with the Salinas government soured when the DEA abducted and hauled a doctor across the border to stand trial in the United States as an accomplice in the Camarena case.[34] A 1995 visit of Secretary of Defense William Perry to Mexico—the first visit in memory—was followed in 1997 by the embarrassing revelation that General Jesús Gutiérrez Rebollo, Mexico's equivalent of the U.S. drug czar, was on the payroll of the Juárez cartel. Even as State Department and narcotics officials talked of greater cooperation and trust, the debates during the annual U.S. certification process brought out some of the less varnished and downright hostile feelings in Congress.

As others areas of cooperation with Mexico blossomed—trade and investment, transboundary water management, and even in small ways border monitoring—the drug war remained a disruptive issue, undermined by mutual suspicions and political calculations on both sides of the border. While billions of dollars in U.S. aid headed to South America, Mexico was largely shunted aside, even as it increasing fell within the drug trafficking line of fire. U.S. security assistance to its southern neighbor totaled less than US$40 million a year (and in many years significantly less than that) until 2008.[35] As U.S. special forces organized repeated operations in the jungles of Colombia and the altiplano of Bolivia and Peru, they barely made contact with their Mexican counterparts.

This distance began to diminish with the election of Felipe Calderón to Mexico's highest office. In the fall of 2006, even as losing presidential candidate Andrés Manuel López Obrador rallied his faithful supporters in Mexico City's Zócalo, Calderón was calling on Washington. At a small private dinner, he shocked the gathered East Coast establishment with a few short sentences. He intimated that the infiltration of organized crime had reached shocking levels, and that unless he did something the next presidential candidate would likely come from within their ranks. He then stated, matter of factly, that he was going to war—with or without the United States—against the narcotraffickers.

Calderón's warning, combined with an already worrisome uptick in violence, jolted America awake. The geographic realities of the drug trade brought many around to the fact that the United States had to be part of the solution. President Bush's 2007 trip to Guatemala and Mexico set U.S. resolve, as the real fear in his counterparts' voices brought home the urgency more than any intelligence report ever could. Calderón, in turn, took almost revolutionary steps to reach out to Mexico's northern neighbor, shaking off the decades-old policy of holding the United States at bay. This mutual evolution paved the way for the Merida Initiative.

Merida was an attempt at starting anew. It brought Mexicans and Americans together first to decide what to do, and then to begin doing it. With Mexico's military at the negotiating table (and with advice from the Colombians), the initial emphasis was heavy on equipment—helicopters, ion scanners, surveillance aircraft, and high-tech communications systems. Less was allocated to the day-to-day police efforts to fight crime or for "institution building" on the prosecution side. During the negotiation process there was surprisingly little anti-American rancor in Mexico, as most politicians hoped for change. Though there would be a few hiccups getting through the U.S. Congress, the initiative, committing US$1.3 billion over three years, passed by a wide margin in June 2008. In the following months, the first orders were placed.

Many would later criticize Merida for not having a comprehensive strategy. It is true; the final list of equipment and programs looked something of a grab bag—a bit for everyone. But a more charitable view can see that after more than twenty years, Mexico and the United States finally again took a seat at the same table, and agreed to start a new and ongoing discussion.

Three years later, the Obama administration would continue Merida, simultaneously shifting and expanding the focus. While maintaining the hunt for kingpins and drugs, U.S.-Mexico security cooperation extended to incorporate the border, working to make it easier for legal flows and harder for illegal flows to get through, and to strengthen communities, especially those hit hardest by drug violence. U.S. funds shifted away from hardware—helicopters, speedboats, mobile gamma-radiation inspections trucks, and hundreds of polygraph units—to software—training, institution building, and community outreach. In part this reflected the delivery of promised equipment. But it was also recognition of the complicated realities of Mexico's drug war—and the real limits of military equipment in turning the tide.

Despite advances, cooperation still faces high barriers. Some are political, in particular the hay to be made in Mexico by painting opponents as U.S. lackeys. Others are more fundamental, reflecting the conflicting priorities of the two governments, as stopping drug flows and reducing violence are not one and the same. But the most difficult barrier has been building the trust necessary to move forward together, which reflects the fundamental problem with which Mexico struggles today.

Mexico's Corruption Challenge

The Achilles' heel of Mexico's security is corruption, compounded by impunity. Corruption permeates day-to-day life, from the traffic cop milking drivers at a stoplight to elected officials handing out government jobs and contracts. A 2010 Transparency International report estimates that Mexicans pay over 200 million bribes for basic government services each year—nearly two for every man, woman, and child in the country—at a cost of roughly US$3 billion.[36] For the average citizen the maxim becomes "Él que no transa no avanza" or roughly, "If you don't cheat, you won't get ahead." This culture of corruption enables and encourages Mexico's criminals, leaving little legal incentive for them to mend their ways.

Much of Mexico's corruption stems from the inherent weakness of its law enforcement. For decades under the PRI, the police and courts were a part of the party machine, instruments of social control rather than providers of protection or justice. For those supportive of the party, infractions could often be overlooked or scuttled. But for dissenters, the long arm of the law on the streets and in the courtroom—whether warranted or not—was an effective instrument of fear and intimidation.[37] This long-standing political manipulation left weak tools for those trying to counter day-to-day corruption, much less aggressive crime networks.

Further hampering crime fighters' abilities are the sorry state of Mexico's police forces in general. The typical officer rarely finishes high school. He or she works long hours and risks mortal danger, and yet the average salary is just over US$600 a month, and in some states it is half that—hardly enough to buy life's necessities, and certainly not enough to save for the future.[38] Officers frequently have to pay for the job's basic requirements—uniforms, bullets, and gasoline—out of their own pockets. Worse for those aspiring to stay on the straight and narrow is a notorious system of payments up the chain of command, in which officers are expected to share extracurricular earnings with their superiors (who then pass along a portion to their own superiors). Law enforcement economics can have a Ponzi feel—a giant pyramid scheme enslaving the underlings but enriching the top. Police jobs are made all the harder by the weak links to local communities, which widely distrust the cops.[39] The combination of low pay, high risk, and diminished social status weeds out the optimistic, idealistic, and able. Though professionalism varies between federal, state, and local levels, and from location to location, overall it is fair to say that few upstanding citizens place police officer among their first career choices, and many must see it as a last resort.

But if the police are bad, the courts are possibly worse. More than 80 percent of crimes are never reported, as citizens either do not want to waste their time or are suspicious of the justice system.[40] Their perceptions are justified, as only one in every five reports is fully investigated, and far fewer are prosecuted.[41] The ability to prosecute cases seems to diminish with the seriousness of the crime (and hence the need to build a case). Of the few actually convicted, the majority are guilty of (often petty) theft, caught in the act of stealing.[42] Those who commit serious crimes that weigh more heavily on the population—kidnapping, extortion, embezzlement, murder—are less likely to face prosecution. In the end, just one or two out of every hundred crimes ends in a conviction, providing no legal deterrence to a life of crime.[43]

Though it can be difficult to convince prosecutors to investigate and move cases forward, once they do the chances of acquittal are slim, even when the only evidence is at best circumstantial or collected under duress (read torture). Defense attorneys are only able to ensure the rules of the court are followed; they are prohibited from cross-examining witnesses or contesting the prosecutor's evidence. Judges routinely fail to attend court proceedings.[44] Even when present, they often refuse to consider the evidence fully, more concerned with paperwork than with the life at stake in front of them. Once caught within the web, citizens have no effective way to defend themselves legally against prosecutors or other agents of the *Ministerio Público*. As a result, when convictions do occur, they can entail grave miscarriages of justice.

Mexico's successive administrations have tried to take on these challenges and find ways to make the third branch of government function. Amid public worries over crime and outrage over police corruption, President Zedillo upped police and public safety budgets, expanded the role of the military in counternarcotics efforts, and created a new Federal Preventive Police (PFP), bringing together police and intelligence officers from multiple federal security agencies.[45] He also purged the notoriously corrupt Federal Judicial Police, filling the empty posts with military officials.[46] Fox began his term by disbanding this same force, and replacing it with a new Federal Investigative Agency, modeled on the U.S. Federal Bureau of Investigation (FBI). He also created an entirely new Ministry of Public Security to oversee the PFP, removing the corps from the purview of the Interior Ministry. Calderón was perhaps the most ambitious, staking his presidency on the issue of security. At the crux of his "New Security Model" was a newly minted federal police with expanded responsibilities under the command of the autonomous secretary of public security (SSP).

Police Reform

At every chance the federal police force shows off its new headquarters, located off the busy Constituyentes thoroughfare in the heart of Mexico City. The noisy traffic outside belies the privacy of the facility behind the white iron gates. From the street it has a vague feel of a school or business campus—sloping green lawns criss-crossed by sidewalks and dotted with sizable pine trees leading up to a sprawling, off-white concrete building. Only the large Mexican flag, and the plaque of the SSP—complete with eagle and snake in its talons—hints at its public purpose. Few approach the formal street entrance on foot, but the guards at the main driveway are busy, waving through the regulars after a quick ID check, and fully stopping and interrogating visitors like ourselves.

Once through the initial checkpoint, our small group of researchers continues up the hill, across the cobblestones to a second officer. Disembarking at the entrance to a four-story parking garage, we follow a flagstone path that weaves its way through tufted grass to the main administrative building, a modern mix of glass, marble, concrete, and steel. Inside, rows upon rows of translucent office windows line a massive interior courtyard filled with greenery.

Though seemingly open, it is all well secured—each set of glass entrances penetrable only to vetted employees with the appropriately programmed ID card. Stepping through one of the dozens of unmarked doors, we move away from the marble and grass, and more practical office gear emerges—cubicles, carpet, wooden conference tables, and chairs. Coffee and packaged cookies appear as members of the secretary's staff brief us on the efforts to overhaul the federal police force and the progress so far.

They explain that their model comprises three essential parts. Perhaps most important are the human components and the efforts to make sure that "Mexico's finest" live up to the moniker. To do so, they beefed up the force's size from fewer than ten thousand to over thirty-five thousand officers. They pushed through a constitutional change, giving the federal police more powers than they previously had, including the ability to investigate crimes, rather than just "preventing" them as beat cops. But most fundamentally, they worked to change how one becomes and what it means to be a police officer in Mexico.

This involves new ways of recruiting, vetting, training, and promoting, all with the goal of creating a truly professional police force. Pay rates far exceed what state and local cops earn, and promotions depend on education, skills, and groundwork rather than kickbacks. College-educated recruits now number near seven thousand, unheard of in the past. They spend six months after college training at the San Luis Potosí academy and in the field, studying interviewing techniques, forensics, evidence collection, and trial testimony—all alongside policing basics taught by instructors from around the world, based on international training standards. The federal police also keeps a closer watch on its active members than do other sectors of law enforcement, as vetting goes beyond a one-time drug test to involve psychological examinations, financial investigations, home visits, and ongoing polygraphs.

A second element of the overhaul effort is technology—led by the much-heralded *Plataforma México*, a comprehensive national crime database. To get a real taste of what this means, we head to the bunker. Another weighty cement and glass entrance greets us, this time graced by a large water fountain, as does a spectacular view. To the left the land slopes down steeply, opening up a glimpse of the Periférico—Mexico City's beltway— and the neighborhoods of Navarte, Benito Juárez, and beyond, seemingly miles and miles of houses and buildings. We enter, descend, and arrive at the threshold—a large space filled with only a translucent desk long enough for three receptionists. A massive seal underfoot is encircled by the words *Secretaría de Seguridad Pública*. Though underground, the lobby is brilliant with the sun pouring through a large skylight. The sound of the fountain, now just above, forces our guide to shout his introductory remarks. From there we go through more glass doors into darkness, and then down to a control room full of black padded office chairs, headphones (for simultaneous translation), and screens built into a center console. In the corner stand three flags—the red, green, and white of the Mexican flag, the royal blue and white of the SSP, and the dark blue seven-point star on a sea of white of the new federal police.

The thoroughly air-conditioned room, two floors below ground, is encased in glass and girded by steel. Just feet away—through impenetrable glass—lay rows and rows of computers, double- and triple-screened, with analysts gazing intently at the numbers, pictures, and search results that appear. Towering over the dozens of bent heads are huge screens—their content ranging from CNN to radar tracking maps, infrared world weather patterns, and the streetscape of a busy road in Tijuana. This control room is the heart of *Plataforma México*. Its goal is to make information easily accessible, searchable, and actionable for law enforcement across the nation. In a demonstration, our guide pulls up the rap sheet of Jaime González Durán, a Zeta founder better known as "the Hummer." But he follows with information available on the (presumably law-abiding) neighbor of one of our group—rattling off his name, address, driver's license number, and house deed as a testament to the database's informational reach.

Though a police facility, the Constituyentes headquarters maintains a military air. Hair is cropped close, the blue uniforms all neatly pressed. And as we walk through the facility with Genaro García Luna, the SSP's head, those within the sea of occupied cubicles silently but simultaneously rise to their feet to salute their commander.

This visible discipline is in part the culture of professionalism and pride the government is working so hard to instill. But it is also due to the origins of the new federal police force. A large percentage is ex-military. At the start they were "on loan," enabling the federal police to nearly triple its numbers in two short years. By 2008, most were forced to make a decision—retire from the army or marines to join the police officially or return to their old posts. Judging by the numbers, most traded in their camouflage for police blues.

These impressive national headquarters are matched by several new Command, Control, Communication, and Computer Centers (C4) in strategic states. Mirroring their U.S. military counterparts, each is equipped with its own mini *Plataforma México*, with the goal to collect, analyze, and act on criminal information in real time. Perhaps the biggest difference at the local centers is the constant murmur of hotline operators taking the pulse of local streets, the sound of each new 0-6-6 (Mexico's version of 9-1-1) call mixing in with the efficient clicking of keyboards as these front-line workers diligently enter each complaint into the ever-growing national database.

The final part of Calderón's plan was revamping the federal prison system, which is seen mostly as a revolving door for powerful criminals and a training ground for those just starting out. It envisioned expanding and upgrading the current overcrowded and run-down facilities and professionalizing the staff. Perhaps tellingly, no one offers to take us on a prison tour or suggests that we talk with a warden. The reported numerous escapes and open door for imprisoned assassins (who seem to come and go at will, handed guns along the way, often by prison staff)—suggest the very long way this branch of the justice system has to go.

Uneven Progress

For all its improvements, some do not see the new federal police in such a glowing light. Overall the recruit's educational levels have increased, but the force still struggles to entice skilled and, some would argue, competent candidates. The challenge is so great that positions go unfilled. And the force has not been immune to corruption—in August 2010 it dismissed about 10 percent of its newly minted ranks on charges of malfeasance. Nor has it escaped human-rights complaints, with evidence confirming its participation in acts of torture, arbitrary detention, and even extrajudicial killings.[47] The technological rhetoric does not always match the reality either. Data on the submission of basic crime reports are uneven and sobering, if not downright dismal. Sources show that many municipalities and states submit less than one report a month. No matter how sophisticated the analytical and computer-generated tools are, the outputs are only as good as those inputs.

Other analysts see the new federal police as just one more revamp—a name change, a new logo—that fails to get at the heart of the rot. Active internal affairs boards, merit-based promotion standards, and improved crime reporting—all necessary for the police to successfully police themselves—still lag.

The transformation of the federal police should be seen as equivalent to a step or two forward, then often a step back. Yet even with the most optimistic take—the right people, the right equipment, the right facilities, and the right training—the challenges remain momentous. The federal police represent only 10 percent of law enforcement in Mexico. The vast majority of officers work at the state and local levels. As one moves down the chain from national to local, the situation deteriorates. For the local beat cop, few fancy operation centers or training academies exist. Everyday necessities—guns, bullets, Kevlar vests, patrol cars—are in short supply. The lack of capacity is often matched by a distinct lack of interest in enforcing the law. In many towns, police are seen as more of a problem than a solution, notorious for their corruption. Although, in at least their partial defense, the local police are often in a no-win situation. Not only is the pay often abysmal for a local policeman or woman, but the criminals know where they and their families live.

Mexico's federal government hasn't forgotten the local component. It actively recruits local forces by offering juicy carrots of equipment and funding in return for meeting basic standards.[48] Some municipalities have bitten, but the number still represents just a fraction of the over two thousand individual departments.

Consistent supervision, much less transformation, remains out of the federal government's hands. Local police salaries and direction remain just that—local. Some municipalities and cities—notably in Querétaro, Chihuahua, and Monterrey—have developed innovative ways to strengthen their police: raising salaries, creating citizen oversight committees, and even handing out mortgages to otherwise ineligible officers.[49] But in other places governors and mayors willingly dole out millions of pesos a month for fancy office spaces or public-relations junkets, while objecting to relatively small increases for the public workers asked to put their lives on the line each day.

During his term Calderón tried to centralize these myriad law enforcement entities into thirty-two state-level forces. Like many other potential reforms, it foundered on the political rocks. But it is unclear if centralization would actually solve Mexico's problem. In the end, all security is local, a maxim as true south of the border as north of it. Yes, well-armed and well-funded drug gangs can easily overwhelm a dozen local officers. But the number of forces is not necessarily the problem in Mexico. The United States has some eighteen thousand separate police forces, but few criticize the number, or think these local teams increase crime rates. Instead, we see these small forces as a foundation of U.S. democracy, images of local community policemen and women as American as baseball and apple pie. Rather than the structure, it is the norms and incentives—both within and outside of the officer corps—that dictate the outcomes, including levels of violence and crime.

ELUSIVE JUSTICE

Under way, but even less advanced, are changes to Mexico's court systems. In 2008, Mexico passed a wide-ranging package of constitutional and legislative reforms that, when enacted, will fundamentally transform Mexico's judicial system. The new legal framework introduces oral trials, the presumption of innocence, access to an adequate defense, and it strengthens due process. It also establishes alternative arbitration and plea bargaining options to help streamline the process, helping prosecutors prioritize their time and resources more strategically. It bolsters investigation and prosecution tools against organized crime, making it easier to tap phones and to hold suspects, effectively suspending habeas corpus for especially serious crimes.[50]

All told, the reforms promise to change the basic nature of the system and the roles of the main actors—judges, prosecutors, police, defense attorneys, defendants, and victims—in ways that should increase transparency and accountability and improve justice more generally. But since the passage of the 2008 reforms, not enough has been done to make this design a reality. Though state governments were given eight years to fully implement the new system, the task is monumental. Before the 2016 deadline, court rooms need to be built or renovated to provide enough space for open trials. Judges, prosecutors, and lawyers need to relearn their jobs. Law school courses have to be revamped, so that the next generation of lawyers, judges, and court officials understands its role and work. Police need to be taught to collect and preserve evidence admissible in the new court of law.

Yet even basic steps forward, such as establishing federal guidelines for reforms to state-level constitutions and laws—have been delayed. Many states have yet to begin the process of passing the legislative reforms necessary to move toward the new system, and fewer have embarked on implementing the new procedures. The pace of follow-through has been so slow that many analysts and activists, including those who worked so hard to achieve judicial reform in the first place, are beginning to worry whether the deadline will pass, and leave judicial reform successful just on paper, not in practice.

Other failings stem from the weakness of Mexico's Attorney General's office, the PGR. As you wander the halls of its main office, the lack of urgency, order, mission, and morale is palpable. Despite its vital role in administering and delivering justice, it remains a bureaucratic backwater. Notorious case backlogs cripple the agency. Unlike other systems, which have separate bodies to sort through criminal complaints, the PGR handles the whole process from start to finish. All cases are treated equally, requiring PGR staff to wade through every complaint and all the compiled evidence to determine the admissibility of each case.[51] This process makes it impossible to prioritize heinous crimes over run-of-the-mill shoplifting and burdens an already overstretched and underfunded staff.

But the problems extend beyond bureaucratic process. Corruption is a pervasive problem for Mexico's supposed crime fighters. Detectives, public prosecutors, and other staff often revert to bribes to offset limited resources and enormous caseloads, or simply for their own personal gain. Victims routinely have to pay police to begin investigations, while suspects can often counteroffer to have cases dismissed. In 2011, seven hundred PGR employees, almost 4 percent of its staff, were under investigation for acts of corruption that included perjury, embezzlement, and the falsification of official documents.[52] Some experts believe that "not only do they [the judiciary] allow crime to go unpunished because of their incompetence ... but in some instances they have actually been 'captured' by criminals."[53]

Over half of the PGR's eighteen-thousand-member staff occupy administrative roles. Active prosecutions fall on the shoulders of roughly 2500 men and women at the federal level.[54] In 2010, there were only three federal prosecutors on staff in Ciudad Juárez, even though drug-related murders (a federal crime) numbered in the thousands. The relatively skeletal staff lacks the necessary training and equipment to do its job well. To date, the PGR's investigative police and prosecutors have shown themselves unable to routinely investigate a charge, gather evidence, compile a case, or even secure the scene of the crime. Yet a lasting rule of law requires these basic building blocks.

While just a decade ago the Mexican government allocated slightly more funds to the justice sector than to its public security agency, today the attorney general's total budget (of roughly US$1 billion) is just over a third that of the secretary of public security.[55] Repeated losses on the bureaucratic battlefield denied the PGR not only resources—making it a poor cousin to the police—but also confused its mandate. With the 2008 security reform, the PGR lost its monopoly on criminal investigations. The federal police now boast roughly 4500 detectives, almost level with the PGR's 4900 investigators. During the new federal police's Pygmalion moment, the fights between the PGR and SSP were legendary. Undoubtedly hard feelings remain, creating further barriers to closer cooperation.

Even if able to overcome the professional jealousies, how the new federal police and Attorney General's office will work together remains undefined. In the SSP's official version of its "New Security Model," the PGR is barely mentioned.[56] In real life, the gap is just as apparent. Investigators and legal staff at the SSP rarely talk to their counterparts, and often do not even know where or to whom they should send their collected evidence and information.

These unbridged chasms show up in the crime data. While operations and arrests have grown exponentially, successful prosecutions and convictions are still rare. The most high-profile embarrassments—ones to which the Attorney General's office presumably dedicated significant resources and talent—illuminate the extent of the challenge. One dramatic case involved Sandra Ávila Beltrán, dubbed by the media as "Queen of the Pacific." She was arrested and marched before the cameras in 2007 on organized crime, drug trafficking, and money laundering charges. Government officials touted her long illicit lineage: niece to the famed Mexican drug trafficking godfather Miguel Ángel Félix Gallardo (in prison in Mexico for participating in the murder of DEA agent Enrique Camarena, among other crimes), wife or girlfriend to more than one high-ranking drug lord, and even a character in a popular *narcocorrido* (a Mexican musical genre that recounts drug exploits).[57]

Despite the federal police's assertions that she smuggled nine tons of cocaine north, the case fell apart, and Mexico's courts exonerated her of the most serious charges. The PGR's bungling had further ramifications, as the courts initially ruled that Ávila could not be extradited and tried by U.S. prosecutors, who appeared to have a great deal more evidence against her than their Mexican counterparts (having put her Colombian boyfriend and accomplice away for six years on the same charges a few years before).[58]

As telling was the 2011 arrest of Jorge Hank Rhon on illegal gun charges. Most in Mexico were ready to believe the worst about the former Tijuana mayor, scion of one of the PRI's most recognized and notorious political bosses, and reported billionaire with business interests including hotels, casinos, and racetracks. His name had for years been associated with the illegal trafficking of exotic animals, organized crime, and even alleged murder.[59] Here, too, the prosecution's case quickly crumbled, thrown out due to insufficient evidence. The incompetence of the PGR was so great that it did something many thought impossible: made the infamous Hank Rhon seem a victim. Justice in Mexico continues to fall through these cracks.

The U.S. Role: Guns, Money, and Demand

In the end, Mexico's security will depend on Mexicans. But U.S. actions can either help or harm these homegrown efforts. Sealing the border will not fix these problems, and would be virtually impossible, to boot. There is, in the end, no way to "fix" border security without fixing security in Mexico more broadly. Spending billions in unilateral outlays for border walls, troops, and equipment will just make things more dire in Mexico—fueling this vicious cycle. It will also limit some of the most effective tools for combating transnational crime, including cross-border intelligence sharing and law enforcement cooperation.

Focusing solely on Mexico lets the United States ignore its responsibility for the dangers to the south, and its role in the rising mayhem. Instead, the United States needs to get its own house in order and enforce its own laws when dealing with the guns, money, and demand that fuel the violence.

Even though it is against U.S. law to sell weapons to foreign nationals or "straw buyers"—those who use their clean criminal records to purchase guns for others—Mexico is awash in illegal U.S. arms. Analysts estimate that some twenty thousand guns head south each year—roughly 70 percent of all illegal weapons in Mexico.[60] AK-47–style and AR-15 assault rifles are among the favored models, as are FN Herstal Five-seveN tactical pistols, better known as "cop killers" since with the right bullets they can pierce Kevlar vests.[61]

In 2011 a scandal broke surrounding the Alcohol, Tobacco, Firearms, and Explosives Bureau's (ATF) Fast and Furious investigation. The operation was supposed to identify and dismantle complex criminal networks by tracking arms sales to Mexican drug traffickers. The plan was that the ATF would willfully turn a blind eye and allow guns "to walk" across the border, then follow their trail in order to nab the bigger fish in these operations. Poorly conceived to start, it then went horribly wrong. Some guns were equipped with tracking devices rigged from cheap parts bought at the local Radio Shack. But the surveillance was never able to penetrate more than fifty miles south of the border, and agents quickly lost track of the guns.[62] The weapons soon enough began to appear at the sites of multiple murders, and in the hands of some of Mexico's better-known hitmen.[63] When two AK-47–style guns followed by Fast and Furious showed up at the Arizona murder site of Border Patrol agent Brian Terry, whistleblowers finally brought the operation down. The ensuing investigations, testimonies, and reports show that during the year long operation the ATF lost track of over one thousand guns.[64]

Exhaustive congressional hearings and investigations opened a window into the shadowy world of the border-centered gun trade, and showed that the United States is effectively arming both sides of the conflict today. While a case study in poor judgment and execution, the episode reveals the mounting frustrations among dedicated ATF officers desperate to find some way to stem the steel river of guns heading south. Sheer numbers make this an uphill battle. There are nearly seven thousand licensed shops or individuals in the Southwest border states alone.[65] Budget and personnel restrictions (promoted by legislators bent on limiting the active enforcement of gun laws) also hamper the ATF's reach. With a staff of roughly five thousand— just half of whom are special agents—the ATF is lucky to review a gun shop or license owner once every five years, and the average is closer to ten.[66] Added to this are frequent gun shows enabling informal "private sales," which do not require the seller to ask for identification, file background checks, or keep a record of the purchase—making them even more difficult to supervise, and therefore doubly attractive to aspiring gun runners.[67]

Onerous rules—such as the Tiahrt amendments—further tie investigators' hands, preventing them from requiring gun shops to review their inventories for stolen or lost guns, or developing a paper trail on suspects.[68] Missing, too, are legal tools, such as specific gun-trafficking statutes, to aid prosecutors in their efforts to build a case. These limits leave the ATF less able to enforce U.S. laws, and enable the cartels to easily replenish their arsenals, threatening Mexican and U.S. citizens alike.

Money also spurs violence. Revenue estimates vary so much that they obscure more than they explain, but official sources put Mexican drug traffickers' U.S. earnings somewhere between US$8 billion and US$23 billion each year.[69] More conservative estimates—such as those done by RAND—put the money that returns to Mexico in the realm of US$6 billion.[70] This money then goes to pay off Mexican officials—the requisite *plata*, or silver, that greases the drug economy's destructive wheels. It also arms the drug cartels—paying for guns and ammunition—with the complementary *plomo*, or lead, to use against those who stand in the way.

Beyond these direct effects, in some places this money undermines legitimate businesses and trade. To repatriate and "clean" the billions of dollars in revenue, cartels invest in seemingly legal front businesses such as travel agencies, car dealerships, textile factories, race tracks, and even accounting services. Local businesses often do not dare take on the newcomers, nor can they hope to compete with the steep discounts they provide. And with Mexico now tightly regulating dollar deposits, drug operations are increasingly resorting to trade-based money laundering. In these schemes criminals buy a good—anything from computer parts to food, fabrics to precious metals—in the United States, and then export it to Mexico. Traffickers on the other side receive their earnings through the sale of the product. Some of these entrepreneurs boost their revenue per transaction by slightly inflating the value of the goods, enabling them to show Mexican tax authorities that the money in their accounts came from the presumed sale of goods worth the amount stated on their customs form.[71]

To make this work, traffickers need to find suppliers willing to take cash and ask few questions. The United States attorney for the Southern District of New York claimed that Vikram Datta, the owner of a chain of perfume stores along the U.S.-Mexico border, was one such man.[72] An FBI investigation found that Datta was receiving lump sums of cash from drug traffickers and, in exchange, exported millions of dollars worth of perfume to Mexico.

Selling these fragrances to Mexican consumers, the cartels both repatriated and "cleaned" their profits.[73]

Going after illicit funds is one of the more effective ways to attack drug trafficking; lost revenue hits the larger operation at its core. The United States is increasing the use of the Kingpin Act (which allows U.S. investigators to freeze assets and impose sanctions on drug trafficking dons). Cash seized along the southwestern border averages some US$300 million a year. Yet this is just 5 percent of the most conservative estimate of the overall money flows (and much lower than official figures).[74]

In the end, law enforcement efforts alone will not be enough, as supply is fueled by demand. In the Mexican drug runners' case, the vast U.S. market fuels their violent business. Surveys rank the United States as the largest consumer of marijuana and cocaine in the world and reveal that just under 9 percent of those twelve and older reported using an illicit drug in the previous month.[75] On this count, the United States has done relatively little to change the status quo. Roughly two-thirds of the money spent by the U.S. government in the war on drugs goes to the supply side. Of those funds spent at home, the largest amount goes to domestic law enforcement (US$9.3 billion), followed by treatment programs (US$8.7 billion), and then much less to prevention programs (US$1.4 billion) such as DARE and "this is your brain on drugs" style commercials.[76]

Studies show that treatment programs, particularly when focused on heavy drug users, are by far the most cost-efficient part of current U.S. policy—some three times as effective as preventive programs and punitive measures. And every dollar spent on substance-abuse rehabilitation reduces the costs of associated crime by somewhere between four and seven dollars.[77] Perhaps even more promising are programs—such as Hawaii's HOPE—that actually enforce probation rules, locking up (for a short time) those committing even minor infractions. The program has cut probationers' reincarceration in half, and reduced their chances of using drugs again by more than 70 percent.[78] Yet these public health approaches consistently lose out to a criminal enforcement model.

MEXICAN SOCIETY IN THE BALANCE

In the fight against the cartels, Mexico (and the United States for that matter) has a potential ally, a potent but latent weapon that cannot be matched by any cartel. It is the millions of citizens who want to live their lives and raise their families in peace. Not only do they constitute a powerful force, but they are also necessary partners. Without citizen buy-in, any security strategy is doomed to fail.

Polls show that Mexicans overwhelmingly want the government to take on the cartels—even if they do not think it is winning. While support for Calderón waned in the later years of his administration, over half of Mexicans still approved of his job performance, in large part because he confronted the drug cartels.[79]

As the deaths mount, Mexicans are fighting back. On a basic level, they try to help each other stay safe. Tens of thousands post to Twitter accounts, detailing the movements of cartel thugs on local streets and from town to town, providing information—at no small risk to themselves—to help their fellow citizens stay out of harm's way. Piercing the news blackout favored by the criminals, some have paid the ultimate price for their work. The lifeless bodies of two Nuevo Laredo tweeters were bound and hung from a bridge in September 2011, the sign next to them reading "This will happen to all the internet snitches...Be warned, we've got our eye on you."[80] Yet as the violence has spread, so too have citizen actions.

Hundreds of thousands more have poured into the streets to show their solidarity and demand change. The first large-scale antiviolence march occurred in Mexico City in 2004. Frustrated by the robberies, kidnappings, and murders, hundreds of thousands paraded in solemn silence down the streets of the capital—their presence a mute plea for change.[81] Still others joined them in 2008—moved by the kidnapping and murder of fourteen-year-old Fernando Martí. An estimated one million Mexicans flooded the streets of eighty cities, dressed all in white, carrying candles lit in memory of victims, in silent condemnation of attackers, and in implicit reproach of government inaction.[82] In the days and weeks that followed, the political establishment tried to mollify the crowds, signing a seventy-five-point agreement that pledged to root out corruption and fight kidnapping and money laundering.[83] Alejandro Martí, the victim's father and the owner of a well-known chain of sporting goods stores, spoke passionately, and at times tearfully, at the televised signing ceremony, urging politicians to resign if they could not deliver, as "getting a salary for a job you aren't doing is also corruption."[84] Yet little changed, and the death toll just climbed higher.

In 2011, Javier Sicilia tapped into the still-simmering frustration. Devastated by his son's murder, the respected poet began what he called a Caravan for Peace. Walking first from the weekend-escape town of Cuernavaca to the capital, he and his growing number of followers slowly moved north to Juárez and the border. Along the way, on the road or at their stops, thousands came to join—families communing in their grief and exasperated neighbors demanding security. In the months to follow, Sicilia became the most visible leader of Mexican society's frustrations, demanding a different government strategy—sending the troops back to the barracks and combating crime by fighting poverty and corruption.[85]

Away from the street, scholars and advocates have done technical studies and surveys to better understand what is happening and better inform efforts for change. Organizations such as Alejandro Martí's Mexico SOS have harnessed these resources, coordinating with other foundations and nonprofit organizations to insert themselves into the national debate and shape the legislative agenda.[86] Others have kept track of government promises, calling to account backsliding on judicial reform, police accountability, and human rights. Well-known business owners and associations have also entered the policy debate, trying to bring management techniques and structures to amplify the disparate voices through umbrella organizations dedicated to security and justice.

This groundswell is encouraging, but it has yet to leave a policy mark. The role for Mexican citizens remains limited. Politicians across the political spectrum seem uneasy about engaging with or championing these independent organizations, still relegating the average Mexican to the status of "client" or victim.

Even as the general public represents Mexico's best security hope, it also symbolizes perhaps its greatest challenge. Though Mexico's middle class is ascending, devastating poverty, persistent inequality, and arbitrary violence remain. Woven into the new landscape of skyscrapers, shiny cars, and iPhones are marginalized millions struggling just to make ends meet.

Emblematic are the "NiNis"—youngsters who are neither working nor in school. They live with little hope on the edges of society, concentrated in many of Mexico's most violent places. Studies count nearly eight million rootless youth between the ages of fifteen and twenty-nine—over 20 percent of Mexico's adolescents.[87] Coming from poorer, less-educated families, they are vulnerable recruits for organized crime, lured in as lookouts, dealers, smugglers, or even assassins with assurances that "más valen cinco años como rey que cincuenta años como buey" or that it is "better to live five years as a king than fifty years as an ox." With much of the social fabric torn by poverty and inequality, immigration, and a climate of fear and insecurity, many choose gangs and crime as a means not just of living but also of identifying.

A few factors are working in Mexico's favor. Demographic shifts should lessen the challenge a bit—as each year fewer youths will hit the streets. A stronger economy should help too—creating more jobs for those just entering the market. But Mexico's government and society will still have to find ways to engage these young people, to help them see beyond the next few years, and to create alternative paths to counter a life of crime.

* * *

Building strong institutions takes decades, and Mexico is arguably only ten years into this process. The end of the PRI broke the previous equilibrium—one of pervasive crime but more limited drug-related violence. Today the situation is still in flux. While the risk of remaining mired in violent impunity continues, Mexico is working to lay the groundwork for a more robust rule of law.

Nurturing strong communities may take even longer—making sure the next generation finds it more worthwhile to invest in its future than live, if briefly, as a gangster or narco-king. Mexico's rising middle is helping transform Mexico's politics and economics, and it has the potential to do the same for its security. But the less fortunate part of Mexico needs to be lifted up as well.

Adrián Cadena picked us up in his red minivan two blocks from the Paso del Norte international bridge—linking the downtowns of El Paso and Ciudad Juárez. After brief introductions, we headed out to Villas de Salvárcar, where his son, Rodrigo Cadena Dávila, was killed along with fourteen others while celebrating a birthday in 2010. Most accounts suggest it was a terrible case of mistaken identity; having driven into the wrong neighborhood, the hitmen confused the students' festivities for a rival group's gathering. Wiretap recordings relayed that the assassins had called back to their main boss, questioning the operation, but his response was to "kill them all anyway." The armed men then separated the girls from the boys, quickly dispatching the latter.

In the two and a half years since his son's death, the mechanic had struggled in his marriage, his work, and his everyday life to move beyond the tragedy. In the first several months he and others benefited from the national attention and the influx of federal funds—receiving counseling and other support. These flows now were just a trickle, leaving the survivors and families mostly on their own. Adrián and others worked to step into this breach, channeling their energies and grief into advocating for those even less fortunate, and into public works for the still-traumatized community.

It was to the most visible symbol of these labors that he first took us on a hot August day. To get to Villas de Salvárcar, the site of the tragedy, we drove for nearly half an hour from downtown, passing hulking industrial parks along the many-laned Avenida de las Torres, the signs outside the high walls announcing major international brands and products—wind turbines, TV screens, auto parts, and beer. Finally turning off the main artery, we headed toward a nondescript neighborhood behind the factories, stopping a few blocks in at the new neighborhood park.

Accustomed to Adrián's visits, the park's caretaker unlocked the gate, and our guide led us to the central cement structure, which holds final words from each victim's family to their loved ones. Rodrigo's plaque reads: "It doesn't matter how many times we fall; what matters is that you know how to get up again." Encircling the monument is a walkway, as well as tall, thin pine trees, one for each youngster now gone.

Once abandoned land, the memorial is part of an active athletic park, complete with basketball courts, football and soccer fields, and an outdoor theater space. Despite temperatures already over 90 degrees, the soccer field was lively, as was an open handball court where exercisers followed two graceful dance instructors, sweating to the beat of festive Tejano music.

Ciudad Juárez is a harbinger of Mexico's future security. Though the death toll has fallen from the 2011 level of some ten murders a day, homicides still range from fifty to one hundred a month, and good governance remains in short supply, suggesting the necessary fix—improving and professionalizing law enforcement and the justice system more generally—is a long, uphill path at best. But the city is also a cradle of civil society involvement and pressure; the efforts such as those of Adrián Cadena build on decades-long initiatives to create a better Juárez. Today, active *mesas de seguridad,* or security roundtables, bring together public officials, business leaders, and engaged residents. Citizen-led organizations have proliferated to overcome the myriad challenges.

Ciudad Juárez is also the crux of deeper bilateral security cooperation. It is here that the U.S. government launched its more expansive efforts to work with Mexico, from funding local projects to keep kids off the streets to backing efforts to come up with strategic development plans for the twin cities of Juárez and El Paso. As the two governments look to move security efforts from the national to the local level, these pilot projects can provide lessons for greater cooperation across the length of the border.

For many, this gritty northern metropolis implies hopelessness. But as a close watcher of the mayhem told me, during the surge in violence not one maquila left—instead more came. And the lessons learned through tragedy have made Juárez now an unlikely leader. Its social activism is a case study for other cities searching for a way to change their—and Mexico's—reality for the better.

DECIDING OUR MUTUAL FUTURE

Ask most Americans—and not a few Mexicans—about Mexico and they will emphasize poverty, corruption, and violence. Though not patently false, these views are misleadingly incomplete. Poverty continues, but the middle class now outnumbers the poor. Corruption is widespread, but Mexico is more transparent today than at any time in its past. Violence, though widespread, is still concentrated, and Mexico is taking steps that, if they continue, will stabilize and deepen its democratic rule of law   the building blocks for long-lasting security. Lost in the headlines, Mexico's real story today is one of fundamental political, economic, and social transformation: from authoritarianism to democracy, from a closed to an open economy, and from a poor society to a middle class nation. Mexico's hard-fought changes are creating a very different country on the southern U.S. border.

The transformations are not all rosy or near completion. Even as Mexico sheds many of the shackles of its past, new problems emerge. Increasingly muscular organized crime joins vested interests and political bosses in threatening Mexico's democratic gains. The privileged, both old and new, unfairly push their advantage at times, stifling entrepreneurship, competitiveness, and ultimately growth. This only exacerbates the already sizeable flow of people north, as millions of go-getters leave in search of a better life.

Their remittances home enable survival, but so far not real economic development. Growing violence threatens nascent advances even as it terrifies Mexico's citizens and families.

Today Mexico stands at a crossroads. It can continue down a path toward a top ten world economy, a stronger democracy, a global voice, and a burgeoning middle class society. Or it can be consumed by its challenges—illegality, bloodshed, and the triumph of might over right—losing much of the ground it has won over the last three decades. The path it takes will depend mostly on Mexico. As the United States has (often painfully) learned in other places, there are severe limits to what it can do. But the United States can make a difference, whether encouraging Mexico along the high road or obstructing its way.

Mexico's successes and failures have never mattered more for the United States. Once distant neighbors, the United States and Mexico are now intimately linked. Perhaps no other nation affects the United States on a day-to-day basis as much as Mexico. Geography, environment, companies, supply chains, people, communities, beliefs, and cultures bind together the two nations and their futures. What happens in Mexico reverberates far and wide north of the Rio Grande. To make the most of the good and to limit the bad from these deep-rooted interconnections, the United States needs to improve its understanding of and change its approach toward its southern neighbor. This means a true partnership between people, markets, economic sectors, and governments.

A Partnership Through People

Leticia Ramírez Carmona's white dress rustled in the light wind as she faced Abraham Hernández Mora. Next to them stood their five-year-old son. Around them curious pedestrians and drivers—inching their way through inspection lanes—became chance witnesses to their matrimonial vows on the halfway mark of International Bridge Number One, the "Gateway to the Americas." As justice of the peace Oscar Liendo pronounced the Mexican and American man and wife, their kiss literally and figuratively spanned the Laredo–Nuevo Laredo border, officially cementing yet another U.S.-Mexican relationship.

Redefining U.S.-Mexico relations should start with people. Today's tough immigration status quo—costing billions of dollars and wrenching apart long-standing communities without stopping the illegality—is a failure.

Recognizing the realities of family ties and labor market needs, the United States should create a more efficient and flexible system that takes into account the fundamental demands that drive today's unlawfulness. The process for families should be streamlined and sped up, creating a legal option that does not entail years apart. For workers, a practical system should take into account supply and demand, enabling a better matching of the fluctuations and needs of America's workplaces with the legal flow of immigrants. The mix of guest workers and more permanent avenues toward citizenship should be adjusted more frequently and fluidly.[1]

After creating a better system, the United States needs a way for the estimated eleven million unauthorized workers already here—half of them Mexican—to come out of the shadows. The only way to overcome this challenge is some sort of legalization. The bar does not have to be low; it can be only for those with clean track records and proven English skills and involve hefty fines for transgressors. But it has to be surmountable. Otherwise, the unlawfulness of today will just continue.

Once the rules are made realistic, the government should enforce them. This will require a mandatory system to check workers' documents. One way would be to improve and expand the current E-Verify system, which allows employers to double-check social security numbers. Going forward, the government should come down hard on errant employers and employees alike, replacing the rare slaps on businesses' wrists with real fines and criminal charges.

Overall, the United States should recognize the benefits of migration, even as it works to reduce the real costs of this illegal influx. This should only get easier, as demographic changes on both sides of the border ease the flow from Mexico and increase the demand for workers in the United States. But the rules still need to be brought in line with the underlying economic and community realities.

A PARTNERSHIP FOR ECONOMIC COMPETITIVENESS

Most days the four bridges joining the cities of Laredo, Texas, and Nuevo Laredo, Tamaulipas, are filled with goods, not bridesmaids. Laredo is now the largest U.S. "inland port" thanks to the explosion of U.S.-Mexico trade since NAFTA. Each day twelve thousand trucks and twelve hundred railcars cross the border here, filled with goods destined for the eastern United States and more than sixty countries beyond.

Yet these ever-increasing volumes can be crushing. Both commercial activity and border wait times have doubled in recent years. On bad days trucks line up for miles and idle for hours. Despite the vast increase in traffic, plans to upgrade and expand Laredo's bridges languish. The lone rail bridge between the two cities is a relic, with just one track dating back to pre–Mexican Revolution days. These physical crossings embody the limits of yesterday's infrastructure for today's bilateral relationship.

Over the past two decades goods from Juárez's expanding maquila businesses have flooded El Paso railway network, headed to destinations such as Kansas City, Chicago, Dallas, Houston, New Orleans, and beyond. The hundred-year-old railroad infrastructure has struggled to keep up with the expanding volume of goods, often resulting in significant delays. The stepped-up activity has taken a toll on life in El Paso as well, as international trains passing through downtown routinely slow transit and often block the only entrance to the historic Chihuahita neighborhood. The problems became so great that companies began sending containers across the border on trucks in order to get them to U.S. railyards on time.

Border congestion may finally see some relief. In 2011, Union Pacific railroad broke ground on a US$400 million project to create a new international railroad border crossing and container facility in Santa Teresa, New Mexico (only thirteen miles from El Paso). When finished, the new crossing and terminal should speed goods, reduce congestion, limit the environmental impact of potentially thousands of idling trucks, and make Mexico more competitive vis-à-vis China and other manufacturers worldwide. As important, it would be one positive step toward recognizing and investing in our mutual future. But the United States and Mexico can and should do more.

A new economic partnership should start with a 180-degree turn from the current policy, building both real and metaphorical roads and bridges instead of walls. More broadly conceived, we need to shift the focus from U.S. to North American competitiveness—helping U.S. businesses, labor unions, and average citizens alike understand that, at least within the neighborhood, a rising tide can lift all boats.

For Mexico to become a world-class economy (boosting North American global competitiveness in the process), it must overcome the domestic barriers that currently limit its potential. Economic monopolies and oligopolies, still limited access to credit, weak infrastructure, and bad schools all hold Mexico back. Here, the United States can help most through invest-ment. Public infrastructure plans from new airports in Baja California and the Caribbean Mayan Riviera to the much-touted Punta Colonet—heralded as the next Pacific megaport and the answer to the maxing-out of the Long Beach and Los Angeles ports in California—will require tens if not hundreds of billions of dollars.[2] So, too, will plans for twelve thousand miles of highways, nine hundred miles of new rail lines, and several major hydroelectric dams.

Less visible but as necessary is improving the ability of goods and ser-vices to move back and forth across the border. This requires upgrading and expanding border crossings to match the ever-growing crush of goods and people. It also means cooperating on how we regulate products, so that makers of air conditioners, light switches, and even nuts and bolts no longer have to engineer two separate models, and do not have to go through the approval process twice. Making regulations more standard and tests univer-sal would lower costs and encourage the regional integration behind much of our mutual competitiveness and growth today.

These investments need to be seen for what they truly are, not just aid for Mexico or even border communities, but an essential keystone for the United States' national economic future. Making Mexico more effi-cient through better infrastructure and expanded border crossings would encourage North American production over wholesale off-shoring to far-away nations, lifting both U.S. trade and export-oriented jobs in the process.[3]

These steps to tear down today's economic obstacles will not lead to the "North American Union" feared by conspiracy theorists, though at times it may mean ceding small aspects of each country's independence for a greater good. It primarily—and necessarily—means embracing and promoting what is already an economic reality.

A PARTNERSHIP FOR SAFETY AND DEMOCRACY

Edgar Valdez Villarreal, better known as La Barbie, shaped Mexico's imagi-nation (and at least for a time its fashion sense, as working class youngsters donned his signature polo shirts) with his criminal exploits. Though his ascendance to Mexico's Most Wanted list—first as the chief enforcer of the Beltrán Leyva cartel and later as a drug kingpin himself—was extraordinary, his background was not. He grew up in Laredo, Texas, one of six children in a typical middle class Mexican American family. At the local United High School he hung with the popular crowd, and played linebacker on a winning Longhorns team. Valdez in fact gained his nickname from his football coach, his good looks leading first to a comparison with Mattel's Ken doll, and then to his more famous blonde female partner, Barbie. Until graduation his path was unremarkable; he was a well-liked guy and a good athlete. In fact, he was not unlike another well-known figure in U.S.-Mexico history, Kiki Camarena. But after graduation their paths diverged. While Camarena would join the marines and then the DEA, becoming a drug war hero and martyr, Valdez would descend into the criminal underworld, becoming a renowned hit man and drug lord. Camarena's death would come to epitomize deep divisions between the United States and Mexico, while Valdez's capture would be the result of close bilateral intelligence sharing and cooperation.

La Barbie began selling marijuana in the 1990s and then moved on to cocaine, making decent money as an independent drug runner. The 1998 bust of his small operation ironically led to his big break. Fleeing to Mexico, he began a dizzying ascent that took him from Nuevo Laredo to Mexico City, Monterrey, Acapulco, and, finally, in 2010, to jail.

Working first for the local Nuevo Laredo don, he turned early against the Gulf cartel and their Zeta assassins, allying himself with the Sinaloa cartel in a failed bid to muscle in and take over the eastern border city. Then, taking the reins of the enforcement arm of the Beltrán Leyva clan, he became a fearsome hit man, known both for his violence and his media savvy; many credit him with popularizing the trend of posting cartel executions on YouTube. At his height, La Barbie moved thousands of kilos of cocaine, managed teams of assassins, and raked in over US$100 million a year. He owned houses, nightclubs, and dozens of expensive watches.[4]

La Barbie's decline came as precipitously as his rise, as intracartel splits, betrayals, and deaths chipped away at his standing and power. On the run from once friends, now sworn enemies, he was finally brought down by intelligence coming from both U.S. and Mexican sources, captured at a safe house just outside Mexico's capital. His start, rise, and final fall were—like his trade—examples of fluid back and forth across the border. Today the only question remaining is where he will serve his time, as his crimes spanned the Rio Grande.

As the United States and Mexico reap the benefits of deeper economic integration, they should together deal with the costs of rising violence. Perhaps the most pressing concern today for both countries and their relationship is security. Violence is terrorizing families, workers, shopkeepers, factory owners, and citizens in far-flung communities throughout Mexico, and there are increasing fears that it is creeping north.

Yet for all the concern, the current U.S. prescription—higher and stronger border walls and more military boots on the ground—misunderstands and in the end will exacerbate the problem. Instead the United States and Mexico need to face the short- and longer-term issues together.

To start, the United States should move beyond the rhetoric to the (more politically difficult) reality of coresponsibility for the drug war. The guns and money flowing south to the drug cartels continue, virtually unimpeded, despite their deadly roles.

The United States also needs to do some soul-searching at home and have a real debate about drugs. After forty-some years of the war on drugs, they just keep coming, with seemingly lower prices and a better selection than ever. Sending billions to far-off lands has not, in fact, stopped drug flows. Continuing on this path seems to fit Albert Einstein's definition of insanity: doing the same thing over and over again and expecting different results.

This does not mean a knee-jerk legalization of drugs. In fact, some of the smartest and most thorough analysts of the issue caution against such a shift. While many see alcohol—its prohibition and then repeal—as the model for drugs, this history holds many rarely discussed societal costs. Some nine million Americans are hooked on alcohol (four times the number of hard-core users of any drug) with devastating effects on their families and friends.[5] Drunk drivers kill over eleven thousand people a year, far more than cocaine and heroin overdoses combined.[6] And the evidence suggests alcohol abuse hits the population at large; roughly half of those in jail today were drinking when they committed their crimes.[7]

How the legalization of marijuana, much less cocaine, heroin, methamphetamines, or other drugs would play out is almost impossible to know. The undoubted rise in abuse, especially of hard drugs (which are both more addictive and more effectively enforced than marijuana) would tax the United States' already overburdened health and prison systems. And illegality in and of itself does not seem to matter as much as drug legalization advocates might suggest; prescription drug abuse is growing faster than any other category, and is the leading cause of overdoses today.[8]

It is not even clear that the escalating violence to the south would end with the legalization of drugs. Mexico's criminals are already diversifying into a host of other businesses—including extortion, kidnapping, and human trafficking. These shifts would only continue if drug profits diminished or disappeared. Whether the gains from ending the illegal drug trade outweigh these costs is unknown. But with no easy answers, it is vital to conduct an honest, science-based discussion of how to diminish the harm from drugs—to individuals, families, and communities throughout the hemisphere.

To counter drug abuse, it is time for the United States to shift its drug policies, moving away from eradication and interdiction abroad and incarceration at home to greater funding for prevention and rehabilitation. Promising pilot programs that deal with addiction should be expanded. One example is Hawaii's HOPE program which, by swiftly punishing parolees who test positive for drugs, has successfully lowered recidivism among a heavy drug-using population.

As America gets its own house in order, there is an important supporting role for the United States regarding Mexico. Security assistance will necessarily be part of this—taking violence, not just drug trafficking, head on.

For sustainable peace and security, Mexico has to establish a stronger rule of law. This means creating a police corps clean enough and courts strong enough to enforce the law. So far, much of the cooperation between our two nations has focused on strengthening Mexico's military. Though it is an important stopgap, Mexico needs to move beyond the military as its solution. The United States should continue to support efforts to professionalize the police. But it can go even further and help Mexico at the most difficult but also most important level: the local one. This assistance should start at the border, through greater cooperation between sheriffs, police chiefs, mayors, council members, and other local officials, as well as chambers of commerce, community organizations, and others trying to make their towns safer. Though replacing the wall with shared actions is perhaps the toughest challenge around—overcoming years of mistrust, known corruption, and worries of infiltration—it is also the most vital.

The other decisive battle is being waged in the courtroom. But the judicial reform implementation remains far from complete. The United States can help push this process along, working with willing government officials and outside reformers to help Mexico meet its deadline. Bringing together lawyers, judges, and legal professors is crucial to the revamping Mexico's whole judicial system. So, too, is hands-on involvement from prosecutors and investigators—à la CSI detectives—helping Mexico's police learn how to collect, preserve, and compile the evidence necessary to identify, prosecute, and put away criminals.

In the end, the best Mexico and the United States can hope for is that organized crime becomes a persistent but manageable law enforcement problem, much as it is in the United States. But this will require true justice for the guilty and innocent alike to return relative safety to all of Mexico's streets.

With the United States' own experience as a guide, cleaning up Mexico's cops and courts will take a couple of decades of hard-fought changes. But until Mexico's third branch of government truly works, security next door will remain fragile.

The United States can also work more closely with citizen groups, cultivating and aiding the budding Grupo Oaxacas or Networks for Oral Trials. The enthusiasm and outpouring from U.S.-based foundations and government programs that occurred during President Fox's tenure have declined as interests shifted, other regions beckoned, and the world economic crisis took its toll. With work still to do, Mexico's own citizens must now lead the charge, taking on autocratic politicians, closed economic sectors, and dysfunctional bureaucracies with the goal of making Mexico's government more open and responsive. Though somewhat more constrained, there is still a vital role for U.S. support.

Some steps are being taken in the right direction. Mexico and the United States are finally beginning to improve border infrastructure, facilitating the half-trillion dollars in trade that crosses between the two nations each year. After years of cautious avoidance we are working together to improve security, sharing information and coordinating efforts to attack the transnational criminal networks that prey on both societies. And in multilateral forums, the United States and Mexico agree more often than not; each is finding in the other a solid partner in the myriad issues reverberating around the world.

Yet these steps are too timid. Discussing immigration remains a taboo in the relationship. Economic ties are also spoken of in hushed whispers. The political mantra of nonintervention hinders discussions and policies that would benefit both sides. Worse, few seem in a hurry to change things. Perhaps as important as any concrete program or initiative is U.S. recognition that this will be a long and difficult process. Mexico's competitiveness, its safety, and its democracy cannot and will not change overnight. But the United States can support Mexico's now like-minded political system, and its leaders—both in and out of government—as they face the singular and shared challenges of today and tomorrow.

As America's neighbor struggles, Washington has yet to truly recognize that what happens to the south is more likely to affect us than what happens almost anywhere else. It remains the most overlooked U.S. foreign policy challenge of our time. Along the border many recognize the gravity, but they are divided on the direction for solutions, the media and local politicians playing up the fears and denying the benefits stemming from these ties. Mexico and the United States are now inextricably united. How to bring out the good and diminish the bad from such a closely bound relationship is the real challenge facing both countries.

By working together more broadly to increase accountability, expand economic and social opportunities, and strengthen the rule of law, the two countries can encourage a more inclusive and stable market-based democracy in Mexico, to the benefit of both. This however will require a conceptual shift, whereby the United States finally recognizes Mexico as a permanent and strategic partner rather than an oft-forgotten neighbor.

The Politics of Partnership

How viable is this vision? It faces inertia bred from outdated images and stubborn stereotypes, as well as pointed opposition from some quarters on both sides of the border. Misunderstandings still undermine U.S.-Mexico relations. When I was traveling with a group of House and Senate staffers in Mexico, more than one said to me that the most eye-opening aspect of the packed four-day trip was how "modern" Mexico's capital seemed. They were taken aback by the broad boulevards, tall buildings, new model cars, and the general bustle; they were surprised by the fact that they found Mexico more cosmopolitan than many of the states and districts from which they hailed.

Conversely, Mexicans too harbor warped impressions, misjudging their counterparts' intentions. One instance occurred in the wake of the

September 11 attacks, when Mexico's leaders shied away from their neighbor, many not realizing that at that moment what the United States needed was not access to Mexico's territory (threatening its sovereignty), but an outpouring of sympathy. Until these basic misunderstandings are overcome, ambitious policy changes will be difficult.

The hurdles to a deeper relationship also include domestic politics. In the United States, policy toward Mexico has been caught in the crosshairs of deep political divides, fodder for partisan skirmishes over immigration, trade, and border control. These issues also divide the political parties themselves. Trade issues divide "blue dogs" from labor Democrats; and migration divides Tea Partiers from Republicans linked to George W. Bush. Add in the discord between the executive and legislative branches, and between federal and local level governments, and shifting the bilateral relationship may seem to many to be an insurmountable task.

U.S.-Mexico issues also attract the focus, and at times ire, of important domestic interest and lobbying groups. Whether the National Rifle Association, the AFL-CIO labor federation, the National Council of La Raza (a Latino advocacy group), or the Federation for Immigration Reform (which works to limit U.S. immigration), each weighs in with policy agendas and campaigns that often ignore the bilateral ramifications.

Mexico grapples with its own domestic politics in foreign policy. Where once Mexico was able to legislate "in fifteen minutes," as noted scholar and former Mexican Ambassador to the United Nations Adolfo Aguilar Zínser used to say (emphasizing the rubber stamp role of Congress under the PRI), today reality is much more complicated. Its three-party system means laws require legislative coalitions. And when the United States is involved, there remains an almost reflexive bristle by some political sectors and leaders, making cooperation all the harder.

Finally, the United States and Mexico have yet to talk honestly (at least publicly) about the good and the bad in the relationship. For decades the U.S. government has had a steadfast policy of not openly criticizing its neighbor. Ambassadors, secretaries of state, and national security advisors have all focused on getting along rather than getting things done. Even in the face of corruption, repression, electoral fraud, and security breaches, the U.S. political establishment (with a few exceptions) stayed silent.[9] This self-imposed ban on publicly talking about the real relationship continues largely to this day. A senior U.S. military officer remarked to me that his policy was always to say that cooperation with Mexico was at its best level ever (even when, in his estimation, it was not).

This reflexive approach stems in part from the long and sensitive history of intervention, and a power asymmetry that continues between the two nations. It comes out of a desire by the United States not to damage the relationship. Why criticize an ally, friend, and neighbor? It also reflects the success of a consistent decades-long Mexican policy of denouncing any criticism as intervention, in the process strengthening its hand in negotiations with the United States.

But this dynamic no longer serves either nation well. It has costs for policymaking and for the bilateral relationship more generally. With the official line virtually unvarying in its sunniness, it can be jarring for those grappling with the more complicated realities on the ground. It sets administrations up for failure, as the media, congressional representatives, citizen groups, and others quickly see and point out the substantial disconnect. And the oversimplifying only encourages the conspiracy theorists, who see behind the rhetoric not diplomatic niceties but diabolical plans.

The United States and Mexico are ready for more grown-up talk, more frank discussions about bilateral strengths and weaknesses. In many areas we should be proud of the increased cooperation and problem solving. But these advances have not occurred across the board, and distinguishing them from the challenges is crucial. Honest discussions would also help bring to the table the very real interests on all sides of complicated binational issues.

Thousands of small, medium, and large businesses benefit from and depend on Mexico. A growing number of American communities are learning about Mexico from the migrants and families in their midst. And Mexican Americans, now some thirty million strong, provide a permanent link. Though a Mexican lobby per se is unlikely to arise, there is a cultural and nostalgic interest that persists. This group has yet to make its increasingly powerful voice heard on bilateral relations.

Public opinion polls show that the views and values of ordinary citizens on both sides of the border are converging. On bilateral issues such as the border wall, and aspects of immigration, the average American and Mexican are not too far apart.[10] These growing interests and moderate outlooks provide an opening and a potential base for enterprising individuals and politicians wanting to redefine U.S.-Mexico relations.

A Spain for the Americas

For well over a century, the U.S. southern strategy (when it has had one) has been to deflect the perceived perils of living next to a large developing country. This has led, at various times, to supporting an authoritarian government, to overlooking the wrongdoing of officials, and to building a concrete wall. But now, having transformed into a top economy and a stable democracy, Mexico could be an able partner—not a problem—for the United States.

What would Mexico's ascent mean for the United States? Today's bilateral tensions, and much of the negative rhetoric, would ease. Northbound immigration would recede, because, given a viable economic choice, more Mexicans would remain at home. In fact, immigration trends might even reverse, with Mexican job-seekers overtaken by American retirees heading south to join the already one-million-strong U.S. expat community. The "giant sucking sound" would be products going south, driven by Mexico's booming middle class and its desire for U.S.-made goods, benefiting American companies and workers alike. And Mexico's stronger democracy—and particularly its rule of law—could make Ciudad Juárez's streets as safe as El Paso's. Crime, as in the United States, would become primarily a local law enforcement problem. All these changes would benefit not just Mexico but also the United States.

Tensions, of course, would not definitively end. An increasingly confident Mexico would become a much more vocal neighbor, one more likely to comment on U.S. shortcomings, whether in the realm of free trade, security, or immigration policy. Yet backed by a booming economy, a large, stable middle class, and a thriving democracy, this back and forth would be one between *amigos*, working together rather than apart.

Yet this path toward a Spanish-style future (or even beyond, given Mexico's larger population and already greater global economic heft) depends on the United States. Mexico's economy remains thoroughly dependent on its northern neighbor—tied by exports, investment, and remittances. Mexico's people are rooted in both places as well. With 10 percent of Mexico's population living in the United States, what happens on one side affects families and communities on the other. Mexico's security will benefit from U.S. cooperation, addressing together the complicated mutual threat posed by organized crime. Together the two neighbors should make the most of their mutual strengths and counteract their weaknesses. What is clear is that our two countries will now rise and fall together, two nations indivisible.

EPILOGUE:
THE RETURN OF THE PRI

On July 1, 2012, the PRI's Enrique Peña Nieto, former governor of the state of Mexico, captured the presidency, winning 38 percent of the vote. In many ways the win was preordained. Peña Nieto had led the polls by double digits for months, bolstered by the full force and resources of the party behind him. If anything, the margin of votes above his nearest rival—6 percent, or just over three million votes—was less than many expected. So too was the PRI's gain of just a plurality—not a majority—in both houses of Congress.

Many heralded the win as a decisive shift, some seeing it for good and others for ill. But perhaps the most notable outcome of the 2012 election was how much didn't change. The PAN, despite a poorly run presidential campaign and a dismal third-place finish, will remain front and center. Still an important congressional force and the party most ideologically in line with the president's inner circle of reformers, the PRI will need to woo the PAN to push forward almost any legislation. The necessity is even greater for the touted issue of energy reform, which will likely require a two-thirds constitutional majority. Coalition politics will remain vital, except now the PAN will wield the crucial swing vote. In the future, as in the recent past, the two parties will shape the nation's agenda.

The PRD too will remain in the game. Though nowhere near his 2006 photo finish, presidential candidate Andrés Manuel López Obrador successfully rallied his faithful and convinced many others from across the socioeconomic spectrum of the left's promise, coming in a solid second place. More decisive and perhaps more illustrative of the PRD's heft was its strong showing in the lower house of Congress (with its allied parties it is now second only to the PRI in its number of seats) and its win in Mexico City—home to a fifth of the nation's population. Here, Miguel Ángel Mancera, a former Mexico City attorney general, swept his nearest rival three to one, winning by over two million votes.[1]

Exit polls show the left's strong support among those comprising Mexico's hopeful future: the young, the urban, and the educated.[2] In nations such as Mexico, with severe inequalities and persistent poverty, a strong left is vital to lead a progressive social agenda. The capital and congressional victories hint at a pragmatic road forward for the PRD, that, if taken, will benefit Mexico's political system and its people.

"I AM 132"

Perhaps the biggest surprise of the 2012 election was the "YoSoy132" ("I Am 132") movement, which began during a Peña Nieto campaign stop at the Iberoamerican University, an exclusive Jesuit school on the western edge of the capital. Armed with banners denouncing Peña Nieto's record as governor, a group of students booed the candidate, who then infamously sought refuge in a bathroom. Embarrassed by the turn of events, Peña Nieto's campaign manager suggested to the media that the hecklers weren't in fact students at all, but instead were political operatives and outside agitators.

The attempted spin backfired, transforming a few placards into a nationwide movement. Three days later, the students posted a YouTube video of 131 of the so-called imposters, each holding their student credential and stating their full name and student ID number. Virally exploding, tens of thousands claimed to be the next in line—"yo soy 132."

From this quixotic beginning, YoSoy132 morphed into a broader phenomenon. It spread from Mexico's elite private universities to its more massive public institutions, and then to the general public. Utilizing both traditional marches as well as social media, YoSoy132 drew in parents, celebrities, and young people from across the country. Though generally anti-PRI, the students and their supporters focused their ire on the system in general. Motivated by the perceived corruption and overwhelming power of the privileged few, YoSoy132 quickly targeted the television media duopoly—Televisa and TV Azteca—repeatedly holding rallies outside the studios (the chanting at times noticeable during Televisa's evening newscasts).

Rather than disappear back into the classroom after the last ballot was cast on July 1, the movement continued. Tens of thousands filled the streets in Mexico City, Tijuana, Monterrey, and Guadalajara, and even U.S. cities such as San Diego, San Francisco, and Austin, to denounce vote buying and other old-school political practices that many believed had skewed the election.

It is too soon to know whether this movement will become an effective and independent force to further open Mexico's political system, or if other similar student- and citizen-led organizations will emerge. But the YoSoy132 movement marks a decided break with Mexico's past. It is the first time Mexico's students have jumped into the political waters in a serious and sustained way since the turbulent 1960s (when they were brutally repressed by the PRI). And the movement's challenges to Mexico's more opaque power structures resonate across partisan lines, a hopeful sign for building a stronger independent civil society to bolster Mexico's democratic system.

THE FUTURE OF MEXICAN DEMOCRACY

YoSoy132's demands give voice to the worries of many—that the PRI's return will reverse Mexico's democratic gains. Indeed, the record in many PRI-run states and municipalities ranks at or near the bottom in terms of budget transparency, according to an annual report by the Mexican Institute for Competitiveness (IMCO).[3] Others point to the still-prominent role played by many of the PRI's old guard, suggesting a return to the party's old tactics. Yet Mexico's democracy today, with all its limitations, can withstand an assault, if one should come.

Mexican democracy has evolved in ways that make a wholesale return to PRI dominance unlikely. The role and power of the legislative and judicial branches have changed dramatically. During the old PRI's heyday, Congress was little more than a rubber stamp, with the PRI's delegates rarely questioning the edicts of their president. Now, Congress is a fulcrum for negotiations and debates between Mexico's three main parties. Unlike the PRI of the past, Peña Nieto and his team will need to work closely with the opposition in order to govern.[4]

Likewise, the Supreme Court is more powerful than in decades past. It now provides a check on the president and on vested interests, and it has become an independent and final arbiter on many political issues—passing judgment on topics as diverse as the constitutionality of new legislation, the rules governing elections, and the jurisdiction of civilian courts over the military.

On a broader scale, over the last twelve years power has been increasingly decentralized, making a return to the PRI's historical hallmark, the "imperial presidency," virtually impossible. Once upon a time, a leader such as Carlos Salinas could dismiss half of the sitting governors during his term without a hint of blowback. Today states and their elected leaders are autonomous, both politically and increasingly economically, from the federal government.

In fact, states wield great power at the national level through their federal senators and representatives. Peña Nieto knows this from his time as the governor of the state of Mexico. Although many scholars argue that this protects rather than erodes the last bastions of authoritarianism in less electorally competitive states—it will nevertheless deter a return to the old political model in which Los Pinos could steamroll regional level executives.

Civil society is stronger in Mexico today too. Mexico has developed a vibrant and fiercely independent press, led by *El Universal*, *Reforma*, and *La Jornada*. Mexican voters and society have also gained a stronger voice, using social media and information now publicly available through Mexico's freedom of information law to shame corrupt bureaucrats and politicians.

Challenges do remain for Mexico's democracy, as lawmakers and activists alike continue to struggle against deep-rooted interests with a limited tool set for ensuring open, accountable, and responsive government. A forward-looking democratic administration could push the doors open further by investing in political reforms that encourage elected officials to be more accountable to their constituents, fully implementing the country's judicial reforms, and ensuring the continuation of a free press and active civil society. All these moves would benefit the country's economy, politics, and society. But even a misaligned government—one that fought to roll back gains in transparency and openness and that delayed efforts to take on systematic corruption—would slow rather than end this evolving process. In Mexico the fundamentals of democracy are here to stay.

Mexico's Path Forward

Mexican commentators, academics, and policymakers have generally agreed on a long list of changes necessary for Mexico to become more productive and competitive and to better the lives of its citizens. These include reforms to Mexico's energy sector, tax system, and labor code, as well as many of its political rules. While these "cures" are widely accepted, the ability to make them happen remains in doubt. Deep sectarian divides, political wrangling, powerful governors, vested interests, and the ever-present need for coalition politics threaten gridlock. And too often Mexico's long-term public needs are sacrificed for short-term political and personal gains.

Looking forward, social inclusion remains one of Mexico's biggest challenges. Mexico has come a long way from the repression of the 1960s, the lost decade of the 1980s, and even the asymmetric opening of the 1990s. Today it is an emerging middle-class nation. And many of the trends are moving in the right direction; per capita income has increased from a little over US$6000 in 1990 to over US$15,000 in 2011, and, while still high, inequality has fallen fairly steadily during the last decade.[5] Social policies such as *Oportunidades* (which provides conditional cash transfers to low-income families who keep their children in school) and *Seguro Popular* (providing health insurance to over fifty million Mexicans) have expanded what has been a traditionally small and frail social safety net.

Yet despite these efforts, millions of Mexicans continue to live on the margins. According to the government agency CONEVAL, there were over ten million citizens living in extreme poverty in 2010, and another forty million without adequate income or access to basic health care, housing, and education.[6] Even more live in fear of the spreading crime and violence, threatening themselves, their families, and their fragile economic gains.

The two socioeconomic worlds clash in the cities, on the border, and even on Mexico's scenic beaches. How to lift these tens of millions from poverty is a vital test for the nation. Its success will have serious ramifications for the United States as well, shaping immigration flows (as tens of thousands head north each year searching for a way to provide the basics for themselves and their kin), crime rates, and even the very stability of our neighbor.

The structural and economic reforms on the docket—should they pass—will help ease workers into the formal labor market as well as bring in more investment. But alone they won't solve the problem. To truly transform

Mexico, Peña Nieto and the PRI will have to take on the powerful teachers' union, break up concentrated economic control, spread financial credit more broadly, create a stronger and fairer court and law enforcement system, and diminish the widespread corruption that rewards connections rather than merit.

If Mexico can better the lives of its poorest and strengthen its middle, benefits for all will follow. Its economy will grow faster; its democracy will be stronger. It will also boost its international standing, carving out a prominent place for itself as one of the few emerging economies to transform itself into a developed nation. But if not, the country will stagnate economically, politically, and socially, proving the pessimists right while harming the interests of the majority.

The Evolving Road with the United States

Presidential elections coincide every twelve years between Mexico and the United States, and 2012, even with the reelection of President Obama, ushered in two new administrations. In Washington, some have worried that the PRI's return will affect the bilateral relationship, bringing back the old suspicions and traditional distance. But the world—and Mexico—have changed irrevocably in the intervening years. The last vestiges of the Cold War are gone, replaced by a multipolar world increasingly guided by multilateral organizations and discussions. Mexico too is different, now one of the most globalized economies in the world, and one tightly linked to its northern neighbor.

Tensions between the United States and Mexico won't disappear, but recent shifts hint at the potential for a closer relationship in the coming years. The changing dynamics of immigration—and in particular the combination of declining demographic trends in Mexico and rising Mexican American voting power—have the potential to change the tone of U.S. immigration politics away from the vitriol of the last several years. Though a repeat of the "whole enchilada" of comprehensive reform will likely remain elusive, a shift toward allowing young migrants to stay and keeping immigrant families together has already begun through administrative directives, a fundamental break from the hardening line of the last two decades.

The Trans-Pacific Partnership, or TPP, has perhaps the most potential to deepen and transform the bilateral economic relationship. Developing out of frustration with the slow pace of the Asia Pacific Economic Cooperation (APEC) negotiations as well as the stalling of the WTO's Doha development agenda round of trade negotiations, TPP discussions began between four small but open market nations—Brunei, Chile, New Zealand, and Singapore—in 2005. In 2008, the United States, along with Australia, Peru, Vietnam, and later Malaysia, joined the founders, aspiring to create a new twenty-first century style free trade agreement—one that built on previous agreements to encompass intellectual property, services, government procurement, and even regulatory frameworks. In 2012, Canada and Mexico entered the negotiations, amplifying the TPP's scope (to represent nearly 30 percent of world GDP) and ultimately its potential importance.

The incorporation of all of North America into the TPP means Mexico, the United States, and Canada will pivot together toward Asia, creating what may become the most dynamic global economic bloc in the coming decades. And by moving beyond the now conflictual symbolism of NAFTA, it reinforces the already solid North American supply chains and production platforms.

The coming years under these new administrations will bring turning points in the efforts to improve security, to deepen economic ties, to resolve the pressures on cross-border families, and to cooperate on the global stage. Whatever the policies and their outcomes, the permanent economic, political, security, and personal links will influence the two countries' futures; for the United States and Mexico's relations there is much to lose, but much more to gain.

NOTES

CHAPTER 1

1. Cambridge Systematics, Inc., "El Paso Regional Ports of Entry Operations Plan" (2011).
2. Mauricio Rodríguez, "Desde 2008 a la Fecha, Suman 9 Mil Homicidios en Juárez," *Proceso,* December 1, 2011, http://www.proceso.com.mx/?p=28982.
3. For instance, Freedom House's 2010 "Countries at the Crossroads" report lists Mexico as one of the top three performers in the hemisphere, along with Argentina and Brazil. Freedom House's 2012 "Freedom in the World" report counts Mexico as an "established democracy," with a free and fair electoral process and a generally well-functioning and transparent government. *The Economist* positions Mexico among "flawed democracies," its second-highest ranking. The Polity index places Mexico solidly in the "democracy" category, and the 2010 Bertelsmann Transformation Index describes Mexico as an "advanced democracy." For more information on these indices, please see chapter 5. Jake Dizard and Christopher Walker, "Countries at a Crossroads: The Vulnerable Middle" (Freedom House, 2010); Arch Puddington, "Freedom in the World 2012" (Freedom House, 2012); Economist Intelligence Unit, "Democracy Index 2011: Democracy Under Stress" (2011); Bertelsmann Stiftung, "Bertelsmann Transformation Index" (2010), http://www.bti-project.org/index/status-index/; Polity, "Polity IV Country Report: Mexico" (2010).
4. Alan Riding, *Distant Neighbors: A Portrait of the Mexicans* (New York: Vintage, 1989).
5. The U.S. Bureau of Consular Affairs estimates that there are over one million Americans living in Mexico, somewhere between one sixth and one fourth of all Americans living abroad. The 2010 Mexican census puts this number slightly lower, at 740,000. Scholars, including Sheila Croucher, suggest that tens—and perhaps hundreds—of thousands of "illegal" U.S. citizens live in Mexico, accounting for some of the difference between the two nations' official figures. While the majority of these are Americans of Mexican origin or descent, a strong percentage are Anglo-Americans, working, playing, or retiring in Mexico. For more see: Sheila Croucher, *The Other Side of the Fence: American Migrants in Mexico* (Austin: UT Austin

Press, 2009), 45–52; Instituto Nacional de Estadística y Geografía, "Informativo Oportuno: Los Nacidos en Otro País Suman 961,121 Personas" (2011); U.S. Department of State, "Background Note: Mexico," Bureau of Western Hemisphere Affairs, http://www.state.gov/r/pa/ei/bgn/35749.htm.

6. In 2011, South Dakota sent 27 percent of its exports to Mexico, Nebraska sent 25 percent, and New Hampshire sent 22 percent. See: "Foreign Trade, 2011" (U.S. Census Bureau, Foreign Trade Division, Dissemination Branch, 2011).

7. Federal Bureau of Investigation, "National Drug Threat Assessment: Emerging Trends" (2011), 8.

8. The Woodrow Wilson Center Mexico Institute's 2011 report calculates these figures using a general equilibrium model. Christopher Wilson, "Working Together: Economic Ties Between the United States and Mexico" (Washington, DC: Woodrow Wilson International Center for Scholars, Mexico Institute, 2011).

CHAPTER 2

1. Timothy J. Henderson, *A Glorious Defeat: Mexico and Its War with the United States* (New York: Hill and Wang, 2007), 53, 62–63, 140.

2. For a more in-depth discussion of the factors that ultimately led to the Mexican American War, see Henderson, *A Glorious Defeat*, 75–101.

3. Edward S. Wallace, "The United States Army in Mexico City," *Military Affairs* 13, no. 3 (1949), 160–161.

4. Historical evidence shows that U.S. ambassador to Mexico Henry Lane Wilson acted on his own with the coup plotters to orchestrate President Francisco Madero's demise. Once Washington became aware of his actions, he was recalled and replaced with the less interventionist John Lind. See: Karl M. Schmitt, *Mexico and the United States, 1821–1973: Conflict and Coexistence* (Hoboken: John Wiley, 1974), 3–4.

5. Mitchell Yockelson, "The United States Armed Forces and the Mexican Punitive Expedition: Part 1," *Prologue Magazine* 29, no. 3 (1997); Robert Freeman Smith, "Latin America, the United States and the European Powers, 1830–1930," in *The Cambridge History of Latin America*, ed. Leslie Bethel (Cambridge, UK: Cambridge University Press, 1986), 107.

6. Bertha Ulloa, *La Revolución Intervenida* (Mexico City: El Colegio de Mexico, 1969).

7. Benjamin Runkle, *Wanted Dead or Alive: Manhunts from Geronimo to Bin Laden* (New York: Palgrave MacMillan, 2011), 89–90.

8. Noel Mauer, "The Empire Struck Back: The Mexican Oil Expropriation of 1938 Reconsidered" (Cambridge, MA: Harvard Business School, 2010), 13.

9. In 1926, ownership within the Mexican oil industry was 56 percent American, 25 percent English, and a mere 4 percent Mexican. See: Merrill Rippy, *Oil and the Mexican Revolution* (Leiden, Netherlands: E. J. Brill, 1972), 182, 233, 227.

10. Jonathan C. Brown, "Why Foreign Oil Companies Shifted Their Production from Mexico to Venezuela During the 1920s," *American Historical Review* 90, no. 2 (1985), 362, 369.

11. Maria del Mar Rubio, "The Role of Mexico in the First Oil Shortage: 1918–1922, an International Perspective" (Barcelona: Universitat Pompeu Fabra, 2005).

12. Rippy, *Oil and the Mexican Revolution*, 53, 56; Brown, "Why Foreign Oil Companies Shifted Their Production"; Harold E. Davis, "Mexican Petroleum Taxes," *Hispanic American Historical Review* 12, no. 4 (1932), 412.

13. Mauer, "The Empire Struck Back," 7; L. H. Woolsey, "The Expropriation of Oil Properties by Mexico," *American Journal of International Law* 32, no. 3 (1938).

14. As part of his "good neighbor" policy (and his fears of a coming European war), U.S. President Franklin Roosevelt was reluctant to take a strong stand on the oil expropriation, worried that an intervention would strengthen the influence of forces hostile to the United States and its allies. For more information see: Rippy, *Oil and the Mexican Revolution*.

15. There are a number of influential scholars and books on U.S.-Mexico relations that emphasize these hostile interactions, including Robert Pastor and Jorge Castañeda, *Limits to Friendship: The United States and Mexico* (New York: Vintage, 1989); Enrique Krauze, *Mexico: Biography of Power* (New York: HarperCollins, 1997); Riding, *Distant Neighbors* (New York: Vintage, 1989); Josefina Vázquez and Lorenzo Meyer, *The United States and Mexico* (Chicago: University of Chicago Press, 1985).

16. Schmitt, *Mexico and the United States, 1821–1973*.

17. General Porfirio Díaz governed from 1876 to 1880, then passed the presidency for four years to Manuel González, a loyalist. In 1884, Díaz resumed official control, which he then held for the following twenty-seven years. Roger D. Hansen, *The Politics of Mexican Development* (Baltimore: Johns Hopkins University Press, 1971), 14.

18. Juan Carlos Moreno-Brid and Jaime Ros, *Development and Growth in the Mexican Economy: A Historical Perspective* (New York: Oxford University Press, 2009), 58, 61.

19. Ibid., 60–61.

20. Stephen Haber, Armando Razo, and Noel Maurer, *The Politics of Property Rights: Political Instability, Credible Commitments, and Economic Growth in Mexico, 1876–1929* (Cambridge, UK: Cambridge University Press, 2003), 193, 248; Krauze, *Mexico: Biography of Power*; Hansen, *The Politics of Mexican Development*.

21. Paul Ganster and David E. Lorey, *The U.S.-Mexican Border into the Twenty-First Century*, 2nd ed. (Lanham: Rowman and Littlefield, 2008), 39; Irwin Unger and Debi Unger, *The Guggenheims: A Family History* (New York: HarperCollins, 2005).

22. Jonathan C. Brown, *Oil and Revolution in Mexico* (Berkeley: University of California Press, 1993), 162–163.

23. Mark Wasserman, "Foreign Investment in Mexico, 1876–1910: A Case Study of the Role of Regional Elites," *The Americas* 36, no. 1 (1979), 7–10.

24. Stephen Haber, *Industry and Underdevelopment: The Industrialization of Mexico, 1890–1940* (Stanford: Stanford University Press, 1995), 28.

25. Haber, Razo, and Maurer, *The Politics of Property Rights*, 248.

26. Richard Bath, "Resolving Water Disputes," *Proceedings of the Academy of Political Science* 34, no. 1 (1981), 181–188.

27. Brian Delay, *War of a Thousand Deserts: Indian Raids and the U.S.-Mexican War* (New Haven: Yale University Press, 2008), 198–205.

28. Rachel St. John, *Line in the Sand: A History of the Western U.S.-Mexico Border* (Princeton: Princeton University Press, 2011), 63. For an overview of Mexico's railroad system, see Robert A. Trennert Jr., "The Southern Pacific Railroad of Mexico," *Pacific Historical Review* 35, no. 3 (August 1966), 265–266.

29. St. John, *Line in the Sand*, 203.

30. Dennis Gilbert, "Rewriting History: Salinas, Zedillo and the 1992 Textbook Controversy," *Mexican Studies/Estudios Mexicanos* 13, no. 2 (1997), 283–288.

31. U.S. agricultural growers worried both about labor shortages and the leverage they might give to union organizers, and so pushed Washington to increase immigration opportunities. For more information see: Debra Cohen, *Bracero* (Chapel Hill: University of North Carolina Press, 2011), 21.

32. Stephen R. Niblo, *War, Diplomacy, and Development: The United States and Mexico, 1938–1954* (Wilmington: Scholarly Resources, 1995), 191. These investments in many ways replaced trade, which remained fairly limited due to Mexico's import-substitution industrialization policies (high tariff barriers and the like) that encouraged domestic production.

33. W. Dirk Raat, *Mexico and the United States: Ambivalent Vistas* (Athens: University of Georgia Press, 2004), 166; Niblo, *War, Diplomacy, and Development*, 191.

34. George W. Grayson, *The Mexico-U.S. Business Committee: Catalyst for the North American Free Trade Agreement* (Rockville: Montrose, 2007), 116.

35. Joyce C. Vialet and Barbara McClure, "Temporary Worker Programs, Background and Issues" (Congressional Research Service, 1980); Philip Martin, "Braceros: History, Compensation," *Rural Migration News* 12, no. 2 (2006).

36. Many scholars note this shift in U.S.-Mexico relations, including Jorge I. Domínguez and Rafael Fernández de Castro, *United States and Mexico: Between Partnership and Conflict* (New York: Routledge, 2001); Susan Kaufman Purcell, "The Changing Nature of US-Mexican Relations," *Journal of Interamerican Studies and World Affairs* 39, no. 1 (1997); Clint E. Smith, *Inevitable Partnership: Understanding Mexico-U.S. Relations* (Boulder: Lynne Rienner, 2000).

37. See: Domínguez and Fernández de Castro, *United States and Mexico*, 31.

38. Ibid., 132–133.

39. Denise Dresser, "Exporting Conflict: Transboundary Consequences of Mexican Politics," in *The California-Mexico Connection*, ed. Abraham F. Lowenthal and Katrina Burgess (Stanford: Stanford University Press, 1993); Meg Sullivan, "Revolution of Words: Oxnard Activists Drive Home View that Mexican Presidential Election was Stolen," *Los Angeles Times*, November 17, 1988; Joseph Thesken, "Mexican Vote Protested Here," *San Diego Tribune*, August 15, 1988.

40. As a part of this new strategy, officially called the Programa Paisano, the Salinas government created the Program for Mexican Communities Living Abroad (known by its Spanish acronym, PCME), under the auspices of the Mexican Foreign Ministry. The growing network of Mexican consulates in the United States managed the PCME's outreach efforts, including organizing migrants into home-town associations (HTAs), creating Latino soccer leagues, and providing literacy and other basic education programs. President Vicente Fox renamed the PCME the Institute

for Mexicans Abroad (IME) and added an advisory board comprising one hundred migrant leaders, responsible for shaping the administration's diaspora policy and coordinating with Mexican American political groups. For more on the Mexican government's relations with its diaspora, see David Ayón, "Taming the Diaspora: Migrants and the State, 1986–2006," in *Mexico's Democratic Challenges*, ed. Andrew Selee and Jacqueline Peschard (Washington, DC: Woodrow Wilson International Center for Scholars, 2010); Alexandra Délano, *Mexico and its Diaspora in the United States: Policies of Emigration since 1848* (Cambridge, UK: Cambridge University Press, 2011).

41. Alfredo Corchado, "Zedillo Vows to Vanquish Mexico Woes," *Dallas Morning News*, April 6, 1995.
42. Guadalupe González, Ferran Martínez i Coma, and Jorge A. Schiavon, "México, las Américas y el Mundo" (Mexico City: Centro de Investigación y Docencia Económicas, 2008), 119.
43. Pew Global Attitudes Project, "Most Mexicans See Better Life in U.S." (Washington, DC: Pew Research Center, 2009).
44. González, Martínez i Coma, and Schiavon, "México, las Américas y el Mundo."
45. Baby Center, "Los 100 Nombres Más Populares de México," http://www.babycenter.com.mx/pregnancy/nombres/nombres_populares_2010/.
46. Marshall Bouton et al., "Global Views 2008: Anxious Americans Seek a New Direction in U.S. Foreign Policy" (Chicago: Chicago Council on Global Affairs, 2009), 27; John E. Reilly, "American Public Opinion and U.S. Foreign Policy" (Chicago: Chicago Council on Foreign Relations, 1995), 26.
47. Roberto Newell, "Restoring Mexico's International Reputation" (Washington, DC: Woodrow Wilson International Center for Scholars, Mexico Institute, 2011).
48. Ibid.
49. U.S. Senate, *Comprehensive Immigration Reform Act of 2006*, 109th Congress, S.2611.
50. William L. Painter and Jennifer Lake, "Homeland Security Department: FY2012 Appropriations" (Washington, DC: Department of Homeland Security, 2011), 21.
51. Richard Verrier, "Cinepolis Plans to Expand Luxury Cinema Concept in Southland," *Los Angeles Times*, October 25, 2011; Emily Bryson York, "Sara Lee Bread Business Sale: Getting to Know Bimbo," *Chicago Tribune*, November 9, 2010; Cemex, "About Us: United States of America," http://www.cemex.com/AboutUs/UnitedStates.aspx.
52. Joyce A. Martin et al., "Births: Final Data for 2008," *National Vital Statistics Reports* 59, no. 1 (2010), 8, 28.
53. According to the 2010 Mexican census there were some 20 million Mexicans living in northern border states (out of a total 112 million). In the United States, 72 million Americans (out of a little over 300 million) live in states along the southern border. U.S. Census Bureau, "State and Country Quickfacts," http://quickfacts.census.gov/qfd/index.html; Instituto Nacional de Estadística y Geografía, "Población, Hogares y Vivienda," http://www.inegi.org.mx/Sistemas/temasV2/Default.aspx?s=est&c=17484.
54. David Ayón, "The Impact of Mexican Migration and Border Proximity on Local Communities" (Houston: Rice University, James A. Baker III Institute for Public Policy, 2009).

CHAPTER 3

1. Immigration Policy Center, "Who and Where the DREAMers Are," July 31, 2012, http://www.immigrationpolicy.org/just-facts/who-and-where-dreamers-are.
2. Steven A. Camarota, "Estimating the Impact of the DREAM Act," Center for Immigration Studies, 2010, http://www.cis.org/dream-act-costs.
3. While Mexican immigration has been falling, Central American immigration to the United States has seen a recent surge. Between October 2011 and May 2012, the number of non-Mexican migrants apprehended along the southern border (57,000, with most from Central America) more than doubled from the same time period the year before (27,000). Many blame the growing security problems in Central America for pushing immigrants north through Mexico to the United States. This increase, however, is still smaller in absolute terms than the decline in recent years in the number of Mexican detained along the border. And, even with this rise, the number of Central Americans caught today is still lower than during the mid-2000s. Lesley Sapp, "Apprehensions by the U.S. Border Patrol: 2005–2010" (U.S. Department of Homeland Security, 2011); Olga R. Rodriguez, "Central American Migrants Flood North through Mexico to U.S.," *Huffington Post,* June 13, 2012, http://www.huffingtonpost.com/2012/07/13/central-americans-in-the-united-states_n_1671551.html.
4. As one of the longest and most extensive guest-worker programs in history, the Bracero program has been the subject of numerous studies and evaluations. On the positive side, scholars find it was less exploitative than previous approaches, while also satisfying U.S. demand for cheap farm labor. Wages and working conditions were better than under informal agreements (and, some suggest, even better than unauthorized immigrants' conditions today). Though research also finds that many employers still violated the rules, withheld social security, skirted minimum-wage laws, and hired illegal migrants. These abuses, combined with pressure from unions and human rights groups, led the Johnson administration to end the program in 1964. For more in-depth accounts see: Jorge Durand, *Braceros: Las Miradas Mexicana y Estadounidense* (Senado de la República, LX Legislatura, 2007); Ernesto Galarza, *Merchants of Labor: The Mexican Bracero Story* (Santa Barbara: McNally & Loftin, 1972).
5. Jeanne Batalova, "Mexican Immigrants in the United States," Migration Policy Institute, 2008, http://www.migrationinformation.org/USfocus/display.cfm?id=679.
6. Jeffrey S. Passel and D'Vera Cohn, "Mexican Immigrants: How Many Come, How Many Leave" (Washington, DC: Pew Hispanic Center, 2009).
7. Elizabeth Grieco and Edward N. Trevelyan, "Place of Birth of the Foreign-Born Population: 2009" (U.S. Census Bureau, 2010).
8. U.S. Customs and Border Patrol, "Border Patrol Staffing by Fiscal Year" (2011); U.S. Customs and Border Patrol, "Enacted Border Patrol Program Budget by Fiscal Year" (2011).
9. U.S. Customs and Border Patrol, "Total Illegal Alien Apprehensions by Fiscal Year" (2011).
10. Mexican Migration Project, "Graph 8: Probability of Apprehension on an Undocumented Border Crossing, 1980–2010," October 2011, http://mmp.opr.princeton.edu/results/008apprehension-en.aspx; Jezmin Fuentes et al., "Impacts of

U.S. Immigration Policies on Migration Behavior," in *Impacts of Border Enforcement on Mexican Migration: the View from Sending Communities*, ed. Wayne A. Cornelius and Jessa M. Lewis (La Jolla: Center for Comparative Immigration Studies, 2007).

11. U.S. Customs and Border Patrol, "Total Illegal Alien Apprehensions by Fiscal Year."

12. Douglas S. Massey, Jorge Durand, and Nolan J. Malone, *Beyond Smoke and Mirrors: Mexican Immigration in an Era of Economic Integration* (New York: Russell Sage Foundation, 2002).

13. Chris McGreal, "The Battle of the U.S.-Mexico Frontier," *The Guardian*, February 20, 2011.

14. Fuentes et al., "Impacts of U.S. Immigration Policies on Migration Behavior," 57.

15. In 2011 over 1600 bills were introduced (though many fewer passed) to address immigration issues at the state and local levels. See Brooke Meyer and Ann Morse, "Immigration-Related Laws and Resolutions in the States" (Washington, DC: National Conference of State Legislatures, 2011).

16. Andrew Malcolm, *Los Angeles Times*, "In Her Own Words: Gov. Jan Brewer on Mexico Joining Lawsuit Against Arizona's Illegal Immigrant Law," 2010.

17. Dana Blanton, "Fox News Poll: Arizona Was Right to Take Action on Immigration," *Fox News*, May 7, 2010, http://www.foxnews.com/us/2010/05/07/fox-news-pol l-arizona-right-action-immigration/#ixzz1ZM20KNWT; Jeffrey M. Jones, "More Americans Favor Than Oppose Arizona Immigration Law," *Gallup*, 2010, http:// www.gallup.com/poll/127598/americans-favor-oppose-arizona-immigration-law. aspx.

18. U.S. Supreme Court, "Arizona et al. *v.* United States" (2012).

19. *New York Times*, "D.I.Y. Immigration Reform," March 20, 2011; Alfonso Aguilar, "Utah's New Immigration Outlook," *Politico*, March 11, 2011, http://www.politico. com/news/stories/0311/51104.html.

20. James C. McKinley and Julia Preston, "U.S. Can't Trace Foreign Visitors on Expired Visas," *New York Times*, October 11, 2009.

21. Brady McCombs, "July Migrant Deaths Could Set Record," *Arizona Daily Star*, July 16, 2010; U.S. Government Accountability Office, "Border-Crossing Deaths Have Doubled Since 1995; Border Patrol's Efforts to Prevent Deaths Have Not Been Fully Evaluated" (2006).

22. James C. McKinley Jr., "An Arizona Morgue Grows Crowded," *New York Times*, July 29, 2010.

23. James Pinkerton, "Fake Documents for Immigrants Swamp Houston," *Houston Chronicle*, May 2, 2008; U.S. Department of Homeland Security, Office of the Press Secretary, "Joint Task Forces Created in 10 Cities to Combat Document and Benefit Fraud" (2006).

24. Alan Zarembo, "Coyote Inc.," *Newsweek*, August 29, 1999; Geovana Ruano, "Sasabe: The New Destination toward Death and Insult for Immigrants," *Yuma Sun* [Arizona], March 10, 2008.

25. Douglas S. Massey, "Backfire at the Border: Why Enforcement without Legalization Cannot Stop Illegal Immigration" (Washington, DC: Center for Trade and Policy Studies, CATO Institute, 2005); Scott Borger, "Estimates of the Cyclical Inflow of

Undocumented Migrants to the United States" (San Diego: Center for Comparative Immigration Studies, University of California, San Diego, 2009).

26. Pew Hispanic Center, "The Mexican-American Boom: Births Overtake Immigration" (Pew Research Center, 2011), 9; Michael S. Rendal, Peter Brownell, and Sarah Kups, "Declining Return Migration from the United States to Mexico in the Late-2000s Recession" (RAND Corporation, 2010).

27. Betsy Cavendish and Maru Cortazar, "Children at the Border: the Screening, Protection and Repatriation of Unaccompanied Mexican Minors" (Appleseed, 2011); U.S. Department of State, "Annual Report of Immigrant Visa Applicants in the Family-Sponsored and Employment-Based Preferences" (2011).

28. U.S. Department of Homeland Security, "Removals Involving Illegal Alien Parents of United States Citizen Children" (Office of Inspector General, 2009); U.S. Immigration and Customs Enforcement, "Deportation of Parents of U.S.-Born Citizens" (Washington, DC: U.S. Department of Homeland Security, 2012), 4.

29. Anne Gorman, "A Family's Painful Split Decision," Los Angeles Times, April 27, 2007.

30. U.S. Department of Homeland Security, "FY2013 Budget in Brief" (2011); Marshall Fitz, Gebe Martinez, and Madura Wijewardena, "The Costs of Mass Deportation: Impractical, Expensive, and Ineffective" (Center for American Progress, 2010).

31. Thomas Jefferson, The Writings of Thomas Jefferson: Being His Autobiography, Correspondence, Reports, Messages, Addresses, and Other Writings, Official and Private, vol. 4 (Washington, DC: Taylor and Maury, 1854), 394.

32. John F. Kennedy, A Nation of Immigrants, Rev. and enlarged ed. (New York: HarperCollins, 1964).

33. Miriam Jordan, "Immigration Audit Takes Toll," Wall Street Journal, March 15, 2011.

34. Nathan Deal, "Statement on the Status of Agricultural Workforce in Georgia," Georgia State Government, July 14, 2011, http://gov.georgia.gov/00/press/deta il/0,2668,165937316_165937374_172486990,00.html.

35. Reid J. Epstein, "Georgia Immigrant Crackdown Backfires," Politico, June 22, 2011, http://www.politico.com/news/stories/0611/57551.html.

36. Samuel Addy, "A Cost-Benefit Analysis of the New Alabama Immigration Law" (University of Alabama, Center for Business and Economic Research, 2012).

37. Raul Hinojosa-Ojeda and Marshall Fitz, "Revitalizing the Golden State: What Legalization over Deportation Could Mean to California and Los Angeles County" (Washington, DC: Center for American Progress, Immigration Policy Center, 2011); Judith Gans, "Immigrants in Arizona: Fiscal and Economic Impacts" (University of Arizona, Udall Center for Studies in Public Policy, 2008).

38. Jason Marczak, et al., Americas Society, "The Economic Impact of Immigrant-Related Local Ordinances" (New York, 2011).

39. Paul Vitello, "Immigration Issues End a Pennsylvania Grower's Season," New York Times, April 2, 2008.

40. Garance Burke, "Despite Economy, Farm Jobs Still Go Begging," Associated Press, September 27, 2010.

41. There is an economic debate about the extent to which immigration affects the real wage earnings of U.S. workers. Following work done by Rachel M. Friedberg and

Jennifer Hunt ("The Impact of Immigrants on Host Country Wages, Employment and Growth," *Journal of Economic Perspectives* 9, no. 2, Spring 1995, 23–44), using data from the 1990 census, David Card ("Immigrant Inflows, Native Outflows, and the Local Market Impacts of Higher Immigration," *Journal of Labor Economics* 19, no. 1, January 2001: 22–64) shows that immigration had negligible effects on native workers' salaries. Studies by George Borjas ("The Labor Demand Curve *Is* Downward Sloping: Reexamining the Impact of Immigration on the Labor Market," *Quarterly Journal of Economics* 118, no. 4, 2003: 1335–1374), George Borjas and Lawrence Katz ("The Evolution of the Mexican-Born Workforce in the United States," in *Mexican Immigration to the United States*, edited by George J. Borjas, 13–56, Chicago: University of Chicago Press, 2007), and Borjas ("Making it in America: Social Mobility in the Immigrant Population," NBER Working Papers, no. 12088, Washington, DC: National Bureau of Economic Research, 2006) contest these claims, arguing that immigration has a statistically significant negative impact on native workers' wages from 1983 to 2000, and hits the less-educated cohort particularly hard in the short term. More recent calculations, such as those done by Gianmarco Ottaviano and Giovanni Peri ("Rethinking the Effects of Immigration on Wages: New Data and Analysis from 1990–2004," *Immigration Policy in Focus* 5, no. 8, October 2006, 1–7), that use more nuanced econometric models, find little effect.

42. Gianmarco Ottaviano and Giovanni Peri, "Immigration and National Wages: Clarifying the Theory and the Empirics" (Cambridge, MA: National Bureau of Economic Research, 2008).

43. Eduardo Porter, "Cost of Illegal Immigration May Be Less than Meets the Eye," *New York Times*, April 16, 2006.

44. Susan Aud, Mary Ann Fox, and Angelina Kewal Ramani, "Status and Trends in the Education of Racial and Ethnic Groups" (National Center for Educational Statistics and the United States Department of Education, 2010); Porter, "Cost of Illegal Immigration May Be Less Than Meets the Eye."

45. Jason Marczak, et al., Americas Society, "Economic Impact of Immigrant-Related Local Ordinances."; Giovanni Peri, "Immigrants, Skills, and Wages: Measuring the Economic Gains from Immigration," *Immigration Policy Center: In Focus* 5, no. 3 (2006); Giovanni Peri, "How Immigrants Affect California Employment and Wages" (San Francisco: Public Policy Institute of California, 2007).

46. Raul Hinojosa-Ojeda, "Raising the Floor for American Workers: The Economic Benefits of Comprehensive Immigration Reform" (Washington, DC: Immigration Policy Center, 2010), 10.

47. Robert I. Lerman, "An Overview of Economic, Social, and Demographic Trends Affecting the U.S. Labor Market" (Washington, DC: U.S. Department of Labor, 1999).

48. Philip Martin, *Importing Poverty? Immigration and the Changing Face of Rural America* (New Haven: Yale University Press, 2009), 54.

49. Eduardo Porter, "Here Illegally, Working Hard and Paying Taxes," *New York Times*, July 19, 2006.

50. Ketchup outpaces salsa in volume sold, but salsa sales (measured by dollars) are higher than for ketchup. Carl Bialik, "Ketchup vs. Salsa: By the Numbers," *Wall*

Street Journal, September 20, 2007, http://blogs.wsj.com/numbersguy/ketchup-vs-salsa-by-the-numbers-191/.

51. Susan Leigh Dieterlen, "Mexican-American Landscapes in Small Midwestern Cities: Mixed Methods Development of a Typology" (PhD diss., University of Michigan, 2009).

52. John B. Thomas, "A Tale of Two Cities," *Indianapolis Monthly*, November 2006, 58.

53. Guillermo Baralt, *If It's Goya It Has to Be Good: The First 75 Years* (Barcelona: Editorial Revés, 2011); Goya Foods, "Goya Foods Celebrates Its 75th Anniversary Serving the Community," October 7, 2010, http://www.goya.com/english/PressRoom/press_release.html?lid=44.

54. David M. Kennedy, "Can We Still Afford to Be a Nation of Immigrants?" *The Atlantic*, November 1996.

55. Simon Romero and Janet Elder, "Hispanics in the U.S. Report Optimism," *New York Times*, August 6, 2003.

56. Dowell Myers and John Pitkin, "Immigrants Today: New Evidence Shows the Latest Immigrants to America are Following our History's Footsteps" (Center for American Progress, 2010), http://www.americanprogress.org/wp-content/uploads/issues/2010/09/pdf/immigrant_assimilation.pdf.

57. Shirin Hakimzadeh and D'Vera Cohn, "English Usage Among Hispanics in the United States" (Washington, DC: Pew Research Center, Pew Hispanic Center, 2007). According to Pew surveys, about half of second-generation Mexicans are bilingual, and half are English-dominant.

58. Mark Hugo Lopez, "Latinos and Education: Explaining the Attainment Gap" (Washington, DC: Pew Research Center, Pew Hispanic Center, 2009).

59. Mark Schneider, "The Costs of Failure Factories in American Higher Education" (Washington, DC: American Enterprise Institute for Public Policy Research, 2008).

60. Economist James Smith points out the flaws of using cross-sectional studies (e.g., comparing the kids and grandkids of Mexican immigrants within a particular year), and instead conducts a longitudinal analysis (which enables one to parse out inter-generational mobility). With these methods, he finds both education and wage gaps close over time. Tomás R. Jiménez and David Fitzgerald cite other studies that work with existing data in similar ways, and that also find positive intergenerational effects. See James P. Smith, "Assimilation across the Latino Generations," *American Economic Review* 93, no. 2 (2003); Tomás R. Jiménez and David Fitzgerald, "Mexican Assimilation: A Temporal and Spatial Reorientation" (Center for Comparative Immigration Studies, 2007).

61. Pew Hispanic Center, "Between Two Worlds: How Young Latinos Come of Age in America" (Washington, DC: Pew Research Center, 2009), 11.

62. Jiménez and Fitzgerald, "Mexican Assimilation"; Smith, "Assimilation across the Latino Generations."

63. Scholars posit a couple of reasons for this continued discrepancy. One is that the higher individuals of Mexican origin climb on the socioeconomic scale, the less likely they are to identify themselves as Mexican. A second reason is that since Mexicans often start low on the education ladder, and the undocumented status of many puts up further barriers, it may take more than three generations to reach

parity with other groups. Jiménez and Fitzgerald, "Mexican Assimilation," 348; Brian Duncan and Stephen Trejo, "Intermarriage and the Intergenerational Transmission of Ethnic Identity and Human Capital for Mexican Americans," *Journal of Labor Economics* (2011); Richard Alba and Tariqul Islam, "The Case of the Disappearing Mexican Americans: An Ethnic-Identity Mystery," *Population Research and Policy Review* 28, no. 2 (2009).

64. Betty Maxfield, "Army Demogaphics" (Office of Army Demographics, 2010).

65. Justin Berton, "Latinos Enlisting in Record Numbers," *San Francisco Chronicle*, May 15, 2006.

66. iCasualties, "Iraq Coalition Casualties: Military Fatalities," http://icasualties.org/ Iraq/Fatalities.aspx.

67. Pew Hispanic Center, "Between Two Worlds," 42.

68. Roberto Suro, "The Hispanic Family in Flux" (Washington, DC: Brookings Institution, 2007); Robert J. Sampson, Jeffrey D. Morenoff, and Stephen Raudenbush, "Social Anatomy of Racial and Ethnic Disparities in Violence," *American Journal of Public Health* 95, no. 2 (2005).

69. Alan Wolfe, "Native Son: Samuel Huntington Defends the Homeland," *Foreign Affairs* (2004).

70. Suro, "Hispanic Family in Flux."

71. William and Mary professor Graham C. Ousey and George Washington University's Charis E. Kubrin came to similar conclusions. In their paper "Exploring the Connection between Immigration and Violent Crime Rates in U.S. Cities, 1980–2000," *Social Problems* 56, no. 3 (2009), they found that in U.S. cities where immigration increased, violent crime rates decreased, even while taking into consideration factors such as demographic transitions or drug markets. Eyal Press, "Do Immigrants Make Us Safer," *New York Times Magazine*, December 3, 2006.

72. Parsing out by ethnicity, Mexican immigrants and their children are less violent than both whites and blacks (though the gap between whites and Mexicans is smaller than the one between Mexicans and blacks). See Robert J. Sampson, "Rethinking Crime and Immigration," *Contexts*, Winter 2008, 9; Sampson, Morenoff, and Raudenbush, "Social Anatomy of Racial and Ethnic Disparities in Violence."

73. Deportation is not an active factor in reducing the number of incarcerated immigrants. Under most state laws, undocumented criminals convicted of violent and nonviolent crimes must complete the minimum sentence before deportation proceedings begin. Some states, however, are looking to pass or have passed laws that allow the deportation of nonviolent offenders before they complete their sentence. Steven A. Camarota and Jessica M. Vaughan, "Immigration and Crime: Assessing a Conflicted Issue" (Center for Immigration Studies, 2009); Mike Ward, "Lawmakers Discuss Deporting Foreign Convicts," *Austin American-Statesman*, 2010.

74. Rubén G. Rumbaut and Walter A. Ewing, "The Myth of Immigrant Criminality and the Paradox of Assimilation: Incarceration Rates among Native and Foreign-Born Men" (Washington, DC: Immigration Policy Center, 2007); Sampson, "Rethinking Crime and Immigration," 32.

75. Press, "Do Immigrants Make Us Safer."

76. Christopher Dickey, "Reading, Ranting, and Arithmetic," *Newsweek*, May 26, 2010. Sampson, "Rethinking Crime and Immigration."

77. Batalova, "Mexican Immigrants in the United States."
78. Kevin Kenny, "Irish Immigrants in the United States," *America.gov*, February 13, 2008, http://www.america.gov/st/peopleplace-english/2008/February/2008030 7131416ebyessedo0.6800043.html; Roger Daniels, *Coming to America: A History of Immigration and Ethnicity in American Life* (New York: Harper Perennial, 1992), 189.
79. Pablo Fajnzylber and J. Humberto López, "Close to Home: The Development Impact of Remittances in Latin America" (Washington, DC: World Bank, 2007); Jeffrey Passel and D'Vera Cohn, "Mexico: Migrants, Remittances, 3x1," *Migration News* 16, no. 4 (2009); Manuel Orozco, "Remittances to Latin America and the Caribbean: Issues and Perspectives on Development" (Washington, DC: Organization of American States, 2004).
80. Raúl Hernández-Coss, "The U.S.–Mexico Remittance Corridor: Lessons on Shifting from Informal to Formal Transfer Systems" (Washington, DC: World Bank, 2005), 4, 31.
81. U.S. Department of State, "U.S. Relations with Mexico: Fact Sheet," Bureau of Western Hemisphere Affairs, June 25, 2012, http://www.state.gov/r/pa/ei/bgn/35749.htm.
82. Andrés Bermúdez's tenure was not without its controversies or problems. Some felt the international attention he received had gone to his head; others were disappointed that he was not able to single-handedly transform the local system. Still, Bermúdez's efforts opened a political door for immigrants. See Michael Peter Smith and Matt Bakker, *Citizenship Across Borders: The Political Transnationalism of el Migrante* (Ithaca: Cornell University Press, 2008); Sam Quinones, *Antonio's Gun and Delfino's Dream: True Tales of Mexican Migration* (Albequerque: University of New Mexico Press, 2008).
83. Pew Global Attitudes Project, "Opinion of the United States," Pew Research Center, 2012, http://www.pewglobal.org/database/?indicator=1.
84. B. Lindsay Lowell, "U.S.-Mexican Relations: Changes in the U.S.-Mexican Relationship, North America and Immigration" (paper presented at the Executive Seminar on Mexico, Washington, DC, August 2011).
85. Passel and Cohn, "Mexican Immigrants: How Many Come, How Many Leave"; U.S. Customs and Border Patrol, "Total Illegal Alien Apprehensions by Fiscal Year."
86. Damien Cave, "Better Lives for Mexicans Cut Allure of Going North," *New York Times*, July 6, 2011.
87. Jeffrey Passel, D'Vera Cohn, and Ana Gonzalez-Barrera, "Net Migration from Mexico Falls to Zero—and Perhaps Less" (Washington, DC: Pew Research Center, 2012); Cave, "Better Lives for Mexicans Cut Allure of Going North."
88. World Bank, "World Development Indicators" (2011).
89. Gordon H. Hanson and Craig McIntosh, "The Demography of Mexican Migration to the U.S.," *American Economic Review: Papers & Proceedings* 99, no. 2 (2009).
90. Barry Bluestone and Mark Melnik, "After the Recovery: Help Needed, the Coming Labor Shortage and How People in Encore Careers Can Help Solve It" (Boston: Northeastern University, Kitty and Michael Dukakis Center for Urban and Regional Policy, 2010); Linda Levine, "Retiring Baby-Boomers = A Labor Shortage" (Washington, DC: Congressional Research Service, 2008).

91. Thomas L. Friedman, "A Gift for Grads: Start-Ups," *New York Times,* June 9, 2010, A25.

92. Rachel Konrad, "Immigrants Behind 25 Percent of Tech Startups," *Associated Press,* January 3, 2007; Vivek Wadhwa et al., "America's New Immigrant Entrepreneurs," Master of Engineering Management Program, Duke University; School of Information, University of California, Berkeley (January 4, 2007).

93. The steady increase, albeit uneven, of the foreign-born immigrant population in the United States for the past forty years and its growing percentage as a part the U.S. labor market make it likely that these low-skilled jobs will increasingly be filled by immigrants. While making up only about 16 percent (22.5 million people) of the total U.S. civilian workforce in 2010, foreign-born immigrants make up approximately 50 percent of the population in the United States that does not have a high-school degree (10 million out of roughly 22 million workers over twenty-five years old). For more information see Jeanne Batalova and Aaron Terrazas, "Frequently Requested Statistics on Immigrants and Immigration in the United States," *Migration Policy Institute,* 2010, http://www.migrationinformation.org/feature/display.cfm?ID=818; U.S. Census Bureau, "Educational Attainment in the United States: 2011" (2012); U.S. Department of Labor, "Labor Force Characteristics of Foreign-Born Workers Summary," *Bureau of Labor Statistics,* 2011, http://www.bls.gov/news.release/forbrn.nr0.htm; Drew Liming and Michael Wolf, "Job Outlook by Education, 2006–16," *Occupational Outlook Quarterly* 52, no. 2 (Fall 2008).

94. A survey done by University of Texas researchers found that 86 percent of U.S. migrants living in Mexico don't plan to return to live in the United States again. See Croucher, *Other Side of the Fence,* 23–65.

95. Ibid., 65.

CHAPTER 4

1. David Shirk, *Mexico's New Politics: The PAN and Democratic Change* (Boulder: Lynne Rienner, 2005).

2. Elana Poniatowska, *Nada, Nadie—Las Voces del Temblor* (Mexico City: Ediciones Era, 1988).

3. Vikram K. Chand, *Mexico's Political Awakening* (Notre Dame: University of Notre Dame Press, 2000), 208–212.

4. Ibid., 102, 172.

5. Carolyn Lesh, "250,000 Protest Vote in Mexico," *Chicago Tribune,* July 17, 1988.

6. Julia Preston and Samuel Dillon, *Opening Mexico: The Making of a Democracy* (New York: Farrar, Straus and Giroux, 2004), 175–176.

7. Todd Eisenstadt, *Courting Democracy in Mexico: Party Strategies and Electoral Institutions* (New York: Cambridge University Press, 2004), 176–177.

8. Denise Dresser, "Bringing the Poor Back In: National Solidarity as a Strategy of Regime Legitimation," in *Transforming State-Society Relations in Mexico: The National Solidarity Strategy,* ed. Wayne Cornelius, Ann Craig, and Jonathan Fox (La Jolla: Center for U.S.-Mexican Studies, University of California, San Diego, 1994).

9. Kenneth F. Greene, *Why Dominant Parties Lose: Mexico's Democratization in Comparative Perspective* (Cambridge, UK: Cambridge University Press, 2007).

10. Shirk, *Mexico's New Politics: The PAN and Democratic Change,* 169–207; Kathleen Bruhn, *Taking on Goliath: The Emergence of a New Left Party and the Struggle for Democracy in Mexico* (University Park: Pennsylvania State University Press, 1997).

11. According to Mexico's constitution, no sitting cabinet minister or active government official can run for the presidency within six months of the election. Since Luis Donaldo Colosio was killed within this time period most of the former presidential hopefuls were unable to step in as candidates. Though Ernesto Zedillo had never been seriously mentioned as a potential candidate, he had resigned from his position as the secretary of education and so was one of the only members of Salinas's team able to assume the candidacy.

12. There is an extensive literature on Mexico's democratization, with scholars prioritizing different variables in their explanations for the country's political opening. For instance, Kenneth Greene (*Why Dominant Parties Lose*) focuses on economic resources, and argues that the privatization of state-owned enterprises and the shrinking of the state more generally in the late 1980s and early 1990s diminished the PRI's financial advantage over opposition parties, ultimately ending its electoral dominance. Todd Eisenstadt (*Courting Democracy in Mexico*) emphasizes the actions of opposition parties through both institutional and extra-institutional (e.g., back-room negotiations) means following disputed elections to force concessions that then chipped away at the ruling party's hegemony. David Shirk (*Mexico's New Politics*) highlights party building within the PAN, and argues that its track record of innovative local governance paved the way for the party's victory in the 2000 federal election. Others, such as Beatriz Magaloni and Vikram Chand, look to society to explain the opening. Magaloni ("Weak and Powerful Courts under Autocracy: The Case of Mexico," Paper presented at the conference "The Politics of Courts in Authoritarian Regimes." University of Pennsylvania Law School, August 30–31, 2006) shows how the economic crisis in the mid-1990s generated widespread public discontent, shifting voter support away from the "known devil" to a relative unknown: the PAN's 2000 presidential candidate, Vicente Fox. Chand (*Mexico's Political Awakening*) emphasizes the role of civil society organizations pushing for greater openness, competition, and ultimately the system's democratization.

13. Joseph Klesner, "The Structure of the Mexican Electorate," in *Mexico's Pivotal Democratic Election: Candidates, Voters, and the Presidential Campaign of 2000* (Stanford: Stanford University Press, 2004), 103; Susan Ferriss, "Younger Voters are Key to Win in Mexico," *Austin American-Statesman,* May 17, 2000, A1.

14. Susan Ferriss, "Mexico's Fox Closes Gap in Bid to End 71-Year Presidential Era," *Austin American-Statesman,* May 22, 2000.

15. Laurence Iliff, "PRI Machine, People of 'Campo' Vital to Mexican's Presidential Bid; Labastida Battling to Extend Party's Decades of Dominance," *Dallas Morning News,* April 18, 2000.

16. Geoffrey Mohan, "Mexican Party's Uphill Struggle; PRI is Trying to Remake Itself," *Newsday,* April 27, 2000.

17. Jorge Castañeda, *Mañana Forever: Mexico and the Mexicans* (New York: Knopf, Borzoi Books, 2011), 171–174.

18. Edward Alden, *The Closing of the American Border* (New York: HarperCollins, 2008).

19. Juan Francisco Escobedo, "Movilización de Opinión Pública en México: El Caso del Grupo Oaxaca y de la Ley Federal de Acceso a la Información Pública," *Derecho Comparado de la Información* (July–December 2003), 64–92.
20. *Reforma*, "Juan Ciudadano: Se Cayó el Sistema," November 27, 2000.
21. Greg Michener, "The Surrender of Secrecy: Explaining the Emergence of Strong Access to Information Laws in Latin America" (PhD diss, University of Texas at Austin, 2010), 28.
22. Jonathan Fox and Libby Haight, "Transparency Reforms: Theory and Practice," in *Mexico's Democratic Challenges*, ed. Andrew Selee and Jacqueline Peschard (Washington, DC: Woodrow Wilson Center Press, 2010), 140–141.
23. Instituto Federal de Acceso a la Información, "Mexican Experience in Access to Public Information" (Access to Public Information Seminar, São Paolo, Brazil, 2011).
24. Miguel Sarre Iguíniz, "The National Human Rights Commission," in *Mexico's Right to Know Reforms: Civil Society Perspectives*, ed. Jonathan Fox (Santa Cruz: University of California, Santa Cruz, Center for Global, International and Regional Studies, 2007), 42–43, 139.
25. Jeffrey Weldon, "Political Sources of Presidencialismo in Mexico," in *Presidentialism and Democracy in Latin America*, ed. Scott Mainwaring and Matthew Shugart (Cambridge, UK: Cambridge University Press, 1997), 225–258.
26. Roderic Ai Camp, "Democracy Redux? Mexico's Voters and the 2006 Presidential Race," in *Consolidating Mexico's Democracy: The 2006 Presidential Campaign in Comparative Perspective* ed. Jorge Domínguez and Chappell Lawson (Baltimore: Johns Hopkins University Press, 2009), 40–49.
27. BBC News, "Mexico's Lopez Obrador 'Sworn In'," November 21, 2006, http://news.bbc.co.uk/2/hi/6166908.stm.
28. Rafael Ch and Marien Rivera, "Numeros Rojos del Sistema Penal" (Centro de Investigación para el Desarrollo AC, 2011).
29. Catalina Pérez Correa, "Front Desk Justice: Inside and Outside Criminal Procedure in Mexico City," *Mexican Law Review* 1, no. 1 (2008).
30. Roberto Hernández and Geoffrey Smith, "Presunto Culpable" (Cinépolis, 2011).
31. Hector Tobar, "Judicial Overhaul in Mexico OKd," *Los Angeles Times*, March 7, 2008.
32. María Hernández, José del Tronco, and Gabriela Sánchez, *Un Congreso Sin Mayorías: Mejores Prácticas en Negociación y Construcción de Acuerdos* (Facultad Latinoamericana de las Ciencias Sociales, 2009), 236; Michael Campbell Taylor, "Civic Alliance: The Emergence of a Political Movement in Contemporary Mexico" (BA thesis, Harvard University, 1995).
33. Carlos Nataren, "Notes on Criminal Process and Constitutional Reform in Mexico Today," *Mexican Law Review* 4, no. 1 (2011), 120.
34. Ibid., 24.
35. Bertelsmann Stiftung, "Bertelsmann Transformation Index," http://www.bti-project.org/index/status-index/.
36. Cámara de Diputados, "Sesión Ordinaria del Martes 18 de Octubre" (2011).
37. Jodi Finkel, "Judicial Reform as Insurance Policy: Mexico in the 1990s," *Latin American Politics and Society* 47, no. 1 (2005), 93; Jodi Finkel, "Supreme Court Decisions on Electoral Rules after Mexico's 1994 Judicial Reform: An Empowered Court," *Journal of Latin American Studies* 35, no. 4 (2003), 777–799.

38. Raymundo Riva Palacio, "A Culture of Collusion: The Ties that Bind the Press and the PRI," in *The Culture of Collusion: An Inside Look at the Mexican Press*, ed. William A. Orme Jr. (Miami: University of Miami North South Center Press, 1996), 22.

39. Chappell Lawson, *Building the Fourth Estate: Democratization and the Rise of a Free Press in Mexico* (Berkeley: University of California Press, 2002); Sallie Hughes, *Newsrooms in Conflict: Journalism and the Democratization of Mexico* (Pittsburgh: University of Pittsburgh Press, 2006). 42.

40. Elisabeth Malkin, "Mexican Court's Media Ruling Shows Support for Competition," *New York Times*, June 6, 2007; Andrea Becerril, "La Ley Televisa, una Imposición Previa a las Elecciones de 2006, Según Creel," *La Jornada*, May 5, 2007.

41. Guadalupe Chávez Méndez, "La Lectura Masiva en Mexico: Apuntes y Reflexiones Sobre la Situación que Presenta esta Práctica Social," *Estudios Sobre las Culturas Contemporaneas* 11, no. 21 (2005), 72–73.

42. María Fernanda Somuano, *Sociedad Civil Organizada y Democracia en Mexico* (Mexico City: Colegio de Mexico, 2011), 55–56; Hector Tobar, "Fox Leaves Mexico's 'Dirty' Past Unsettled," *Los Angeles Times*, November 30, 2006.

43. Andrew Reding, "Perspective Series: Mexico Democracy and Human Rights" (U.S. Department of Justice, 1995), 66.

44. Jonathan Fox, *Accountability Politics: Power and Voice in Rural Mexico* (New York: Oxford University Press, 2007), 121–124.

45. *El Universal*, "Perfil: José Antonio Ríos Granados," October 2, 2007.

46. Juan Pardinas, "El Actor de Tultitlán," *Reforma*, October 7, 2007.

47. *Proceso*, "Sólo 30% de Portales Cumple con Transparencia," July 18, 2011.

48. Jonathan Fox, *Mexico's Right-to-Know Reforms: Civil Society Perspectives* (Washington, DC: Woodrow Wilson International Center for Scholars, 2007).

49. George W. Grayson, "Vigilantism: Increasing Self-Defense against Runaway Violence in Mexico?" Foreign Policy Research Institute, October 2009, http://www.fpri.org/enotes/200910.grayson.vigilantismmexico.html.

50. Organisation for Economic Cooperation and Development (OECD), "ICT Database and Eurostat, Community Survey on ICT Usage in Households and by Individuals" (2010).

51. Agustina Giraudy, "Subnational Undemocratic Regime Continuity After Democratization: Argentina and Mexico in Comparative Perspective" (PhD diss, University of North Carolina, Chapel Hill, 2009), 150.

CHAPTER 5

1. This measure reflects relative purchasing power parity, or PPP, which accounts for differences in exchange rates and the costs of goods between countries (i.e., what each currency can purchase within its own country). In 2011 the World Bank reported Mexico's PPP per capita as US$15,000, compared to the United States' US$48,000. When measuring just GDP using current U.S. dollars as the benchmark (and not taking into consideration purchasing power), Mexico falls further behind, with US$10,000 per capita in 2011 (U.S. numbers stay the same). World Bank, "World Development Indicators" (2011).

2. Martin Ravallion, "The Developing World's Bulging (but Vulnerable) 'Middle Class'" (Washington, DC: World Bank Development Research Group, 2009).

3. A group of economists from the Brookings Institution utilize a measure of the global middle class using the poverty line in Portugal and Italy—the lowest-income advanced European countries—as the lower limit of the global middle, and twice the average income in Luxembourg, the richest European nation, as the upper limit. Their calculation "excludes those who are considered poor in the poorest advanced countries and those who are considered rich in the richest advanced country." This translates roughly to between US$4000 and US$37,000 per person. Tailoring it more specifically to the Mexican context, the scholars Luis de la Calle and Luis Rubio set the annual earnings range for the middle class between US$7000 and US$85,000. See Homi Kharas, "The Emerging Middle Class in Developing Countries" (Organisation for Economic Cooperation and Development, 2010); Homi Kharas and Geoffrey Gertz, "The New Global Middle Class: A Cross-Over from West to East" (Washington, DC: Brookings Institution, Wolfensohn Center for Development, 2010), 17, 24–25, 48–49, 66, 86–87; Mauricio Cárdenas, Homi Kharas, and Camila Henao, "Latin America's Global Middle Class" (Washington, DC: Brookings Institution, 2011); Luis de la Calle and Luis Rubio, *Clasemediero: Pobre No Más, Desarollado Aún No* (Mexico City: Centro de Investigación para el Desarrollo, 2010).

4. Estimations of Mexico's poor vary significantly, depending on methodology. The OECD puts the number of poor Mexicans at 23 million; Mexican researchers Luis de la Calle and Luis Rubio estimate 29 million are poor; while the World Bank's two dollar a day mark (considered by many as the extreme poor) would include only 5.6 million. See OECD, "Economic Surveys: Mexico" (2011); Consejo Nacional de Evaluación de la Política de Desarrollo Social, "Estados Unidos Mexicanos: Medición de Pobreza 2010 a Nivel Nacional" (2010); Julio Boltvinik, "Economía Moral," *La Jornada*, April 13, 2012; de la Calle and Rubio, *Clasemediero*.

5. U.S. Census Bureau, "U.S. Trade in Goods with Mexico: 1992" (Washington, DC: Foreign Trade Division, Dissemination Branch, 2011).

6. Gary Clyde Hufbauer and Jeffrey J. Schott, *NAFTA Revisited: Achievements and Challenges* (Washington, DC: Institute for International Economics, 2005), 1–5.

7. George W. Grayson, *The Mexico-U.S. Business Committee: Catalyst for the North American Free Trade Agreement* (Rockville: Montrose, 2007).

8. In their 1989 book *Limits to Friendship: The United States and Mexico*, prominent observers of U.S.-Mexico bilateral relations Robert Pastor and Jorge Castañeda projected that a NAFTA style agreement wouldn't come to fruition. Larry Rohter, "North American Trade Bloc? Mexico Rejects Such an Idea," *New York Times*, November 24, 1988; Pastor and Castañeda, *Limits to Friendship*.

9. Among ordinary Mexicans in 1990, 80 percent endorsed completely open free trade, compared to 55 percent of Canadians and 40 percent of Americans. Mexico's high number of free-trade proponents has been attributed to government-backed mass media, presenting highly positive predictions of what NAFTA would bring to ordinary Mexicans. Ronald F. Inglehart, Neil Nevitte, and Miguel Basañez, *The North American Trajectory* (New York: Aldine de Gruyter, 1996), 39.

10. Strom Cronan Thacker, *Big Business, The State, and Free Trade: Constructing Coalitions in Mexico* (Cambridge, UK: Cambridge University Press, 2000), 183.

11. Adolfo Aguilar Zinser, "Authoritarianism and North American Free Trade: The Debate in Mexico," in *The Political Economy of North American Free Trade* ed. Richard Grinspun and Maxwell A. Cameron (New York: St. Martin's, 1993).

12. John W. Warnock, *The Other Mexico: The North American Triangle Completed* (Montreal: Black Rose, 1995), 155.

13. James Risen and James Gerstenzang, "President Plays Let's Make a Deal as NAFTA Vote Nears," *Los Angeles Times*, November 7, 1993; Michael Ross, "Clinton Sends NAFTA to Congress After Reaching Deals," *Los Angeles Times*, November 4, 1993.

14. U.S. Census Bureau, "Foreign Trade, 2011."

15. U.S. Census Bureau, "Quarterly Financial Report (QFR), Manufacturing, Mining, Trade, and Selected Service Industries, Historical QFR Data," http://www.census.gov/econ/qfr/historic.html.

16. John J. Audley, Demetrios G. Papademetriou, Sandra Polaski, and Scott Vaughan, "NAFTA's Promise and Reality: Lessons From Mexico for the Hemisphere" (Carnegie Endowment for International Peace, 2004); Pierre S. Pettigrew, Robert B. Zoellick, and Luis Ernesto Derbez, "NAFTA at Eight: A Foundation of Economic Growth" (Office of the United States Trade Representative, 2002).

17. J. F. Hornbeck, "NAFTA at Ten: Lessons from Recent Studies" (Congressional Research Service, 2004).

18. Every export dollar generates only about US$1.80 in Mexico compared with US$2.30 in Brazil and US$3.30 in the United States. *The Economist*, "Mexico's Economy: Bringing NAFTA Back Home," October 28, 2010.

19. World Bank, "World Development Indicators."

20. John Scott, "Subsidios Agrícolas en México: Quién Gana, y Cuánto," in *Subsidios para la Desigualdad: Las Políticas Públicas del Maíz en México a Partir del Libre Comercio*, ed. Jonathan Fox and Libby Haight (Mexico City: Woodrow Wilson International Center for Scholars, Mexico Institute, 2010).

21. Ignacio Alvarado Álvarez and Evangelina Hernández, "Depredan Procampo Políticos y Narcos," *El Universal*, July 27, 2009.

22. Alejandro Nadal and Timothy A. Wise, "Los Costos Ambientales de la Liberalización Agrícola," in *Globalización y Medio Ambiente: Lecciones Desde las Américas*, ed. Liane Schalatek (Santiago, Chile: Heinrich Böll Foundation North America, 2005).

23. Christopher B. Barry, Gonzalo Castañeda, and Joseph B. Lipscomb, "The Structure of Mortgage Markets in Mexico and Prospects for Their Securitization," *Journal of Housing Research* 5, no. 2 (1994), 187.

24. Pablo Camacho-Gutiérrez and Vanessa Gonzalez, "Mexico's Current Account Deficit: A Time Series Analysis," *International Journal of Business Research*, no. 2 (2009).

25. Office of the U.S. Trade Representative, "Study on the Operation and Effect of the North American Free Trade Agreement" (Washington, DC: 1997).

26. Mexico Secretaría de Comercio y Fomento Industrial, "Exportaciones Totales de México a América del Norte (1993–1999)," http://www.rmalc.org.mx/tratados/tlcan/mexandat.pdf.

27. Measured in PPP terms. World Bank, "World Development Indicators."

28. U.S. Census Bureau, "U.S. Trade in Goods with Mexico: 1992."

29. Ninety-three percent of Mexicans have televisions, 82 percent have refrigerators, 66 percent have washing machines, and 65 percent have mobile phones. Instituto Nacional de Estadística y Geografía, "Censo de Población y Vivienda" (2000).

30. María de los Ángeles Moreno-Uriegas, "Participación Laboral de la Mujer en México," *Revista de Enfermería del IMSS* 8, no. 3 (2000).

31. Instituto Nacional de Estadística y Geografía, "Mujeres y Hombres en México" (2005).

32. World Bank, "World Development Indicators."

33. Angel Gurría, "El Acuerdo de Cooperación México OCDE para Mejorar la Calidad de la Educación en las Escuelas Mexicanas" (Mexico City, October 19, 2010); Instituto Nacional de Estadística y Geografía, "Servicios Educativos" (2010).

34. *Businessweek*, "Learning Is Earning," March 13, 2006.

35. Eduardo Salazar, "Extraordinario el Crecimiento de Universitarios: Fox," *Esmas*, November 29, 2004; Mexicanos Primero, "Contra la Pared: Estado de la Educación en Mexico" (2009).

36. Roy Campos, "México: Dónde Vivir, Descansar, Vacacionar, Trabajar o Estudiar" (Consulta Mitofsky, 2010).

37. de la Calle and Rubio, *Clasemediero*.

38. Ibid., 24–25.

39. M. Angeles Villarreal, "NAFTA and the Mexican Economy" (Congressional Research Service, 2010).

40. In 1996, Mexico's Gini coefficient was 54.3. It had decreased to 49.8 by 2006. OECD, "Growing Income Inequality in OECD Countries: What Drives it and How Can Policy Tackle It" (Paris, 2011).

41. Tina Grant, "Grupo Elektra, SA de CV," in *International Directory of Company Histories*: vol. 39 (Chicago: St. James, 2001).

42. Homex, "Nuestros Mercados," http://www.homex.com.mx/ri/index.htm.

43. Instituto Nacional de Estadística y Geografía, "Censo de Población y Vivienda."

44. Sociedad Hipotecaria Federal, "Comparecencia ante Diputados y Senadores" (2010), 9.

45. Banco Azteca, "¿Quienes Somos?" http://www.bancoazteca.com.mx/PortalBancoAzteca/publica/conocenos/historia/quienes.jsp.

46. Noel Randewich, "Wal-Mart's Mexico Bank Aims at First-time Savers," *Reuters*, June 18, 2010, http://www.reuters.com/article/2010/06/18/walmart-mexico-id USN1812635420100618.

47. Maria Alejandra Moreno, "Regulador Emite Reglas sobre Corresponsales Bancarios," *Business News Americas*, December 5, 2008.

48. Oxford Analytica, "Mexico: Banking Continues Steady Recovery," December 2, 2010, http://www.oxan.com/display.aspx?ItemID=DB164552.

49. Asli Demirgüc-Kunt, Thorsten Beck, and Patrick Honohan, "Finance for All?: Policies and Pitfalls in Expanding Access" (Washington, DC: World Bank, 2008), 20–25.

50. OECD, "Perspectivas OCDE: México Políticas Clave para un Desarrollo Sostenible" (2010).

51. Dave Graham, "Slim's Telmex Not Planning to Take Part in TV Auction," *Reuters*, June 9, 2012, http://www.reuters.com/article/2012/06/09/us-slim-tv-idUSBRE8580E020120609.

52. The regulatory agency has cited abuses in local telephone services, access or inter-connection services, domestic long-distance service, and international long dis-tance service. Angelina Mejía Guerrero, "Telmex no es un Monopolio, Resuelve Juzgado," *El Universal*, October 12, 2006.

53. Rafael del Villar, "Competition and Equity in Telecommunications," in *No Growth Without Equity: Inequality, Interests, and Competition in Mexico*, ed. Santiago Levy and Michael Walton (Washington, DC: World Bank, 2009), 333–335.

54. Office of the U.S. Trade Representative, "U.S. Wins WTO Telecommunications Case Against Mexico" (2004).

55. Hepsi Swarna and Saradhi Kumar Gonela, "Mexican Telecom Industry: (Un) Wanted Monopoly" (IBS Case Development Centre, 2009).

56. World Bank, "World Development Indicators."

57. Ibid.

58. Ibid.

59. Gobierno de Mexico, "National Infrastructure Program of Mexico," Mexico City, July 2007.

60. Juan Carlos Moreno-Brid and Jaime Ros, *Development and Growth in the Mexican Economy: A Historical Perspective* (New York: Oxford University Press, 2009), 240–241.

61. OECD, "ICT Database and Eurostat, Community Survey on ICT Usage in Households and by Individuals" (2010).

62. World Bank, "World Development Indicators"; Moreno-Brid and Ros, *Development and Growth in the Mexican Economy*, 240–241.

63. To put this into comparative perspective with the United States (one of the advanced economies with the least amount of social mobility), 42 percent of children born into the bottom 20 percent remain there. For a Pew study on economic mobility, see Pew Charitable Trusts, "Pursuing the American Dream: Economic Mobility of Families Across Generations" (Washington, DC, 2012).

64. "Resultados de la Encuesta ESRU," *Fundación Espinosa Rugarcía*, 2008, http://www.movilidadsocial.org/content/resultados-encuesta-esru.

65. Carlos J. McCadden M. and Raúl Bravo Aduna, "La Clase Media Mexicana," *Este País*, December 2008, 213.

66. Mexico Secretaría de Educación Pública, "General Statistical Indicators for the 2008–2009 Academic Term" (Mexico City, 2010).

67. OECD, "Comparing Countries' and Economies' Performance" (2010).

68. Jeffrey Puryear, "Reform in Mexico Forces Debate on Sale of Teaching Positions," *Latin America Advisor*, November 24, 2008; Iván Barrera, "El Registro de Maestros," *Mexicanos Primero*, May 18, 2011, http://www.mexicanosprimero.org/maestros/blog-mexicanos-primero/326-el-registro-de-maestros.html; Maria Teresa Tatto, "Education Reform and the Global Regulation of Teachers' Education, Development and Work: A Cross-Cultural Analysis," *International Journal of Educational Research* 45, nos. 4–5 (2006); National Center for Fair and Open Testing, "Teachers Boycott Tests," http://www.fairtest.org/teachers-boycott-tests.

69. OECD, "Factbook 2011–2012, Economic, Environmental and Social Statistics" (2011).

70. Carla Pederzini, "Labor Market and Emigration from Mexico during the World Economic Recession" (2011).
71. World Bank, "World Development Indicators."
72. Instituto Nacional para el Federalismo y el Desarrollo Municipal, "Estado de Chiapas" (2005).
73. The set of policies designed to deal with the Latin American debt crisis and then guide economic opening is often referred to as the "Washington Consensus," and includes deregulation, trade liberalization, fiscal discipline, and the privatization of state-owned entities. See John Williamson, "What Washington Means by Policy Reform," in *Latin American Adjustment: How Much Has Happened* (Washington, DC: Institute for International Economics, 1990). For a strong critique of this economic model, see James Petras, "Alternatives to Neoliberalism in Latin America," *Latin American Perspectives* 24, no. 1 (1997).
74. Guillermo E. Perry et al., "Poverty Reduction and Growth: Virtuous and Vicious Circles" (World Bank, 2006).
75. Gerardo Esquivel uses a current monetary income-based version of the Gini index. The OECD's numbers, which calculate the Gini after cash-transfers and taxes, show a similar trend, from 0.45 in the mid-1980s to 0.52 in the mid-1990s. Gerardo Esquivel, "The Dynamics of Income Inequality in Mexico since NAFTA" (Mexico City: El Colegio de Mexico, 2008), 8; OECD, "StatExtracts" (2011).
76. David Fairris, "Unions and Wage Inequality in Mexico," *Industrial and Labor Relations Review* 56, no. 3 (2003).
77. OECD, "StatExtracts." Esquivel calculates that the Gini fell from 0.53 in 1998 to 0.48 in 2011. Esquivel, "The Dynamics of Income Inequality in Mexico since NAFTA."
78. Joao Pedro Azevedo, Louise Cord, and Carolina Díaz-Bonilla, "On the Edge of Uncertainty: Poverty Reduction in Latin America and the Caribbean during the Great Recession and Beyond" (Washington, DC: World Bank, 2011).
79. For an in-depth evaluation and econometric analysis of the importance of various factors for the declining rates of inequality in Mexico, see Gerardo Esquivel, Nora Lustig, and John Scott, "A Decade of Falling Inequality in Mexico: Market Forces or State Actions" (United Nations Development Programme, 2010). They find that higher wages for low-skilled workers have had the largest effect, followed by a rise in remittances directed to rural areas and government cash transfers to the poorest quintile.
80. Nora Lustig, "Crises and the Poor: Socially Responsible Macroeconomics" (Inter-American Development Bank, Sustainable Development Department, Poverty and Inequality Advisory Unit Working Paper, 2000).
81. *Oportunidades* is regarded as one of the most successful models of redistributive conditional cash transfers, and has been copied in Brazil, Bolivia, and Peru. Evaluations confirm the program's positive effect on health and education indicators, as well as on beneficiary families' savings and investment—key to lifting individuals out of chronic poverty. See Santiago Levy, *Progress Against Poverty, Sustaining Mexico's Progresa-Oportunidades Program* (Washington, DC: Brookings Institution Press, 2006); *Oportunidades*, "Oportunidades Atiende a 5.8 Millones

de Familias en el País," http://www.oportunidades.gob.mx/Portal/wb/Web/oportunidades_atiende_a_58_millones_de_familias_.

82. Wilson, "Working Together."
83. A.T. Kearney Inc., "Offshoring Opportunities Amid Economic Turbulence" (2011).
84. Wilson, "Working Together."
85. Mihir Desai, C. Fritz Foley, and James Hines, "Domestic Effects of the Foreign Activities of US Multinationals" (Cambridge, MA: Harvard Business School, 2008).
86. OECD, "Moving Up the Value Chain: Staying Competitive in the Global Economy" (2007).
87. U.S. labor unions have long battled with Caterpillar. For a discussion see Steven Greenhouse, "At Caterpillar, Pressing Labor While Business Booms," *New York Times*, July 22, 2012.
88. NAFTANow, "Caterpillar Inc.: 'Paving a Brighter Future…,'" http://www.naftanow.org/success/us_en.asp.
89. Juan Carlos Moreno-Brid, "Mexico's Auto Industry After NAFTA: A Successful Experience in Restructuring" (South Bend: Notre Dame University, Kellogg Institute, 1996).
90. James M. Rubenstein and Thomas Klier, "Restructuring of the Auto Industry: Geographic Implications of Outsourcing" (Chicago: Industry Studies Association, 2009).
91. San Luis Corporación, "Annual Report" (2009).
92. Nemak, "Our Facilities," http://www.nemak.com/facilities.html.
93. José G. Vargas-Hernández and Mohammad Reza Noruzi, "Internationalization Strategies Followed by Three Mexican Pioneer Companies—Grupo Modelo, Grupo Bimbo, and Cemex: Issues and Challenges," *International Journal of Research in Commerce and Management* 2, no. 10 (2011).
94. Bimbo Bakeries U.S.A., "About Us," http://www.bimbobakeriesusa.com/about_us/our_history.html.
95. M. Luis Herrera-Lasso, "The Mexico-United States Border: A Fragmented Agenda," *National Strategy Forum* 18, no. 3 (2009).
96. Jean Parcher, "Sistema de Información Geográfica de la Frontera entre México y Estados Unidos" (New York: United States Geological Survey, 2009), 5.
97. Tim Gaynor, "Roof Collapse Injures 17 at U.S.-Mexico Border Crossing," *Reuters*, September 14, 2011, http://www.reuters.com/article/2011/09/14/us-usa-mexico-crossing-idUSTRE78D7JJ20110914; Kristina Davis and Sandra Dibble, "13 Northbound Border Lanes Reopen: Closure Followed Collapse," *UT San Diego*, September 14, 2011, http://www.utsandiego.com/news/2011/sep/14/several-injured-border-crossing-roof-collapse/.
98. Hercules E. Haralambides and Maria P. Londono-Kent, "Supply Chain Bottlenecks: Border Crossing Inefficiencies Between Mexico and the United States," *International Journal of Transport Economics* 31, no. 2 (2004), 172–179.
99. Ibid.
100. Rubenstein and Klier, "Restructuring of the Auto Industry."
101. San Diego Association of Governments and California Department of Transportation, "Economic Impacts of Wait Times at the San Diego–Baja California Border" (2006).

102. U.S. Department of Commerce, "Improving Economic Outcomes by Reducing Border Delays" (International Trade Administration, 2008).

103. Matthew Kirdahy, "Best Cities for Jobs in 2008," January 10, 2008, http://www.forbes.com/2008/01/10/jobs-economy-growth-lead-careers-cx_mk_0110cities.html.

104. *The Economist*, "One River, One Country," September 11, 1997.

105. KYMA 11, "San Luis II Port Complete" (ABC News, 2010).

106. U.S. Customs and Border Patrol, "Securing America's Borders: CBP Fiscal Year 2010 in Review Fact Sheet," March 15, 2011, http://www.cbp.gov/xp/cgov/newsroom/fact_sheets/cbp_overview/fy2010_factsheet.xml.

107. Texas Border Coalition, "White Paper on Border Security" (2009).

108. House Committee on Homeland Security, Subcommittee on Border and Maritime Security, *Using Resources Effectively to Secure Our Border at Ports of Entry—Stopping the Illicit Flow of Money, Guns and Drugs*, 2011.

109. Alex Lee, "Review of Unused Presidential Permit: Laredo, Texas International Railroad Bridge" (Washington, DC: U.S. Department of State Federal Register, 2009).

110. Alexandra Mendoza, "Construction Work Resumes at Border Crossing: Contractor Makes Change to Safeguard Security," *San Diego Red*, September 27, 2011.

111. U.S. Department of Homeland Security, "SENTRI Program Description," Customs and Border Protection, http://www.cbp.gov/xp/cgov/travel/trusted_traveler/sentri/sentri.xml.

112. Halit Yanikkaya, "Trade Openness and Economic Growth: A Cross-Country Empirical Investigation," *Journal of Development Economics*, no. 72 (2003).

113. Lawrence Summers, "The Global Middle Cries Out for Reassurance," *Financial Times*, October 29, 2006.

CHAPTER 6

1. Some independent analysts estimate much higher numbers. A 2012 study by the newspaper *El Diario* calculated more than 80,000 drug-related deaths during Calderón's term, while Molly Molloy, a Latin America specialist at the New Mexico State University Library, puts the number of aggravated homicides closer to 110,000. See Luz del Carmen Sosa, "Son 83 Mil los Asesinatos Registrados en el Sexenio," *El Diario*, August 4, 2012, http://www.diario.com.mx/notas.php?f=2012%2F08%2F04&id=db6aa0610c40288b4ecbcc91f2cb0b63; Molly Molloy, "Mexico's Magical Homicides," *Miami New Times*, July 26, 2012, http://www.miaminewtimes.com/2012-07-26/news/mexico-s-magical-homicides/%5C/.

2. A 2011 report by Human Rights Watch argues that since the Attorney General's office has investigated less than 3 percent of the 35,000 officially identified drug-related homicides from December 2006 to January 2011, there is no evidence to confirm the motives, or even at times the identity of the victims. Human Rights Watch's own investigations uncovered numerous cases of (presumably innocent) murdered civilians who were classified by the government as narco-traffickers (again, without adequate investigation). See Human Rights Watch, "Neither

Rights nor Security: Killings, Torture, and Disappearances in Mexico's 'War on Drugs'" (2011).

3. Arturo Perez, "Gunmen Kill Former Mexico Governor," *Associated Press*, November 21, 2010; Meena Hartenstein, "Mexican Governor Candidate Killed by Gunmen, Calderon Says Assassination Tied to Drug Gang Violence," *New York Daily News*, June 28, 2010; Walter McKay Consulting, "Narco Killings," http://sites.google.com/site/policereform/narco-killings.

4. Fernando Escalante Gonzalbo, "Homicidios 1990–2007," *Nexos*, September 1, 2009.

5. Elena Michel, "El 80% de los Homocidios, en 162 Municipios del País," *El Universal*, August 20, 2011.

6. Viridiana Ríos and David A. Shirk, "Drug Violence in Mexico: Data and Analysis through 2010" (San Diego: Trans-Border Institute, 2011), 1.

7. United Nations Office on Drugs and Crime, "World Drug Report" (2011).

8. The details of the origins, relations, and even number of drug trafficking groups are quite murky and much disputed between scholars, researchers, and journalists that closely follow their operations. In depth accounts of the scope and fluidity of these organizations include Luis Astorga and David A. Shirk ("Drug Trafficking Organizations and Counter-Drug Strategies in the U.S.-Mexican Context." Center for U.S.-Mexican Studies, San Diego; Woodrow Wilson Mexico Institute, Washington, DC; El Colegio de la Frontera Norte, Tijuana; El Colegio de México, Mexico City, 2010), Malcolm Beith, *The Last Narco* (New York: Grove, 2010); Ricardo Ravelo, *Herencia Maldita: El Reto de Calderón y el Nuevo Mapa del Narcotráfico* (Mexico City: Grijalbo, 2007); Ricardo Ravelo, "Los Capos: Las Narco-Rutas de México," 2007).

9. U.S. Department of Justice, "National Drug Threat Assessment" (National Drug Intelligence Center, 2011), 8.

10. Roberto Steiner and Alejandra Corchuelo, "Economic and Institutional Repercussions of the Drug Trade in Colombia" (Universidad de los Andes, Centro de Estudios sobre Desarrollo Económico, 1999); Robert E. Grosse, *Drugs and Money: Laundering Latin America's Cocaine Dollars* (Westport: Praeger, 2001).

11. Beau Kilmer, Jonathan P. Caulkins, Brittany M. Bond, and Peter H. Reuter, "Reducing Drug Trafficking Revenues and Violence in Mexico: Would Legalizing Marijuana in California Help?" (RAND Corporation, 2010), 30; U.S. Government Accountability Office, "Drug Control: US Assistance Has Helped Mexican Counternarcotics Efforts, but Tons of Illicit Drugs Continue to Flow into the United States" (Washington, DC: 2007).

12. During a twenty-two month U.S. federal investigation into Wachovia Bank, begun after finding papers inside a drug-smuggling aircraft in Mexico and receiving testimony from a whistleblower, investigators found that US$380 billion in transactions had not been subject to the required anti-money laundering procedures. In their preliminary investigations of these funds, they estimated that at least US$20 billion came from "suspicious origins." Wachovia chose to settle outside of court for US$110 million with an additional US$50 million fine, before a full investigation was completed. See United States District Attorney's Office, "Wachovia Enters into Deferred Prosecution Agreement" (Southern District of Florida, 2010); Ed Vulliamy, "How a Big U.S. Bank Laundered Billions from Mexico's Murderous Drug Gangs," *The Observer*, April 2, 2011.

13. The AK-47 assault rifle has been copied extensively around the world. Even though Russia retired the AK-47 in 2011, there remain approximately fifty million AK-47s worldwide, and another 100 million weapons that are copies of the AK-47 style. Phillip Killicoat, "Weaponomics: The Global Market for Assault Rifles," *World Bank Research Digest,* April 13, 2007, http://siteresources.worldbank.org/DEC/Resources/84797-1154354760266/2807421-1183396414833/Weaponomics. pdf; Nick Miroff and William Booth, "Mexican Drug Cartels' Newest Weapon: Cold War-Era Grenades Made in U.S.," *Washington Post,* July 17, 2010.

14. Luis Astorga, "Organized Crime and the Organization of Crime," in *Organized Crime & Democratic Governability: Mexico and the U.S.-Mexican Borderlands,* ed. John Bailey and Roy Godson (Pittsburgh: University of Pittsburgh Press, 2000).

15. Carlos Antonio Flores Pérez, *El Estado en Crisis: Crimen Organizado y Política, Desafíos para la Consolidación Democrática* (Mexico City: Centro de Investigaciones y Estudios Superiores en Antropología Social, 2009), 124; Astorga, "Organized Crime and the Organization of Crime," 62.

16. Malgorzata Polanska, "Homicidios por Entidad Federativa y Regiones 1990–2007" (Mexico City: Colectivo de Análisis de la Seguridad con Democracia, 2009).

17. David Carrizales, "Protesta de Agentes de Nuevo León Estuvo a Punto de Terminar en Balacera con Federales," *La Jornada,* June 9, 2009, 8; Julie Watson, "Drug War: Mexican Police Standoff with Mexican Federal Agents," *The Guardian,* June 9, 2009, http://www.guardian.co.uk/world/feedarticle/8549879.

18. Michael McCaul, "Let's Make a Commitment to War on Mexican Cartels: US Should Consider Strategy Used in Colombia," *Austin American-Statesman,* March 20, 2011.

19. Jan Brewer, "Statement on Law Enforcement Shooting in Pinal County," *State of Arizona,* 2010, http://azgovernor.gov/dms/upload/PR_043010_StatementGov Brewer_Shooting.pdf; Devin Dwyer, "Obama Authorizes Deployment of More National Guard Troops Along Border," *ABC News,* May 25, 2010, http://abc-news.go.com/Politics/obama-authorizes-deployment-national-guard-southwest/story?id=10740858.

20. The FBI's statistics do not, however, include drug trafficking or money launder-ing—two crimes that are prevalent along the border. Alan Gomez, Jack Gillum, and Kevin Johnson, "U.S. Border Cities Prove Havens from Mexico's Drug Violence," *USA Today,* July 19, 2011.

21. Andrew Becker and Richard Marosi, "Border Agency's Rapid Growth Accompanied by Rise in Corruption," *Los Angeles Times,* October 16, 2011.

22. *Associated Press,* "Arrests of Corrupt U.S. Border Police Rise," August 9, 2009, http://www.msnbc.msn.com/id/32349677/ns/us_news-crime_and_courts/t/a rrests-corrupt-us-border-police-rise/.

23. Investigations into U.S. Customs and Border Patrol employees have spiked from 244 in 2005 to 870 in 2010. In roughly the same time period, 132 customs employ-ees have either been convicted or indicted on corruption charges. Becker and Marosi, "Border Agency's Rapid Growth Accompanied by Rise in Corruption."; Randal C. Archibold and Andrew Becker, "As Border Efforts Grow, Corruption is on the Rise," *New York Times,* May 27, 2008; Homeland Security News Wire, "Border Agents Corrupted While FBI and DHS Wrangle for Power," June 17, 2011,

http://www.homelandsecuritynewswire.com/border-agents-corrupted-while-fb i-and-dhs-wrangle-power.

24. Felix Belair Jr., "Drug Drive Opens at Mexico Border: U.S. Operation Seeks to Cut Illicit Flow of Marijuana, Heroin and Pep Pills," *New York Times*, September 22, 1969.

25. Juan de Onis, "U.S. Drug Search Irks Diaz Ordaz," *New York Times*, September 30, 1969.

26. Domínguez and Fernández de Castro, *United States and Mexico*, 9, 31–32, 37, 125, 132–133; William O. Walker, *Drug Control in the Americas* (Albequerque: University of New Mexico Press, 1981), 192.

27. Richard Craig, "Operation Condor: Mexico's Antidrug Campaign Enters a New Era," *Journal of Interamerican Studies and World Affairs* 22, no. 3 (1980), 351.

28. Ibid., 348.

29. Elaine Shannon, *Desperados: Latin Drug Lords, U.S. Lawmen, and the War America Can't Win* (New York: Viking, 1988), 1–2, 32, 120, 187, 194–195.

30. Ibid., 194–195; John Ross, *El Monstruo: Dread and Redemption in Mexico City* (New York: Nation, 2009), 297.

31. Carlos Antonio Flores Pérez, "Organized Crime and Official Corruption in Mexico," in *Police and Public Security in Mexico*, ed. Robert A. Donnelly and David A. Shirk (San Diego: University Readers, 2010), 103.

32. U.S. Drug Enforcement Administration, "Kiki and the History of Red Ribbon Week," http://www.justice.gov/dea/ongoing/red_ribbon/redribbon_history. html.

33. White House, "National Security Decision Directive No. 221" (1986).

34. Andreas Lowenfeld, "Kidnapping by Government Order: A Follow-Up," *American Journal of International Law* (1990), 712.

35. Mark P. Sullivan and June S. Beittel, "Mexico-U.S. Relations: Issues for Congress" (Washington, DC: Congressional Research Service, 2009).

36. Transparencia Mexicana, "Executive Summary: National Index of Corruption and Good Governance" (2010), 6.

37. Magaloni, "Weak and Powerful Courts under Autocracy," 10–11; Niels Uildriks, *Mexico's Unrule of Law: Implementing Human Rights in Police and Judicial Reform Under Democratization* (Lanham: Lexington, 2010).

38. Mexico Secretariado Ejecutivo del Sistema Nacional de Seguridad Pública, "Sueldos de Policías Estatales y Municipales" (2011).

39. John Bailey and Jorge Chabat, *Transnational Crime and Public Security: Challenges to Mexico and the United States* (La Jolla: Center for U.S.-Mexican Studies, 2002), 14.

40. Ch and Rivera, "Numeros Rojos del Sistema Penal," 5.

41. Guillermo Zepeda Lecuona, "Criminal Investigation and the Subversion of the Principles of the Justice System in Mexico," in *Reforming the Administration of Justice in Mexico*, ed. Wayne A. Cornelius and David A. Shirk (South Bend: Notre Dame Press, 2007), 141–143.

42. Marien Rivera, "The Fight Worth Fighting: Reforming the Mexican Criminal Justice System" (Centro de Investigación para el Desarrollo AC, 2010); Tobar, "Judicial Overhaul in Mexico OKd."

43. Guillermo Zepeda Lecuona, "Índice de Incidencia Delictiva y Violencia" (Centro de Investigación para el Desarrollo AC, 2008).

44. Transparency International, "Global Corruption Report: Corruption in Judicial Systems" (2007), 226.

45. Daniel Sabat, "Police Reform in Mexico: Advances and Persistent Obstacles" (Washington, DC: Woodrow Wilson International Center for Scholars, Mexico Institute, 2010). Also see: Vivianna Macías and Fernando Castillo, "Mexico's National Public Security System: Perspectives for the New Millennium," in *Transnational Crime and Public Security: Challenges to Mexico and the United States*, ed. John Bailey and Jorge Chabat (La Jolla: Center for U.S.-Mexican Studies, 2002).

46. Sabat, "Police Reform in Mexico."

47. Human Rights Watch, "Neither Rights nor Security," 28.

48. Beth J. Asch, Nicholas Burger, and Mary Manqing Fu, "Mitigating Corruption in Government Security Forces: The Role of Institutions, Incentives, and Personnel Management in Mexico" (RAND Corporation, 2011).

49. Morgan Lee, "Mexico Combats Police Corruption with Mortgages," *USA Today*, September 20, 2008.

50. Miguel Carbonell, "Sobre el Nuevo Artículo 16 Constitucional" (Mexico City: Universidad Nacional Autónoma de México, 2008), 143–145.

51. Guillermo Zepeda Lecuona, "Mexican Police and the Criminal Justice System," in *Police and Public Security in Mexico*, ed. David A. Shirk and Robert Donnelly (San Diego: University Readers, 2009).

52. *Associated Press*, "México: Procuraduría Indaga a 700 Funcionarios por Corrupción," July 21, 2011.

53. Beatriz Magaloni and Guillermo Zepeda, "Democratization, Judicial and Law Enforcement Institutions, and the Rule of Law in Mexico," in *Dilemmas of Political Change in Mexico*, ed. Kevin J. Middlebrook (London: University of London, Institute of Latin American Studies, 2004), 194.

54. Sigrid Arzt, "The Militarization of the Procuraduría General de la República: Risks for Mexican Democracy," in *Reforming the Administration of Justice in Mexico*, ed. Wayne A. Cornelius and David A. Shirk (South Bend: Notre Dame Press, 2007), 165.

55. See Table 3 in Sabat, "Police Reform in Mexico: Advances and Persistent Obstacles."

56. Genaro García Luna, *Para Entender: El Nuevo Modelo de Seguridad para México* (Mexico City: Nostra Ediciones, 2010).

57. James C. McKinley Jr., "In Mexico, a Fugitive's Arrest Captivates the Cameras," *New York Times*, October 12, 2007.

58. Sandra Ávila Beltrán's extradition ruling was overturned in June 2012, when a Mexican court deemed that one of the two U.S. charges—for the 2001 delivery of 100 kilos of cocaine to Chicago—was different from the charges she had faced in Mexico and for which she had been acquitted. *Fox News Latino*, "Mexico's 'Queen of the Pacific' Avoids Extradition," August 10, 2011; *Fox News Latino*, "Mexican Court Approves Extradition of 'Queen of the Pacific,'" June 8, 2012.

59. Josh Kun, "The Island of Jorge Hank Rhon," *LA Weekly*, February 16, 2006.

60. There has been some controversy regarding the actual number and percentage of illegal guns heading from the United States to Mexico. Some argue that the number is relatively small and question Mexico's process of selecting which guns to trace (most guns found in Mexico are not tested). Other reports place the percentage coming from the United States as much higher—near 90 percent. Whatever the actual number and percentage, the presence of these guns in Mexico breaks both Mexican and U.S. laws. U.S. Government Accountability Office, "U.S. Efforts to Combat Arms Trafficking to Mexico Face Planning and Coordination Challenges" (2009); Dianne Feinstein, Charles Schumer, and Sheldon Whitehouse, "Halting U.S. Firearms Trafficking to Mexico" (United States Senate Caucus on International Narcotics Control, 2011); U.S. Department of Justice, "ATF: Mexico" (Bureau of Alcohol, Tobacco, Firearms and Explosives, 2012).

61. Cami McCormick, "The U.S. Guns in Mexico's Drug War," CBS News, March 26, 2009; David Fortier, "Military Ammo Today," Guns and Ammo, 2010, http://www.handgunsmag.com/2010/09/24/ammunition_hg_militarytoday_200811/.

62. U.S. House Committee on Oversight and Government Reform, "House Committee on Oversight and Government Reform Holds a Hearing on the ATF's Mexican Gun-Trafficking Investigation" (2011).

63. Richard A. Serrano, "Fast and Furious Weapons Were Found in Mexico Cartel Enforcer's Home," Los Angeles Times, October 8, 2011.

64. Richard A. Serrano, "Supervisors in ATF Gun Operation are Promoted," Los Angeles Times, August 16, 2011; U.S. House Committee on Oversight and Government Reform, "House Committee on Oversight and Government Reform Holds a Hearing on the ATF's Mexican Gun-Trafficking Investigation" (2011).

65. Vivian S. Chu and William J. Krouse, "Gun Trafficking and the Southwest Border" (Washington, DC: Congressional Research Service, 2009), 15.

66. William J. Krouse, "The Bureau of Alcohol, Tobacco, Firearms and Explosives (ATF), Budget and Operations for FY2011" (Washington, DC: Congressional Research Service, 2011), 12–13.

67. Garen J. Wintemute, Anthony A. Braga, and David M. Kennedy, "Private-Party Gun Sales, Regulations and Public Safety," New England Journal of Medicine (2010), 509.

68. Mayors Against Illegal Guns, "The Tiahrt Amendments," http://www.mayorsagainstillegalguns.org/html/federal/tiahrt.shtml.

69. U.S. Government Accountability Office, "Drug Control: US Assistance Has Helped Mexican Counternarcotics Efforts, but Tons of Illicit Drugs Continue to Flow into the United States," 13.

70. Kilmer et al., "Reducing Drug Trafficking Revenues and Violence in Mexico."

71. Tracy Wilkinson and Ken Ellingwood, "Cartels Use Legitimate Trade to Launder Money, US, Mexico Say," Los Angeles Times, December 19, 2011.

72. U.S. Drug Enforcement Administration, "Perfume Store Owner Charged with Laundering Millions of Dollars for Mexican Narcotics Trafficking Organizations," January 18, 2011, http://www.justice.gov/dea/pubs/states/newsrel/2011/nwk011811.html

73. Vikram Datta was convicted in 2012 for international money-laundering conspiracy and received twenty years in prison. See Chivis Martinez, "The Perfume Man and

Chapo's Stinking Dollars," *InSight Crime,* January 25, 2012, http://www.insightcrime. org/insight-latest-news/item/2125-the-perfume-man-and-chapos-stinking-dollars.

74. U.S. Department of Justice, "National Drug Threat Assessment," 40.

75. U.S. Department of Health and Human Services, "Results from the 2010 National Survey on Drug Use and Health: Summary of National Findings" (2011).

76. Executive Office of the President of the United States, "FY2012 Budget and Performance Summary" (2011).

77. National Institute on Drug Abuse, "Principles of Drug Addiction Treatment: A Research Based Guide," http://www.nida.nih.gov/PODAT/faqs.html#faq4.

78. Pew Center on the States, "The Impact of Hawaii's HOPE Program on Drug Use, Crime and Recidivism" (Washington, DC, 2010); Angela Hawken and Mark Kleiman, "Managing Drug Involved Probationers with Swift and Certain Sanctions: Evaluating Hawaii's HOPE" (U.S. Department of Justice, 2009).

79. Alejandro Moreno and María Antonia Mancillas, "Respaldan Labor de las Fuerzas Armadas," *Reforma,* December 1, 2011.

80. Jessica Satherley, "Tortured, Disemboweled and Hung from a Bridge for Tweeting," *Daily Mail* [London], September 16, 2011.

81. Presidencia de la República de Mexico, "Decenas de Miles de Mexicanos Exigen Seguridad en una Marcha de Silencio," June 27, 2004, http://fox.presidencia.gob. mx/buenasnoticias/?contenido=8487&pagina=343.

82. Patricia Mercado, "Marcha Masiva Contra la Violencia," *BBC News,* August 31, 2008, http://news.bbc.co.uk/hi/spanish/latin_america/newsid_7590000/7590363.stm.

83. *El Universal,* "Publican el Acuerdo Nacional por la Seguridad," August 25, 2008.

84. *CNN Expansion,* "Martí: Si No Pueden, Renuncien," http://www.cnnexpansion. com/actualidad/2008/08/21/marti-si-hay-incapacidad-2018renuncien2019.

85. Jo Tuckman, "Mexican Peace Caravan Led by Poet Javier Sicilia Nears Its Final Stop," *The Guardian,* June 9, 2011.

86. *El Economista,* "Voto Nulo 'Quinta Fuerza Electoral' en México," July 6, 2009; Alejandro Martí, "Por Qué Sí Debe Aprobarse la Ley de Seguridad Nacional," *Animal Político,* August 16, 2011, http://www.animalpolitico. com/blogueros-mexico-sos/2011/08/16/por-que-si-debe-aprobarse-la- ley-de-seguridad-nacional/; "Mexico SOS Iniciativas de Ley," http://mexicosos. org/index.php?option=com_content&view=article&id=96&Itemid=242.

87. OECD, *Employment Outlook 2011* (2012).

CHAPTER 7

1. The numbers for many visa categories are fixed, regardless of the state of the U.S. econ- omy or the need. For instance, the 65,000 annual H1-B visas, for individuals with "highly specialized knowledge," routinely fill up in days if not hours—suggesting the deep chasm between the U.S. immigration system's supply and demand. U.S. Department of State, "Temporary Worker Visas," http://travel.state.gov/visa/temp/types/types_1271.html.

2. Gobierno de Mexico, "National Infrastructure Program of Mexico" (2007).

3. For an expansive view and blueprint of North American economic integration, see Robert Pastor, *The North American Idea: A Vision of a Continental Future* (New York: Oxford University Press, 2011).

4. Vanessa Grigoriadis and Mary Cuddehe, "An American Drug Lord in Acapulco," *Rolling Stone*, August 25, 2011.
5. Kilmer et al., "Reducing Drug Trafficking Revenues and Violence in Mexico." U.S. Department of Health and Human Services, "Results from the 2010 National Survey on Drug Use and Health: Summary of National Findings."
6. Centers for Disease Control and Prevention and National Center for Injury Prevention, "Impaired Driving: Get the Facts," 2011, http://www.cdc.gov/Motorvehiclesafety/Impaired_Driving/impaired-drv_factsheet.html.
7. Jennifer C. Karberg and Doris J. James, "Substance Dependence, Abuse, and Treatment of Jail Inmates, 2002" (U.S. Department of Justice, 2005).
8. Centers for Disease Control and Prevention, "Policy Impact: Prescription Painkiller Overdoses," Centers for Disease Control and Prevention, http://www.cdc.gov/homeandrecreationalsafety/rxbrief/.
9. For an in-depth discussion of this phenomenon during the 1980s and 1990s, see Jacqueline Mazza, *Don't Disturb the Neighbors: The U.S. and Democracy in Mexico, 1980–1995* (New York: Routledge, 2001). In the 1970s, a defining memo by national security advisor Zbigniew Brzezinski laid out a similar strategy for President Jimmy Carter.
10. Zogby Internacional and El Centro de Investigación para el Desarrollo, "Encuesta CIDAC-ZOGBY de Percepciones entre Mexico y Estados Unidos" (Mexico City, 2006).

EPILOGUE

1. *CNN*, "Los Siete Gobernadores Electos Reciben la Constancia de Mayoría," July 8, 2012, http://mexico.cnn.com/nacional/2012/07/08/los-siete-gobernadores-electos-reciben-la-constancia-de-mayoria.
2. Roy Campos, "Mexico: 1 de Julio 2012: Perfil del Votante" (Consulta Mitofsky, 2012).
3. The report, "Índice de Información Presupuestal 2011," by Juan Pardinas finds that PRI-governed states outnumber PAN- or PRD-governed states in terms of having the least transparent budgets. PRI governors did lead some of the most transparent states and municipalities (Colima and Campeche), but they also dominated the lower tier, heading five of the eight worst states, including Querétaro and Tamaulipas (ranked at twenty-ninth and thirty-first respectively, of Mexico's thirty-two states). Juan Pardinas, "Índice de Información Municipal Presupuestal" (Instituto Mexicano para la Competividad AC, 2011).
4. Reprinted by permission of FOREIGN AFFAIRS (June 6, 2012). Copyright (2012) by the Council on Foreign Relations, Inc., www.ForeignAffairs.com. Shannon K. O'Neil, "The Old Guard in a New Mexico: How a Stronger Democracy Will Check the PRI," *Foreign Affairs*, June 6, 2012, http://www.foreignaffairs.com/articles/137677/shannon-k-oneil/the-old-guard-in-a-new-mexico.
5. "World Development Indicators Database: GDP Per Capita (Current US$)" (2011).
6. "Estados Unidos Mexicanos: Medición de Pobreza 2010 a Nivel Nacional" (Consejo Nacional de Evaluación de la Política de Desarrollo Social, 2010).

BIBLIOGRAPHY

A. T. Kearney, Inc. "Offshoring Opportunities Amid Economic Turbulence." 2011.

Addy, Samuel. "A Cost-Benefit Analysis of the New Alabama Immigration Law." Tuscaloosa: University of Alabama, Center for Business and Economic Research, 2012.

Aguilar, Alfonso. "Utah's New Immigration Outlook." *Politico*, March 11, 2011, http://www.politico.com/news/stories/0311/51104.html.

Aguilar Zinser, Adolfo. "Authoritarianism and North American Free Trade: The Debate in Mexico." In *The Political Economy of North American Free Trade*, edited by Richard Grinspun and Maxwell A. Cameron, 205–216. New York: St. Martin's, 1993.

Alba, Richard, and Tariqul Islam. "The Case of the Disappearing Mexican Americans: An Ethnic-Identity Mystery." *Population Research and Policy Review* 28, no. 2 (2009): 109–121.

Alden, Edward. *The Closing of the American Border*. New York: HarperCollins, 2008.

Alvarado Álvarez, Ignacio, and Evangelina Hernández. "Depredan Procampo Políticos y Narcos." *El Universal*, July 27, 2009.

Archibold, Randal C., and Andrew Becker. "As Border Efforts Grow, Corruption Is on the Rise." *New York Times*, May 27, 2008.

Arzt, Sigrid. "The Militarization of the Procuraduría General de la República: Risks for Mexican Democracy." In *Reforming the Administration of Justice in Mexico*, edited by Wayne A. Cornelius and David A. Shirk, 153–174. South Bend: Notre Dame Press, 2007.

Asch, Beth J., Nicholas Burger, and Mary Manqing Fu. "Mitigating Corruption in Government Security Forces: The Role of Institutions, Incentives, and Personnel Management in Mexico." Santa Monica: RAND Corporation, 2011.

Associated Press. "Arrests of Corrupt U.S. Border Police Rise." August 9, 2009, http://www.msnbc.msn.com/id/32349677/ns/us_news-crime_and_courts/t/arrests-corrupt-us-border-police-rise/.

———. "México: Procuraduría Indaga a 700 Funcionarios por Corrupción." July 21, 2011.

Astorga, Luis. "Organized Crime and the Organization of Crime." In *Organized Crime & Democratic Governability: Mexico and the U.S.-Mexican Borderlands*, edited by John Bailey and Roy Godson, 58–82. Pittsburgh: University of Pittsburgh Press, 2000.

Astorga, Luis, and David A. Shirk. "Drug Trafficking Organizations and Counter-Drug Strategies in the U.S.-Mexican Context." Center for U.S.-Mexican Studies, San Diego; Woodrow Wilson Mexico Institute, Washington, DC; El Colegio de la Frontera Norte, Tijuana; El Colegio de México, Mexico City, 2010. http://usmex.ucsd.edu/assets/024/11632.pdf.

Aud, Susan, Mary Ann Fox, and Angelina KewalRamani. "Status and Trends in the Education of Racial and Ethnic Groups (NCES 2010–015)." U.S. Department of Education, National Center for Educational Statistics. Washington, DC: U.S. Government Printing Office, 2010.

Audley, John J., Demetrios G. Papademetriou, Sandra Polaski, and Scott Vaughan. "NAFTA's Promise and Reality: Lessons From Mexico for the Hemisphere." Washington, DC: Carnegie Endowment for International Peace, 2004.

Ayón, David. "The Impact of Mexican Migration and Border Proximity on Local Communities." Houston: Rice University, James A. Baker III Institute for Public Policy, 2009.

———. "Taming the Diaspora: Migrants and the State, 1986–2006." In Mexico's Democratic Challenges, edited by Andrew Selee and Jacqueline Peschard, 231–250. Washington, DC: Woodrow Wilson International Center for Scholars, 2010.

Azevedo, João Pedro, Louise Cord, and Carolina Díaz-Bonilla. "On the Edge of Uncertainty: Poverty Reduction in Latin America and the Caribbean during the Great Recession and Beyond." Washington, DC: World Bank, 2011.

Baby Center. "Los 100 Nombres Más Populares de México." http://www.babycenter.com.mx/pregnancy/nombres/nombres_populares_2010/.

Bailey, John, and Jorge Chabat. Transnational Crime and Public Security: Challenges to Mexico and the United States. La Jolla: Center for U.S.-Mexican Studies, 2002.

Banco Azteca. "¿Quienes Somos?" http://www.bancoazteca.com.mx/PortalBancoAzteca/publica/conocenos/historia/quienes.jsp.

Baralt, Guillermo. If It's Goya It Has to Be Good: The First 75 Years. Barcelona: Editorial Revés, 2011.

Barrera, Iván. "El Registro de Maestros." Mexicanos Primero, May 18, 2011, http://www.mexicanosprimero.org/maestros/blog-mexicanos-primero/326-el-registro-de-maestros.html.

Barry, Christopher B., Gonzalo Castañeda, and Joseph B. Lipscomb. "The Structure of Mortgage Markets in Mexico and Prospects for Their Securitization." Journal of Housing Research 5, no. 2 (1994): 173–204.

Batalova, Jeanne. "Mexican Immigrants in the United States." Migration Policy Institute, 2008, http://www.migrationinformation.org/USfocus/display.cfm?id=679.

Batalova, Jeanne, and Aaron Terrazas. "Frequently Requested Statistics on Immigrants and Immigration in the United States." Migration Policy Institute, 2010, http://www.migrationinformation.org/feature/display.cfm?ID=818.

Bath, Richard. "Resolving Water Disputes." Proceedings of the Academy of Political Science 34, no. 1 (1981): 181–188.

BBC News. "Mexico's Lopez Obrador 'Sworn In.'" November 21, 2006, http://news.bbc.co.uk/2/hi/6166908.stm.

Becerril, Andrea. "La Ley Televisa, una Imposición Previa a las Elecciones de 2006, Según Creel." La Jornada, May 5, 2007.

Becker, Andrew, and Richard Marosi. "Border Agency's Rapid Growth Accompanied by Rise in Corruption." *Los Angeles Times*, October 16, 2011.

Beith, Malcolm. *The Last Narco*. New York: Grove, 2010.

Belair Jr., Felix. "Drug Drive Opens at Mexico Border: U.S. Operation Seeks to Cut Illicit Flow of Marijuana, Heroin and Pep Pills." *New York Times*, September 22, 1969.

Bertelsmann Stiftung. "Bertelsmann Transformation Index," 2010, http://www.bti-project.org/index/status-index/.

Berton, Justin. "Latinos Enlisting in Record Numbers." *San Francisco Chronicle*, May 15, 2006.

Bialik, Carl. "Ketchup vs. Salsa: By the Numbers." *Wall Street Journal*, September 20, 2007, http://blogs.wsj.com/numbersguy/ketchup-vs-salsa-by-the-numbers-191/.

Bimbo Bakeries USA. "About Us." http://www.bimbobakeriesusa.com/about_us/our_history.html.

Blanton, Dana. "Fox News Poll: Arizona Was Right to Take Action on Immigration." *Fox News*, May 7, 2010, http://www.foxnews.com/us/2010/05/07/fox-news-poll-arizona-right-action-immigration/#ixzz1ZM20KNWT.

Bluestone, Barry, and Mark Melnik. "After the Recovery: Help Needed, the Coming Labor Shortage and How People in Encore Careers Can Help Solve It." Boston: Northeastern University, Kitty and Michael Dukakis Center for Urban and Regional Policy, 2010.

Boltvinik, Julio. "Economía Moral." *La Jornada*, April 13, 2012.

Borger, Scott. "Estimates of the Cyclical Inflow of Undocumented Migrants to the United States." San Diego: Center for Comparative Immigration Studies, University of California, San Diego, 2009.

Borjas, George J. "The Labor Demand Curve *Is* Downward Sloping: Reexamining the Impact of Immigration on the Labor Market." *Quarterly Journal of Economics* 118, no. 4 (2003): 1335–1374.

———. "Making it in America: Social Mobility in the Immigrant Population." NBER Working Papers, no. 12088. Washington, DC: National Bureau of Economic Research, 2006.

Borjas, George J., and Lawrence F. Katz. "The Evolution of the Mexican-Born Workforce in the United States." In *Mexican Immigration to the United States*, edited by George J. Borjas, 13–56. Chicago: University of Chicago Press, 2007.

Bouton, Marshall, Gregory Holyk, Steven Kull, and Benjamin Page. "Global Views 2008: Anxious Americans Seek a New Direction in U.S. Foreign Policy." Chicago Council on Global Affairs, 2009.

———. "Statement on Law Enforcement Shooting in Pinal County." *State of Arizona*, 2010, http://azgovernor.gov/dms/upload/PR_043010_StatementGovBrewer_Shooting.pdf.

Brown, Jonathan C. *Oil and Revolution in Mexico*. Berkeley: University of California Press, 1993.

———. "Why Foreign Oil Companies Shifted Their Production from Mexico to Venezuela During the 1920s." *American Historical Review* 90, no. 2 (April 1985): 362–385.

Bruhn, Kathleen. *Taking on Goliath: The Emergence of a New Left Party and the Struggle for Democracy in Mexico*. University Park: Pennsylvania State University Press, 1997.

Burke, Garance. "Despite Economy, Farm Jobs Still Go Begging." *Associated Press*, September 27, 2010.

Businessweek. "Learning Is Earning." March 13, 2006.

Camacho Gutierrez, Pablo, and Vanessa Gonzalez. "Mexico's Current Account Deficit: A Time Series Analysis." *International Journal of Business Research* 9, no. 2 (March 2009): 33–40.

Cámara de Diputados. "Sesión Ordinaria del Martes 18 de Octubre." 2011. http://gaceta.diputados.gob.mx/Gaceta/61/2011/oct/20111018.html.

Camarota, Steven A. "Estimating the Impact of the DREAM Act." Center for Immigration Studies, 2010, http://www.cis.org/dream-act-costs.

Camarota, Steven A., and Jessica M. Vaughan. "Immigration and Crime: Assessing a Conflicted Issue." Washington, DC: Center for Immigration Studies, 2009.

Cambridge Systematics, Inc. "El Paso Regional Ports of Entry Operations Plan." Austin: 2011. http://www.camsys.com/pubs/EPOperations.pdf.

Camp, Roderic Ai. "Democracy Redux? Mexico's Voters and the 2006 Presidential Race." In *Consolidating Mexico's Democracy: The 2006 Presidential Campaign in Comparative Perspective,* edited by Jorge Domínguez and Chappell Lawson, 29–50. Baltimore: Johns Hopkins University Press, 2009.

Campos, Roy. "México: Dónde Vivir, Descansar, Vacacionar, Trabajar o Estudiar." *Consulta Mitofsky,* 2010.

Carbonell, Miguel. "Sobre el Nuevo Artículo 16 Constitucional." 139–152. Mexico City: Universidad Nacional Autónoma de México, 2008.

Card, David. "Immigrant Inflows, Native Outflows, and the Local Market Impacts of Higher Immigration." *Journal of Labor Economics* 19, no. 1 (January 2001): 22–64.

Cárdenas, Mauricio, Homi Kharas, and Camila Henao. "Latin America's Global Middle Class." Washington, DC: Brookings Institution, 2011.

Carrizales, David. "Protesta de Agentes de Nuevo León Estuvo a Punto de Terminar en Balacera con Federales." *La Jornada,* June 9, 2009.

Castañeda, Jorge. *Mañana Forever: Mexico and the Mexicans.* New York: Knopf, Borzoi, 2011.

Cave, Damien. "Better Lives for Mexicans Cut Allure of Going North." *New York Times,* July 6, 2011.

Cavendish, Betsy, and Maru Cortazar. "Children at the Border: the Screening, Protection and Repatriation of Unaccompanied Mexican Minors." Washington, DC: Appleseed Foundation, 2011.

Cemex. "About Us: United States of America." http://www.cemex.com/AboutUs/UnitedStates.aspx.

Centers for Disease Control and Prevention. "Policy Impact: Prescription Painkiller Overdoses." http://www.cdc.gov/homeandrecreationalsafety/rxbrief/.

Centers for Disease Control and Prevention, and National Center for Injury Prevention. "Impaired Driving: Get the Facts." 2011, http://www.cdc.gov/Motorvehiclesafety/Impaired_Driving/impaired-drv_factsheet.html.

Ch, Rafael, and Marien Rivera. "Numeros Rojos del Sistema Penal." Centro de Investigación para el Desarrollo, A.C., 2011.

Chand, Vikram K. *Mexico's Political Awakening.* Notre Dame: University of Notre Dame Press, 2000.

Chávez Méndez, Guadalupe. "La Lectura Masiva en Mexico: Apuntes y Reflexiones Sobre la Situación que Presenta esta Práctica Social." *Estudios Sobre las Culturas Contemporaneas* 11, no. 21 (2005): 71–84.

Chu, Vivian S., and William J. Krouse. "Gun Trafficking and the Southwest Border." Washington, DC: Congressional Research Service, 2009.

CNN Expansion. "Martí: Si No Pueden, Renuncien." http://www.cnnexpansion.com/ actualidad/2008/08/21/marti-si-hay-incapacidad-2018renuncien2019.

CNN, "Los Siete Gobernadores Electos Reciben la Constancia de Mayoría," July 8, 2012, http://mexico.cnn.com/nacional/2012/07/08/los-siete-gobernadores-elec-tos-reciben-la-constancia-de-mayoria.

Cohen, Debra. Bracero. Chapel Hill: University of North Carolina Press, 2011.

Consejo Nacional de Evaluación de la Política de Desarrollo Social. "Estados Unidos Mexicanos: Medición de Pobreza 2010 a Nivel Nacional." 2010.

Corchado, Alfredo. "Zedillo Vows to Vanquish Mexico Woes." Dallas Morning News, April 6, 1995.

Craig, Richard. "Operation Condor: Mexico's Antidrug Campaign Enters a New Era." Journal of Interamerican Studies and World Affairs 22, no. 3 (1980): 345–363.

Croucher, Sheila. The Other Side of the Fence: American Migrants in Mexico. Austin: UT Austin Press, 2009.

Daniels, Roger. Coming to America: A History of Immigration and Ethnicity in American Life. New York: Harper Perennial, 1992.

Davis, Harold E. "Mexican Petroleum Taxes." Hispanic American Historical Review 12, no. 4 (November 1932): 405–412.

Davis, Kristina, and Sandra Dibble. "13 Northbound Border Lanes Reopen: Closure Followed Collapse." UT San Diego, September 14, 2011, http://www.utsandiego.com/news/2011/sep/14/several-injured-border-crossing-roof-collapse/.

de la Calle, Luis, and Luis Rubio. Clasemediero: Pobre No Más, Desarollado Aún No. Mexico City: Centro de Investigación para el Desarrollo, A.C., 2010.

de Onis, Juan. "U.S. Drug Search Irks Diaz Ordaz." New York Times, September 30, 1969.

Deal, Nathan. "Statement on the Status of Agricultural Workforce in Georgia." Georgia State Government, July 14, 2011, http://gov.georgia.gov/00/press/detail/0,2668,1 65937316_165937374_172486990,00.html.

del Carmen Sosa, Luz. "Son 83 Mil los Asesinatos Registrados en el Sexenio." El Diario, August 4, 2012, http://www.diario.com.mx/notas.php?f=2012%2F08%2F04&id= db6aa0610c40288b4ecbcc91f2cb0b63.

del Mar Rubio, Maria. "The Role of Mexico in the First Oil Shortage: 1918–1922, an International Perspective." Barcelona: Universitat Pompeu Fabra, 2005.

del Villar, Rafael. "Competition and Equity in Telecommunications." In No Growth Without Equity: Inequality, Interests, and Competition in Mexico, edited by Santiago Levy and Michael Walton, 321–364. Washington, DC: World Bank, 2009.

Délano, Alexandra. Mexico and its Diaspora in the United States: Policies of Emigration since 1848. Cambridge, UK: Cambridge University Press, 2011.

Delay, Brian. War of a Thousand Deserts: Indian Raids and the U.S.-Mexican War. New Haven: Yale University Press, 2008.

Demirgüç-Kunt, Asli, Thorsten Beck, and Patrick Honohan. "Finance for All?: Policies and Pitfalls in Expanding Access." Washington, DC: World Bank, 2008.

Desai, Mihir, C. Fritz Foley, and James Hines. "Domestic Effects of the Foreign Activities of U.S. Multinationals." Cambridge, MA: Harvard Business School, 2008.

Dickey, Christopher. "Reading, Ranting, and Arithmetic." Newsweek, May 26, 2010.

Dieterlen, Susan Leigh. "Mexican-American Landscapes in Small Midwestern Cities: Mixed Methods Development of a Typology." PhD diss., University of Michigan, 2009.

"D.I.Y. Immigration Reform." *New York Times,* March 20, 2011.

Dizard, Jake, and Christopher Walker. "Countries at a Crossroads: The Vulnerable Middle." Washington, DC: Freedom House, 2010.

Domínguez, Jorge I., and Rafael Fernández de Castro. *United States and Mexico: Between Partnership and Conflict.* New York: Routledge, 2001.

Dresser, Denise. "Bringing the Poor Back In: National Solidarity as a Strategy of Regime Legitimation." In *Transforming State-Society Relations in Mexico: The National Solidarity Strategy,* edited by Wayne Cornelius, Ann Craig, and Jonathan Fox, 143–166. La Jolla: Center for U.S.-Mexican Studies, University of California, San Diego, 1994.

———. "Exporting Conflict: Transboundary Consequences of Mexican Politics." In *The California-Mexico Connection,* edited by Abraham F. Lowenthal and Katrina Burgess, 82–112. Stanford: Stanford University Press, 1993.

Duncan, Brian, and Stephen Trejo. "Intermarriage and the Intergenerational Transmission of Ethnic Identity and Human Capital for Mexican Americans." *Journal of Labor Economics* 29, no. 2 (April 29, 2011): 195–227.

Durand, Jorge. *Braceros: Las Miradas Mexicana y Estadounidense.* Mexico City: Senado de la República, LX Legislatura, 2007.

Dwyer, Devin. "Obama Authorizes Deployment of More National Guard Troops Along Border." *ABC News,* May 25, 2010, http://abcnews.go.com/Politics/obama-authori zes-deployment-national-guard-southwest/story?id=10740858.

The Economist. "Mexico's Economy: Bringing NAFTA Back Home." October 28, 2010.

———. "One River, One Country." September 11, 1997.

Economist Intelligence Unit. "Democracy Index 2011: Democracy Under Stress." 2011.

El Economista. "Voto Nulo 'Quinta Fuerza Electoral' en México." July 6, 2009.

Eisenstadt, Todd. *Courting Democracy in Mexico: Party Strategies and Electoral Institutions.* New York: Cambridge University Press, 2004.

Epstein, Reid J. "Georgia Immigrant Crackdown Backfires." *Politico,* June 22, 2011, http://www.politico.com/news/stories/0611/57551.html.

Escalante Gonzalbo, Fernando. "Homicidios 1990–2007." *Nexos,* September 1, 2009, http://www.nexos.com.mx/?P=leerarticulo&Article=776.

Escobedo, Juan Francisco. "Movilización de Opinión Pública en México: El Caso del Grupo Oaxaca y de la Ley Federal de Acceso a la Información Pública." *Derecho Comparado de la Información* 2 (July–December 2003): 64–92.

Esquivel, Gerardo, Nora Lustig, and John Scott. "A Decade of Falling Inequality in Mexico: Market Forces or State Actions." New York: United Nations Development Programme, 2010.

Esquivel, Gerardo. "The Dynamics of Income Inequality in Mexico since NAFTA." Mexico City: Colegio de Mexico, 2008.

Executive Office of the President of the United States. "FY2012 Budget and Performance Summary." 2011.

Fairris, David. "Unions and Wage Inequality in Mexico." *Industrial and Labor Relations Review* 56, no. 3 (2003): 481–497.

Fajnzylber, Pablo, and J. Humberto López. "Close to Home: The Development Impact of Remittances in Latin America." Washington, DC: World Bank, 2007.

Federal Bureau of Investigation. "National Gang Threat Assessment: Emerging Trends." 2011.

Feinstein, Dianne, Charles Schumer, and Sheldon Whitehouse. "Halting U.S. Firearms Trafficking to Mexico." United States Senate Caucus on International Narcotics Control, 2011.

Ferriss, Susan. "Mexico's Fox Closes Gap in Bid to End 71-Year Presidential Era." *Austin American-Statesman*, May 22, 2000.

———. "Younger Voters are Key to Win in Mexico." *Austin American-Statesman*, May 17, 2000.

Finkel, Jodi. "Judicial Reform as Insurance Policy: Mexico in the 1990s." *Latin American Politics and Society* 47, no. 1 (2005): 87–113.

———. "Supreme Court Decisions on Electoral Rules after Mexico's 1994 Judicial Reform: An Empowered Court." *Journal of Latin American Studies* 35, no. 4 (November 2003): 777–799.

Fitz, Marshall, Gebe Martinez, and Madura Wijewardena. "The Costs of Mass Deportation: Impractical, Expensive, and Ineffective." Washington, DC: Center for American Progress, 2010.

Flores Pérez, Carlos Antonio. *El Estado en Crisis: Crimen Organizado y Política, Desafíos para la Consolidación Democrática*. Mexico City: Centro de Investigaciones y Estudios Superiores en Antropología Social, 2009.

———. "Organized Crime and Official Corruption in Mexico." In *Police and Public Security in Mexico*, edited by Robert A. Donnelly and David A. Shirk, 93–124. San Diego: University Readers, 2010.

Fortier, David. "Military Ammo Today." *Guns and Ammo*. 2010, http://www.handgunsmag.com/2010/09/24/ammunition_hg_militarytoday_200811/

Fox News Latino. "Mexican Court Approves Extradition of 'Queen of the Pacific.'" June 8, 2012.

———. "Mexico's 'Queen of the Pacific' Avoids Extradition." August 10, 2011.

Fox, Jonathan. *Accountability Politics: Power and Voice in Rural Mexico*. New York: Oxford University Press, 2007.

———. *Mexico's Right-to-Know Reforms: Civil Society Perspectives*. Washington, DC: Woodrow Wilson International Center for Scholars, 2007.

Fox, Jonathan, and Libby Haight. "Transparency Reforms: Theory and Practice." In *Mexico's Democratic Challenges*, edited by Andrew Selee and Peschard Jacqueline, 135–161. Washington, DC: Woodrow Wilson Center Press, 2010.

Friedberg, Rachel M., and Jennifer Hunt. "The Impact of Immigrants on Host Country Wages, Employment and Growth." *Journal of Economic Perspectives* 9, no. 2 (Spring 1995): 23–44.

Friedman, Thomas L. "A Gift for Grads: Start-Ups." *New York Times*, June 9, 2010, A25.

Fuentes, Jezmin, Henry L'Esperance, Raul Perez, and Caitlin White. "Impacts of U.S. Immigration Policies on Migration Behavior." In *Impacts of Border Enforcement on Mexican Migration: the View from Sending Communities*, edited by Wayne A. Cornelius and Jessa M. Lewis, 53–74. La Jolla: Center for Comparative Immigration Studies, 2007.

Galarza, Ernesto. *Merchants of Labor: The Mexican Bracero Story*. Santa Barbara: McNally & Loftin, 1972.

Gans, Judith. "Immigrants in Arizona: Fiscal and Economic Impacts." Tucson: University of Arizona, Udall Center for Studies in Public Policy, 2008.

Ganster, Paul, and David E. Lorey. *The U.S.-Mexican Border into the Twenty-first Century*. 2nd ed. Lanham: Rowman and Littlefield, 2008.

García Luna, Genaro. *Para Entender: El Nuevo Modelo de Seguridad para México*. Mexico City: Nostra Ediciones, 2010.

Gaynor, Tim. "Roof Collapse Injures 17 at U.S.-Mexico Border Crossing." *Reuters*, September 14, 2011, http://www.reuters.com/article/2011/09/14/us-usa-mexico -crossing-idUSTRE78D7JJ20110914.

Gilbert, Dennis. "Rewriting History: Salinas, Zedillo and the 1992 Textbook Controversy." *Mexican Studies/Estudios Mexicanos* 13, no. 2 (Summer 1997): 271–297.

Giraudy, Agustina. "Subnational Undemocratic Regime Continuity After Democratization: Argentina and Mexico in Comparative Perspective." PhD diss, University of North Carolina, Chapel Hill, 2009.

Gobierno de Mexico. "National Infrastructure Program of Mexico." Mexico City, July 2007.

Gomez, Alan, Jack Gillum, and Kevin Johnson. "U.S. Border Cities Prove Havens from Mexico's Drug Violence." *USA Today*, July 19, 2011.

González, Guadalupe, Ferran Martínez i Coma, and Jorge A. Schiavon. "México, las Américas y el Mundo." Mexico City: Centro de Investigación y Docencia Económicas, 2008.

Gorman, Anne. "A Family's Painful Split Decision." *Los Angeles Times*, April 27, 2007.

Goya Foods. "Goya Foods Celebrates Its 75th Anniversary Serving the Community." October 7, 2010, http://www.goya.com/english/PressRoom/press_release. html?lid=44.

Graham, Dave. "Slim's Telmex Not Planning to Take Part in TV Auction." *Reuters*, June 9, 2012, http://www.reuters.com/article/2012/06/09/ us-slim-tv-idUSBRE8580E020120609.

Grant, Tina. "Grupo Elektra, SA de CV." In *International Directory of Company Histories*: vol. 39. Chicago: St. James, 2001.

Grayson, George W. *Mexico: Narco-Violence and a Failed State?* New Brunswick: Transaction, 2009.

———. *The Mexico-U.S. Business Committee: Catalyst for the North American Free Trade Agreement*. Rockville: Montrose, 2007.

———. "Vigilantism: Increasing Self-Defense against Runaway Violence in Mexico?" Foreign Policy Research Institute, October 2009, http://www.fpri.org/enotes/200910. grayson.vigilantismmexico.html.

Greene, Kenneth F. *Why Dominant Parties Lose: Mexico's Democratization in Comparative Perspective*. Cambridge, UK: Cambridge University Press, 2007.

Greenhouse, Steven. "At Caterpillar, Pressing Labor While Business Booms." *New York Times*, July 22, 2012.

Grieco, Elizabeth, and Edward N. Trevelyan. "Place of Birth of the Foreign-Born Population: 2009." Washington, DC: U.S. Census Bureau, 2010.

Grigoriadis, Vanessa, and Mary Cuddehe. "An American Drug Lord in Acapulco." *Rolling Stone*, August 25, 2011.

Grosse, Robert E. *Drugs and Money: Laundering Latin America's Cocaine Dollars*. Westport: Praeger, 2001.

Guerrero, Angelina Mejía. "Telmex no es un Monopolio, Resuelve Juzgado." *El Universal,* October 12, 2006.

Gurría, Angel. "El Acuerdo de Cooperación México OCDE para Mejorar la Calidad de la Educación en las Escuelas Mexicanas." October 19, 2010. Mexico City: Organisation for Economic Co-operation and Development.

Haber, Stephen. *Industry and Underdevelopment: The Industrialization of Mexico, 1890–1940.* Stanford: Stanford University Press, 1995.

Haber, Stephen, Armando Razo, and Noel Maurer. *The Politics of Property Rights: Political Instability, Credible Commitments, and Economic Growth in Mexico, 1876–1929.* Cambridge, UK: Cambridge University Press, 2003.

Hakimzadeh, Shirin, and D'Vera Cohn. "English Usage Among Hispanics in the United States." Washington, DC: Pew Research Center, Pew Hispanic Center, 2007.

Hanson, Gordon H., and Craig McIntosh. "The Demography of Mexican Migration to the U.S." *American Economic Review: Papers & Proceedings* 99, no. 2 (May 2009): 22–27.

Hansen, Roger D. *The Politics of Mexican Development.* Baltimore: Johns Hopkins University Press, 1971.

Haralambides, Hercules E., and Maria P. Londono-Kent. "Supply Chain Bottlenecks: Border Crossing Inefficiencies Between Mexico and the United States." *International Journal of Transport Economics* 31, no. 2 (June 2004): 171–183.

Hartenstein, Meena. "Mexican Governor Candidate Killed by Gunmen, Calderon Says Assassination Tied to Drug Gang Violence." *New York Daily News,* June 28, 2010.

Hawken, Angela, and Mark Kleiman. "Managing Drug Involved Probationers with Swift and Certain Sanctions: Evaluating Hawaii's HOPE." U.S. Department of Justice, 2009.

Henderson, Timothy J. *A Glorious Defeat: Mexico and Its War with the United States.* New York. Hill and Wang, 2007.

Hernández, María, José del Tronco, and Gabriela Sánchez. *Un Congreso Sin Mayorías: Mejores Prácticas en Negociación y Construcción de Acuerdos.* Mexico City: Facultad Latinoamericana de las Ciencias Sociales, 2009.

Hernández, Roberto, and Geoffrey Smith. "Presunto Culpable." 87 minutes: Cinépolis, 2011.

Hernández-Coss, Raúl. "The U.S.–Mexico Remittance Corridor: Lessons on Shifting from Informal to Formal Transfer Systems." Washington, DC: World Bank, 2005.

Herrera-Lasso, M. Luis. "The Mexico-United States Border: A Fragmented Agenda." *National Strategy Forum* 18, no. 3 (2009): 7–11.

Hinojosa-Ojeda, Raul. "Raising the Floor for American Workers: The Economic Benefits of Comprehensive Immigration Reform." Washington, DC: Immigration Policy Center, 2010.

Hinojosa-Ojeda, Raul, and Marshall Fitz. "Revitalizing the Golden State: What Legalization over Deportation Could Mean to California and Los Angeles County." Washington, DC: Center for American Progress, Immigration Policy Center, 2011.

Homeland Security News Wire. "Border Agents Corrupted While FBI and DHS Wrangle for Power." June 17, 2011, http://www.homelandsecuritynewswire.com/border-agents-corrupted-while-fbi-and-dhs-wrangle-power.

Homex. "Nuestros Mercados." http://www.homex.com.mx/ri/index.htm.

Hornbeck, J. F. "NAFTA at Ten: Lessons from Recent Studies." Washington, DC: Congressional Research Service, 2004.

House Committee on Homeland Security, Subcommittee on Border and Maritime Security. *Using Resources Effectively to Secure Our Border at Ports of Entry—Stopping the Illicit Flow of Money, Guns and Drugs*, 2011.

Hufbauer, Gary Clyde, and Jeffrey J. Schott. *NAFTA Revisited: Achievements and Challenges*. Washington, DC: Institute for International Economics, 2005.

Hughes, Sallie. *Newsrooms in Conflict: Journalism and the Democratization of Mexico*. Pittsburgh: University of Pittsburgh Press, 2006.

Hugo Lopez, Mark. "Latinos and Education: Explaining the Attainment Gap." Washington, DC: Pew Research Center, Pew Hispanic Center, 2009.

Human Rights Watch. "Neither Rights nor Security: Killings, Torture, and Disappearances in Mexico's 'War on Drugs.'" 2011.

iCasualties. "Iraq Coalition Casualties: Military Fatalities." http://icasualties.org/Iraq/Fatalities.aspx.

Iliff, Laurence. "PRI Machine, People of 'Campo' Vital to Mexican's Presidential Bid; Labastida Battling to Extend Party's Decades of Dominance." *Dallas Morning News*, April 18, 2000.

Immigration Policy Center. "Who and Where the DREAMers Are." July 31, 2012, http://www.immigrationpolicy.org/just-facts/who-and-where-dreamers-are.

Inglehart, Ronald F., Neil Nevitte, and Miguel Basañez. *The North American Trajectory*. New York: Aldine de Gruyter, 1996.

Instituto Federal de Acceso a la Información. "Mexican Experience in Access to Public Information." Access to Public Information Seminar. São Paolo, Brazil, 2011.

Instituto Nacional de Estadística y Geografía. "Censo de Población y Vivienda." Aguascalientes, 2000.

———. "Informativo Oportuno: Los Nacidos en Otro País Suman 961,121 Personas." Aguascalientes, 2011.

———. "Mujeres y Hombres en México." Aguascalientes, 2005.

———. "Población, Hogares y Vivienda." Aguascalientes, http://www.inegi.org.mx/Sistemas/temasV2/Default.aspx?s=est&c=17484.

———. "Servicios Educativos." *Directorio Estadístico Nacional de Unidades Económicas*. Aguascalientes, 2010.

Instituto Nacional para el Federalismo y el Desarrollo Municipal. "Estado de Chiapas." 2005.

Jefferson, Thomas. *The Writings of Thomas Jefferson: Being His Autobiography, Correspondence, Reports, Messages, Addresses, and Other Writings, Official and Private*. Washington, DC: Taylor and Maury, 1854.

Jiménez, Tomás R., and David Fitzgerald. "Mexican Assimilation: A Temporal and Spatial Reorientation." Center for Comparative Immigration Studies, University of California, San Diego, 2007.

Jones, Jeffrey M. "More Americans Favor than Oppose Arizona Immigration Law." *Gallup*, 2010, http://www.gallup.com/poll/127598/americans-favor-oppose-arizona-immigration-law.aspx.

Jordan, Miriam. "Immigration Audit Takes Toll." *Wall Street Journal*, March 15, 2011.

Karberg, Jennifer C., and Doris J. James. "Substance Dependence, Abuse, and Treatment of Jail Inmates, 2002." Washington, DC: U.S. Department of Justice, 2005.

Kaufman Purcell, Susan. "The Changing Nature of US-Mexican Relations." *Journal of Interamerican Studies and World Affairs* 39, no. 1 (Spring 1997): 137–152.

Kennedy, David M. "Can We Still Afford to Be a Nation of Immigrants?" *The Atlantic*, November 1996.

Kennedy, John F. *A Nation of Immigrants.* Revised and enlarged edition. New York: HarperCollins, 1964.

Kenny, Kevin. "Irish Immigrants in the United States." *America.gov Archive*, February 13, 2008, http://www.america.gov/st/peopleplace-english/2008/February/20080 307131416ebyessedo0.6800043.html.

Kharas, Homi. "The Emerging Middle Class in Developing Countries." Paris: Organisation for Economic Cooperation and Development, 2010. http://www. oecd.org/social/povertyreductionandsocialdevelopment/44457738.pdf.

Kharas, Homi, and Geoffrey Gertz. "The New Global Middle Class: A Cross-over from West to East." Washington, DC: Brookings Institution, Wolfensohn Center for Development, 2010.

Killicoat, Phillip. "Weaponomics: The Global Market for Assault Rifles." *World Bank Research Digest*, April 13, 2007, http://siteresources.worldbank.org/DEC/ Resources/84797-1154354760266/2807421-1183396414833/Weaponomics.pdf.

Kilmer, Beau, Jonathan P. Caulkins, Brittany M. Bond, and Peter H. Reuter. "Reducing Drug Trafficking Revenues and Violence in Mexico: Would Legalizing Marijuana in California Help?" Santa Monica: RAND Corporation, 2010.

Kirdahy, Matthew. "Best Cities for Jobs in 2008." January 10, 2008, http://www.forbes. com/2008/01/10/jobs-economy-growth-lead-careers-cx_mk_0110cities.html.

Klesner, Joseph. "The Structure of the Mexican Electorate." In *Mexico's Pivotal Democratic Election: Candidates, Voters, and the Presidential Campaign of 2000*, edited by Jorge I. Domínguez and Chappell H. Lawson, 91–122. Stanford: Stanford University Press, 2004.

Konrad, Rachel. "Immigrants Behind 25 Percent of Tech Startups." *Associated Press*, January 3, 2007.

Krauze, Enrique. *Mexico: Biography of Power.* New York: HarperCollins, 1997.

Krouse, William J. "The Bureau of Alcohol, Tobacco, Firearms and Explosives (ATF): Budget and Operations for FY2011." Washington, DC: Congressional Research Service, 2011.

Kun, Josh. "The Island of Jorge Hank Rhon." *LA Weekly*, February 16, 2006.

KYMA News 11. "San Luis II Port Complete." 1:36: ABC News, 2010.

Lawson, Chappell. *Building the Fourth Estate: Democratization and the Rise of a Free Press in Mexico.* Berkeley: University of California Press, 2002.

Lee, Alex. "Review of Unused Presidential Permit: Laredo, Texas International Railroad Bridge." Washington, DC: U.S. Department of State Federal Register, 2009.

Lee, Morgan. "Mexico Combats Police Corruption with Mortgages." *USA Today*, September 20, 2008.

Lerman, Robert I. "An Overview of Economic, Social, and Demographic Trends Affecting the U.S. Labor Market." Washington, DC: U.S. Department of Labor, 1999.

Lesh, Carolyn. "250,000 Protest Vote in Mexico." *Chicago Tribune*, July 17, 1988.

Levine, Linda. "Retiring Baby-Boomers = A Labor Shortage." Washington, DC: Congressional Research Service, 2008.

Levy, Santiago. *Progress against Poverty, Sustaining Mexico's Progresa-Oportunidades Program*. Washington, DC: Brookings Institution Press, 2006.

Liming, Drew, and Michael Wolf. "Job Outlook by Education, 2006–16." *Occupational Outlook Quarterly* 52, no. 2 (Fall 2008): 2–29.

Lowell, B. Lindsay. "U.S.-Mexican Relations: Changes in the U.S.-Mexican Relationship, North America and Immigration." Paper presented at the Executive Seminar on Mexico, Washington, DC, August 2011.

Lowenfeld, Andreas. "Kidnapping by Government Order: A Follow-Up." *American Journal of International Law* 84, no. 3 (1990): 712–716.

Lustig, Nora. "Crises and the Poor: Socially Responsible Macroeconomics." Inter-American Development Bank, Sustainable Development Department, Poverty and Inequality Advisory Unit Working Paper, 2000.

Macías, Viviana, and Fernando Castillo. "Mexico's National Public Security System: Perspectives for the New Millennium." In *Transnational Crime and Public Security: Challenges to Mexico and the United States*, edited by John Bailey and Jorge Chabat, 53–70. La Jolla: Center for U.S.-Mexican Studies, 2002.

Magaloni, Beatriz, and Guillermo Zepeda. "Democratization, Judicial and Law Enforcement Institutions, and the Rule of Law in Mexico." In *Dilemmas of Political Change in Mexico*, edited by Kevin J. Middlebrook, 168–197. London: University of London, Institute of Latin American Studies, 2004.

Magaloni, Beatriz. "Weak and Powerful Courts under Autocracy: The Case of Mexico." Paper presented at the conference "The Politics of Courts in Authoritarian Regimes." University of Pennsylvania Law School, August 30–31, 2006.

Malcolm, Andrew. "In Her Own Words: Gov. Jan Brewer on Mexico Joining Lawsuit Against Arizona's Illegal Immigrant Law." *Los Angeles Times*, June 22, 2010, http://latimesblogs.latimes.com/washington/2010/06/arizona-jan-brewer-illegal-immigrant-mexico.html.

Malkin, Elisabeth. "Mexican Court's Media Ruling Shows Support for Competition." *New York Times*, June 6, 2007.

Marczak, Jason, Jerónimo Cortina, George Hawley, Aaron Diamond, Chris Nicholson, Richard André, Alexandra Délano, and Lina Salazar. "The Economic Impact of Immigrant-Related Local Ordinances." New York: Americas Society, 2011.

Martí, Alejandro. "Por Qué Sí Debe Aprobarse la Ley de Seguridad Nacional." *Animal Político*, August 16, 2011, http://www.animalpolitico.com/blogueros-mexico-sos/2011/08/16/por-que-si-debe-aprobarse-la-ley-de-seguridad-nacional/.

Martin, Joyce A., Brady E. Hamilton, Paul D. Sutton, Stephanie J. Ventura, T.J. Matthews, and Michelle J.K. Osterman. "Births: Final Data for 2008." *National Vital Statistics Reports* 59, no. 1 (December 8, 2010): 1–72.

Martin, Philip. "Braceros: History, Compensation." *Rural Migration News* 12, no. 2 (April 2006). http://migration.ucdavis.edu/rmn/more.php?id=1112_0_4_0.

———. *Importing Poverty? Immigration and the Changing Face of Rural America*. New Haven: Yale University Press, 2009.

Martinez, Chivis. "The Perfume Man and Chapo's Stinking Dollars." *InSight Crime*, January 25, 2012, http://www.insightcrime.org/insight-latest-news/item/2125-the-perfume-man-and-chapos-stinking-dollars.

Massey, Douglas S. "Backfire at the Border: Why Enforcement without Legalization Cannot Stop Illegal Immigration." Washington, DC: Center for Trade and Policy Studies, CATO Institute, 2005.

Massey, Douglas S., Jorge Durand, and Nolan J. Malone. *Beyond Smoke and Mirrors: Mexican Immigration in an Era of Economic Integration*. New York: Russell Sage Foundation, 2002.

Mauer, Noel. "The Empire Struck Back: The Mexican Oil Expropriation of 1938 Reconsidered." Cambridge, MA: Harvard Business School, 2010.

Maxfield, Betty. "Army Demogaphics." Office of Army Demographics, 2010. http://www.armyg1.army.mil/hr/docs/demographics/fy10_army_profile.pdf.

Mayors Against Illegal Guns. "The Tiahrt Amendments." http://www.mayorsagainstillegalguns.org/html/federal/tiahrt.shtml.

Mazza, Jacqueline. *Don't Disturb the Neighbors: The U.S. and Democracy in Mexico, 1980–1995*. New York: Routledge, 2001.

"Mexico SOS Iniciativas de Ley." http://mexicosos.org/index.php?option=com_content&view=article&id=96&Itemid=242.

McCadden M., Carlos J., and Raúl Bravo Aduna. "La Clase Media Mexicana." *Este País*, December 2008, 10–11.

McCaul, Michael. "Let's Make a Commitment to War on Mexican Cartels: U.S. Should Consider Strategy Used in Colombia." *Austin American-Statesman*, March 20, 2011.

McCombs, Brady. "July Migrant Deaths Could Set Record." *Arizona Daily Star*, July 16, 2010.

McCormick, Cami. "The U.S. Guns in Mexico's Drug War." *CBS News*, March 26, 2009.

McGreal, Chris. "The Battle of the U.S.-Mexico Frontier." *The Guardian*, February 20, 2011.

McKinley Jr., James C. "An Arizona Morgue Grows Crowded." *New York Times*, July 29, 2010.

———. "In Mexico, a Fugitive's Arrest Captivates the Cameras." *New York Times*, October 12, 2007.

McKinley, James C., and Julia Preston. "U.S. Can't Trace Foreign Visitors on Expired Visas." *New York Times*, October 11, 2009.

Mendoza, Alexandra. "Construction Work Resumes at Border Crossing: Contractor Makes Change to Safeguard Security." *San Diego Red*, September 27, 2011.

Mercado, Patricia. "Marcha Masiva Contra la Violencia." *BBC News*, August 31, 2008, http://news.bbc.co.uk/hi/spanish/latin_america/newsid_7590000/7590363.stm.

Mexican Migration Project. "Graph 8: Probability of Apprehension on an Undocumented Border Crossing, 1980–2010," October 2011, http://mmp.opr.princeton.edu/results/008apprehension-en.aspx.

Mexicanos Primero. *Contra la Pared: Estado de la Educación en Mexico*. Mexico City: Mexicanos Primero Visión, 2009.

Mexico Secretaría de Educación Pública. "General Statistical Indicators for the 2008–2009 Academic Term." Mexico City, 2010.

Mexico Secretariado Ejecutivo del Sistema Nacional de Seguridad Pública. "Sueldos de Policías Estatales y Municipales." 2011.

Meyer, Brooke, and Ann Morse. "Immigration-Related Laws and Resolutions in the States." Washington, DC: National Conference of State Legislatures, 2011.

Michel, Elena. "El 80% de los Homocidios, en 162 Municipios del País." *El Universal,* August 20, 2011.

Michener, Greg. "The Surrender of Secrecy: Explaining the Emergence of Strong Access to Information Laws in Latin America." PhD diss, University of Texas at Austin, 2010.

Miroff, Nick, and William Booth. "Mexican Drug Cartels' Newest Weapon: Cold War-Era Grenades Made in U.S." *Washington Post,* July 17, 2010.

Mohan, Geoffrey. "Mexican Party's Uphill Struggle; PRI is Trying to Remake Itself." *Newsday,* April 27, 2000.

Molloy, Molly. "Mexico's Magical Homicides." *Miami New Times,* July 26, 2012, http://www.miaminewtimes.com/2012-07-26/news/mexico-s-magical-homicides/%5C/.

Moreno, Alejandro, and María Antonia Mancillas. "Respaldan Labor de las Fuerzas Armadas." *Reforma,* December 1, 2011.

Moreno, Maria Alejandra. "Regulador Emite Reglas sobre Corresponsales Bancarios." *Business News Americas,* December 5, 2008.

Moreno-Brid, Juan Carlos. "Mexico's Auto Industry After NAFTA: A Successful Experience in Restructuring?" South Bend: Notre Dame University, Kellogg Institute, 1996.

Moreno-Brid, Juan Carlos, and Jaime Ros. *Development and Growth in the Mexican Economy: A Historical Perspective.* New York: Oxford University Press, 2009.

Moreno-Uriegas, María de los Ángeles. "Participación Laboral de la Mujer en México." *Revista de Enfermería del IMSS* 8, no. 3 (2000): 121–124.

Myers, Dowell, and John Pitkin. "Immigrants Today: New Evidence Shows the Latest Immigrants to America are Following our History's Footsteps." Center for American Progress, 2010. http://www.americanprogress.org/wp-content/uploads/issues/2010/09/pdf/immigrant_assimilation.pdf.

Nadal, Alejandro, and Timothy A. Wise. "Los Costos Ambientales de la Liberalización Agrícola." In *Globalización y Medio Ambiente: Lecciones Desde las Américas,* edited by Liane Schalatek, 49–92. Santiago, Chile: Heinrich Böll Foundation North America, 2005.

NAFTANow. "Caterpillar Inc.: 'Paving a Brighter Future...'." http://www.naftanow.org/success/us_en.asp.

Nataren, Carlos. "Notes on Criminal Process and Constitutional Reform in Mexico Today." *Mexican Law Review* 4, no. 1 (2011): 99–124.

National Center for Fair and Open Testing. "Teachers Boycott Tests." http://www.fairtest.org/teachers-boycott-tests.

National Institute on Drug Abuse. "Principles of Drug Addiction Treatment: A Research Based Guide." http://www.nida.nih.gov/PODAT/faqs.html#faq4.

Nemak. "Our Facilities." http://www.nemak.com/facilities.html.

Newell, Roberto. "Restoring Mexico's International Reputation." Washington, DC: Woodrow Wilson International Center for Scholars, Mexico Institute, 2011.

Niblo, Stephen R. *War, Diplomacy, and Development: The United States and Mexico, 1938–1954.* Wilmington: Scholarly Resources, 1995.

Office of the Executive. "Study on the Operation and Effect of the North American Free Trade Agreement." Washington, DC. 1997.

Office of the U.S. Trade Representative. "U.S. Wins WTO Telecommunications Case Against Mexico." Washington, DC. 2004.

O'Neil, Shannon K. "The Old Guard in a New Mexico: How a Stronger Democracy Will Check the PRI." *Foreign Affairs,* June 6, 2012. http://www.foreignaffairs.com/articles/137677/shannon-k-oneil/the-old-guard-in-a-new-mexico.

Oportunidades. "Oportunidades Atiende a 5.8 Millones de Familias en el País." http://www.oportunidades.gob.mx/Portal/wb/Web/oportunidades_atiende_a_58_millones_de_familias_.

Organisation for Economic Cooperation and Development. "Comparing Countries' and Economies' Performance." 2010.

———. "Economic Surveys: Mexico." 2011.

———. *Employment Outlook, 2011.* 2012.

———. "Factbook 2011–2012, Economic, Environmental and Social Statistics." 2011.

———. "Growing Income Inequality in OECD Countries: What Drives it and How Can Policy Tackle It." Paris, 2011.

———. "ICT Database and Eurostat, Community Survey on ICT Usage in Households and by Individuals." 2010.

———. "Moving Up the Value Chain: Staying Competitive in the Global Economy." 2007.

———. "Perspectivas OCDE: México Políticas Clave para un Desarrollo Sostenible." 2010.

———. "StatExtracts." 2011.

Orozco, Manuel. "Remittances to Latin America and the Caribbean: Issues and Perspectives on Development." Washington, DC: Organization of American States, 2004.

Ottaviano, Gianmarco, and Giovanni Peri. "Immigration and National Wages: Clarifying the Theory and the Empirics." Cambridge, MA: National Bureau of Economic Research, 2008.

———. "Rethinking the Effects of Immigration on Wages: New Data and Analysis from 1990–2004." *Immigration Policy in Focus* 5, no. 8 (October 2006): 1–7.

Ousey, Graham C., and Charis E. Kubrin. "Exploring the Connection between Immigration and Violent Crime Rates in U.S. Cities, 1980–2000." *Social Problems* 56, no. 3 (2009): 447–473.

Oxford Analytica. "Mexico: Banking Continues Steady Recovery." December 2, 2010, http://www.oxan.com/display.aspx?ItemID=DB164552.

Painter, William L., and Jennifer Lake. "Homeland Security Department: FY2012 Appropriations." Washington, DC: Department of Homeland Security, 2011.

Parcher, Jean. "Sistema de Información Geográfica de la Frontera entre México y Estados Unidos." *Noveno Conferencia Cartográfica Regional de las Naciones Unidas para América.* New York: United States Geological Survey, 2009.

Pardinas, Juan. "El Actor de Tultitlán." *Reforma,* October 7, 2007.

Passel, Jeffrey S., and D'Vera Cohn. "Mexican Immigrants: How Many Come, How Many Leave." Washington, DC: Pew Research Center, Pew Hispanic Center, 2009.

———. "Mexico: Migrants, Remittances, 3x1." *Migration News* 16, no. 4 (October 2009).

Passel, Jeffrey, D'Vera Cohn, and Ana Gonzalez-Barrera. "Net Migration from Mexico Falls to Zero—and Perhaps Less." Washington, DC: Pew Research Center, 2012.

Pastor, Robert. *The North American Idea: A Vision of a Continental Future.* New York: Oxford University Press, 2011.

Pastor, Robert, and Jorge Castañeda. *Limits to Friendship: The United States and Mexico.* New York: Vintage, 1989.

Pederzini, Carla. "Labor Market and Emigration from Mexico during the World Economic Recession." Presented at conference, "Migration and Development: Comparing Mexico-US and Turkey-Europe," May 6, 2011.

Perez, Arturo. "Gunmen Kill Former Mexico Governor." *Associated Press,* November 21, 2010.

Pérez Correa, Catalina. "Front Desk Justice: Inside and Outside Criminal Procedure in Mexico City." *Mexican Law Review* 1, no. 1 (July-December 2008): 3–32.

Peri, Giovanni. "How Immigrants Affect California Employment and Wages." San Francisco: Public Policy Institute of California, 2007.

———. "Immigrants, Skills, and Wages: Measuring the Economic Gains from Immigration." *Immigration Policy Center: In Focus* 5, no. 3 (March 2006): 1–7.

Perry, Guillermo E., Omar S. Arias, J. Humberto López, William F. Maloney, and Luis Servén. "Poverty Reduction and Growth: Virtuous and Vicious Circles." Washington, DC: World Bank, 2006.

Petras, James. "Alternatives to Neoliberalism in Latin America." *Latin American Perspectives* 24, no. 1 (1997): 80–91.

Pettigrew, Pierre S., Robert B. Zoellick, and Luis Ernesto Derbez. "NAFTA at Eight: A Foundation of Economic Growth." Washington, DC: Office of the United States Trade Representative, 2002.

Pew Center on the States. "The Impact of Hawaii's HOPE Program on Drug Use, Crime and Recidivism." Washington, DC: Pew Research Center, 2010.

Pew Charitable Trusts. "Pursuing the American Dream: Economic Mobility of Families Across Generations." Washington, DC: Pew Research Center, 2012.

Pew Global Attitudes Project. "Most Mexicans See Better Life in U.S." Washington, DC: Pew Research Center, 2009.

———. "Opinion of the United States." Washington, DC: Pew Research Center, 2012, http://www.pewglobal.org/database/?indicator=1.

Pew Hispanic Center. "Between Two Worlds: How Young Latinos Come of Age in America." Washington, DC: Pew Research Center, 2009.

———. "The Mexican-American Boom: Births Overtake Immigration." Washington, DC: Pew Research Center, 2011.

Pinkerton, James. "Fake Documents for Immigrants Swamp Houston." *Houston Chronicle,* May 2, 2008.

Polanska, Malgorzata. "Homicidios por Entidad Federativa y Regiones 1990–2007." In *Atlas de la Seguridad y la Defensa de México 2009,* edited by Raúl Benítez Manaut, Abelardo Rodríguez Sumano, and Armando Rodríguez Luna, 122–125. Mexico City: Colectivo de Análisis de la Seguridad con Democracia, 2009.

Polity. "Polity IV Country Report: Mexico." 2010. http://www.systemicpeace.org/polity/Mexico2010.pdf.

Poniatowska, Elana. *Nada, Nadie—Las Voces del Temblor.* Mexico City: Ediciones Era, 1988.

Porter, Eduardo. "Cost of Illegal Immigration May Be Less than Meets the Eye." *New York Times,* April 16, 2006.

———. "Here Illegally, Working Hard and Paying Taxes." *New York Times,* July 19, 2006.

Presidencia de la República de Mexico. "Decenas de Miles de Mexicanos Exigen Seguridad en una Marcha de Silencio." June 27, 2004, http://fox.presidencia.gob.mx/buenasnoticias/?contenido=8487&pagina=343.

Press, Eyal. "Do Immigrants Make Us Safer." *New York Times Magazine,* December 3, 2006.

Preston, Julia, and Samuel Dillon. *Opening Mexico: The Making of a Democracy.* New York: Farrar, Straus and Giroux, 2004.

Proceso. "Sólo 30% de Portales Cumple con Transparencia." July 18, 2011.

Puddington, Arch. "Freedom in the World 2012." Freedom House, 2012. http://www.freedomhouse.org/article/freedom-world-2012-arab-uprisings-and-their-global-repercussions.

Puryear, Jeffrey. "Reform in Mexico Forces Debate on Sale of Teaching Positions." *Latin America Advisor,* November 24, 2008.

Quinones, Sam. *Antonio's Gun and Delfino's Dream: True Tales of Mexican Migration.* Albequerque: University of New Mexico Press, 2008.

Raat, W. Dirk. *Mexico and the United States: Ambivalent Vistas.* Athens: University of Georgia Press, 2004.

Randewich, Noel. "Wal-Mart's Mexico Bank Aims at First-time Savers." *Reuters,* June 18, 2010, http://www.reuters.com/article/2010/06/18/walmart-mexico-idUSN1812635420100618.

Ravallion, Martin. "The Developing World's Bulging (but Vulnerable) 'Middle Class.'" Washington, DC: World Bank Development Research Group, 2009.

Ravelo, Ricardo. *Los Capos: Las Narco-Rutas de México.* Mexico City: RH Español, 2007.

———. *Herencia Maldita: El Reto de Calderón y el Nuevo Mapa del Narcotráfico.* Mexico City: Grijalbo, 2007.

Red Mexicana de Acción Frente al Libre Comercio. "Exportaciones Totales de México a América del Norte (1993–1999)." http://www.rmalc.org.mx/tratados/tlcan/mexandat.pdf.

Reding, Andrew. "Perspective Series: Mexico Democracy and Human Rights." Washington, DC: U.S. Department of Justice, 1995.

Reforma. "Juan Ciudadano: Se Cayó el Sistema." November 27, 2000.

Reilly, John E. "American Public Opinion and U.S. Foreign Policy." Chicago: Chicago Council on Foreign Relations, 1995.

Rendal, Michael S., Peter Brownell, and Sarah Kups. "Declining Return Migration from the United States to Mexico in the Late-2000s Recession." Santa Monica: RAND Corporation, 2010.

"Resultados de la Encuesta ESRU." *Fundación Espinosa Rugarcía.* 2008, http://www.movilidadsocial.org/content/resultados-encuesta-esru.

Riding, Alan. *Distant Neighbors: A Portrait of the Mexicans.* New York: Vintage, 1989.

Ríos, Viridiana, and David A. Shirk. "Drug Violence in Mexico: Data and Analysis through 2010." San Diego: Trans-Border Institute, 2011.

Rippy, Merrill. *Oil and the Mexican Revolution.* Leiden, Netherlands: E. J. Brill, 1972.

Risen, James, and James Gerstenzang. "President Plays Let's Make a Deal as NAFTA Vote Nears." *Los Angeles Times,* November 7, 1993.

Riva Palacio, Raymundo. "A Culture of Collusion: The Ties that Bind the Press and the PRI." In *The Culture of Collusion: An Inside Look at the Mexican Press,* edited by William A. Orme Jr., 21–32. Miami: University of Miami, North South Center Press, 1996.

Rivera, Marien. "The Fight Worth Fighting: Reforming the Mexican Criminal Justice System." Mexico City: Centro de Investigación para el Desarrollo, A.C., 2010.

Rodríguez, Mauricio. "Desde 2008 a la Fecha, Suman 9 Mil Homicidios en Juárez." *Proceso,* December 1, 2011, http://www.proceso.com.mx/?p=28982.

Rodriguez, Olga R. "Central American Migrants Flood North through Mexico to U.S." *Huffington Post,* June 13, 2012, http://www.huffingtonpost.com/2012/07/13/central-americans-in-the-united-states_n_1671551.html.

Rohter, Larry. "North American Trade Bloc? Mexico Rejects Such an Idea." *New York Times,* November 24, 1988.

Romero, Simon, and Janet Elder. "Hispanics in the U.S. Report Optimism." *New York Times,* August 6, 2003.

Ross, John. *El Monstruo: Dread and Redemption in Mexico City.* New York: Nation, 2009.

Ross, Michael. "Clinton Sends NAFTA to Congress After Reaching Deals." *Los Angeles Times,* November 4, 1993.

Ruano, Geovana. "Sasabe: The New Destination toward Death and Insult for Immigrants." *Yuma Sun* [Arizona], March 10, 2008.

Rubenstein, James M., and Thomas Klier. "Restructuring of the Auto Industry: Geographic Implications of Outsourcing." Chicago: Industry Studies Association, 2009.

Rumbaut, Rubén G., and Walter A. Ewing. "The Myth of Immigrant Criminality and the Paradox of Assimilation: Incarceration Rates among Native and Foreign-Born Men." Washington, DC: Immigration Policy Center, 2007.

Runkle, Benjamin. *Wanted Dead or Alive: Manhunts from Geronimo to Bin Laden.* New York: Palgrave MacMillan, 2011.

Sabat, Daniel. "Police Reform in Mexico: Advances and Persistent Obstacles." Washington, DC: Woodrow Wilson International Center for Scholars, Mexico Institute, and Trans-Border Institute, University of San Diego, 2010.

Salazar, Eduardo. "Extraordinario el Crecimiento de Universitarios: Fox." *EsMas,* November 29, 2004. www.esmas.cohttp://www.systemicpeace.org/polity/Mexico2010.pdf.

Sampson, Robert J. "Rethinking Crime and Immigration." *Contexts* 7, no. 1, Winter 2008: 28–33.

Sampson, Robert J., Jeffrey D. Morenoff, and Stephen Raudenbush. "Social Anatomy of Racial and Ethnic Disparities in Violence." *American Journal of Public Health* 95, no. 2 (February 2005): 224–232.

San Diego Association of Governments and California Department of Transportation. "Economic Impacts of Wait Times at the San Diego–Baja California Border." 2006.

San Luis Corporación. "Annual Report." Mexico City, 2009.

Sapp, Lesley. "Apprehensions by the U.S. Border Patrol: 2005–2010." Washington, DC: U.S. Department of Homeland Security, 2011.

Sarre Iguíniz, Miguel. "The National Human Rights Commission." In Mexico's Right to Know Reforms: Civil Society Perspectives, edited by Jonathan Fox 134–139. Santa Cruz: University of California, Santa Cruz, Center for Global, International and Regional Studies, 2007.

Satherley, Jessica. "Tortured, Disemboweled and Hung from a Bridge for Tweeting." Daily Mail [London], September 16, 2011.

Schmitt, Karl M. Mexico and the United States, 1821–1973: Conflict and Coexistence. Hoboken: John Wiley & Sons, 1974.

Schneider, Mark. "The Costs of Failure Factories in American Higher Education." Washington, DC: American Enterprise Institute for Public Policy Research, 2008.

Scott, John. "Subsidios Agrícolas en México: Quién Gana, y Cuánto." In Subsidios para la Desigualdad: Las Políticas Públicas del Maíz en México a Partir del Libre Comercio, edited by Jonathan Fox and Libby Haight, 73–127. Mexico City: Woodrow Wilson International Center for Scholars, Mexico Institute, 2010.

Serrano, Richard A. "Fast and Furious Weapons Were Found in Mexico Cartel Enforcer's Home." Los Angeles Times, October 8, 2011.

———. "Supervisors in ATF Gun Operation are Promoted." Los Angeles Times, August 16, 2011.

Shannon, Elaine. Desperados: Latin Drug Lords, U.S. Lawmen, and the War America Can't Win. New York: Viking, 1988.

Shirk, David. Mexico's New Politics: The PAN and Democratic Change. Boulder: Lynne Rienner, 2005.

Smith, Clint E. Inevitable Partnership: Understanding Mexico-U.S. Relations. Boulder: Lynne Rienner, 2000.

Smith, James P. "Assimilation across the Latino Generations." American Economic Review 93, no. 2 (May 2003): 315–319.

Smith, Michael Peter, and Matt Bakker. Citizenship Across Borders: The Political Transnationalism of el Migrante. Ithaca: Cornell University Press, 2008.

Smith, Robert Freeman. "Latin America, the United States and the European Powers, 1830–1930." In The Cambridge History of Latin America, edited by Leslie Bethel, 955–958. Cambridge, UK: Cambridge University Press, 1986.

Sociedad Hipotecaria Federal. "Comparecencia ante Diputados y Senadores." 2010.

Somuano, María Fernanda. Sociedad Civil Organizada y Democracia en Mexico. Mexico City: Colegio de Mexico, 2011.

St. John, Rachel. Line in the Sand: A History of the Western U.S.-Mexico Border. Princeton: Princeton University Press, 2011.

Steiner, Roberto, and Alejandra Corchuelo. "Economic and Institutional Repercussions of the Drug Trade in Colombia." Bogotá: Universidad de los Andes, El Centro de Estudios sobre Desarrollo Económico, 1999.

Sullivan, Mark P., and June S. Beittel. "Mexico-U.S. Relations: Issues for Congress." Washington, DC: Congressional Research Service, 2009.

Sullivan, Meg. "Revolution of Words: Oxnard Activists Drive Home View that Mexican Presidential Election was Stolen." *Los Angeles Times*, November 17, 1988.

Summers, Lawrence. "The Global Middle Cries Out for Reassurance." *Financial Times*, October 29, 2006.

Suro, Roberto. "The Hispanic Family in Flux." Washington, DC: Brookings Institution, 2007.

Swarna, Hepsi, and Saradhi Kumar Gonela. "Mexican Telecom Industry: (Un)wanted Monopoly." IBS Case Development Centre, 2009.

Tatto, Maria Teresa. "Education Reform and the Global Regulation of Teachers' Education, Development and Work: A Cross-Cultural Analysis." *International Journal of Educational Research* 45, nos. 4–5 (2006): 231–241.

Taylor, Michael Campbell. "Civic Alliance: The Emergence of a Political Movement in Contemporary Mexico." BA thesis, Harvard University, 1995.

Texas Border Coalition. "White Paper on Border Security." Washington DC, 2009.

Thacker, Strom Cronan. *Big Business, The State, and Free Trade: Constructing Coalitions in Mexico*. Cambridge, UK: Cambridge University Press, 2000.

Thesken, Joseph. "Mexican Vote Protested Here." *San Diego Tribune*, August 15, 1988.

Thomas, John B. "A Tale of Two Cities." *Indianapolis Monthly*, November 2006.

Tobar, Hector. "Fox Leaves Mexico's 'Dirty' Past Unsettled." *Los Angeles Times*, November 30, 2006.

———. "Judicial Overhaul in Mexico OKd." *Los Angeles Times*, March 7, 2008.

Transparencia Mexicana. "Executive Summary: National Index of Corruption and Good Governance." 2010.

Transparency International. "Global Corruption Report: Corruption in Judicial Systems." 2007.

Trennert Jr., Robert A. "The Southern Pacific Railroad of Mexico." *Pacific Historical Review* 35, no. 3 (August 1966): 265–284.

Tuckman, Jo. "Mexican Peace Caravan Led by Poet Javier Sicilia Nears its Final Stop." *The Guardian*, June 9, 2011.

Uildriks, Niels. *Mexico's Unrule of Law: Implementing Human Rights in Police and Judicial Reform Under Democratization*. Lanham: Lexington, 2010.

Ulloa, Bertha. *La Revolución Intervenida*. Mexico City: El Colegio de Mexico, 1969.

Unger, Irwin, and Debi Unger. *The Guggenheims: A Family History*. New York: HarperCollins, 2005.

United States District Attorney's Office. "Wachovia Enters into Deferred Prosecution Agreement." Southern District of Florida, 2010.

El Universal. "Perfil: José Antonio Ríos Granados." October 2, 2007.

———. "Publican el Acuerdo Nacional por la Seguridad." August 25, 2008.

United Nations Office on Drugs and Crime. "World Drug Report." 2011.

U.S. Census Bureau. "Educational Attainment in the United States: 2011." Washington, DC: 2012.

———. "Foreign Trade, 2011." Washington, DC: Foreign Trade Division, Dissemination Branch, 2011.

———. "Quarterly Financial Report (QFR), Manufacturing, Mining, Trade, and Selected Service Industries, Historical QFR Data." http://www.census.gov/econ/qfr/historic.html.

———. "State and Country Quickfacts." http://quickfacts.census.gov/qfd/index.html.

———. "U.S. Trade in Goods with Mexico: 1992." Washington, DC: Foreign Trade Division, Dissemination Branch, 2011.

U.S. Customs and Border Patrol. "Border Patrol Staffing by Fiscal Year." 2011.

———. "Enacted Border Patrol Program Budget by Fiscal Year." 2011.

———. "Securing America's Borders: CBP Fiscal Year 2010 in Review Fact Sheet." Published electronically March 15, 2011, http://www.cbp.gov/xp/cgov/newsroom/fact_sheets/cbp_overview/fy2010_factsheet.xml.

———. "Total Illegal Alien Apprehensions by Fiscal Year." 2011.

U.S. Department of Commerce. "Improving Economic Outcomes by Reducing Border Delays." International Trade Administration, 2008.

U.S. Department of Health and Human Services. "Results from the 2010 National Survey on Drug Use and Health: Summary of National Findings." 2011.

U.S. Department of Homeland Security. "Joint Task Forces Created in 10 Cities to Combat Document and Benefit Fraud." Office of the Press Secretary, 2006.

———. "FY2013 Budget in Brief." 2011.

———. "Removals Involving Illegal Alien Parents of United States Citizen Children." Office of Inspector General, 2009.

———. "SENTRI Program Description." Customs and Border Protection, http://www.cbp.gov/xp/cgov/travel/trusted_traveler/sentri/sentri.xml.

U.S. Department of Justice. "ATF: Mexico." Bureau of Alcohol, Tobacco, Firearms and Explosives, 2012.

———. "National Drug Threat Assessment." National Drug Intelligence Center, 2011.

U.S. Department of Labor. "Labor Force Characteristics of Foreign-Born Workers Summary." Bureau of Labor Statistics. Published electronically 2011, http://www.bls.gov/news.release/forbrn.nr0.htm.

U.S. Department of State. "Annual Report of Immigrant Visa Applicants in the Family-Sponsored and Employment-Based Preferences." 2011.

———. "U.S. Relations with Mexico: Fact Sheet" Bureau of Western Hemisphere Affairs, June 25, 2012, http://www.state.gov/r/pa/ei/bgn/35749.htm.

———. "Temporary Worker Visas." http://travel.state.gov/visa/temp/types/types_1271.html.

U.S. Drug Enforcement Administration. "Kiki and the History of Red Ribbon Week." http://www.justice.gov/dea/ongoing/red_ribbon/redribbon_history.html.

U.S. Drug Enforcement Administration. "Perfume Store Owner Charged with Laundering Millions of Dollars for Mexican Narcotics Trafficking Organizations." Published electronically January 18, 2011, http://www.justice.gov/dea/pubs/states/newsrel/2011/nwk011811.html.

U.S. Government Accountability Office. "Border-Crossing Deaths Have Doubled Since 1995; Border Patrol's Efforts to Prevent Deaths Have Not Been Fully Evaluated." Washington, DC, 2006.

———. "Drug Control: U.S. Assistance Has Helped Mexican Counternarcotics Efforts, but Tons of Illicit Drugs Continue to Flow into the United States." Washington, DC, 2007.

———. "U.S. Efforts to Combat Arms Trafficking to Mexico Face Planning and Coordination Challenges." Washington, DC, 2009.

U.S. House Committee on Oversight and Government Reform. "House Committee on Oversight and Government Reform Holds a Hearing on the ATF's Mexican Gun-Trafficking Investigation." 2011.

U.S. Immigration and Customs Enforcement. "Deportation of Parents of U.S.-Born Citizens." Washington, DC: U.S. Department of Homeland Security, 2012.

U.S. Senate. *Comprehensive Immigration Reform Act of 2006.* 109th Congress, S.2611.

U.S. Supreme Court. "Arizona et al. v. United States." *11–182,* 2012.

Vargas-Hernández, José G., and Mohammad Reza Noruzi. "Internationalization Strategies Followed by Three Mexican Pioneer Companies—Grupo Modelo, Grupo Bimbo, and Cemex: Issues and Challenges." *International Journal of Research in Commerce and Management* 2, no. 10 (2011): 1–7.

Vázquez, Josefina, and Lorenzo Meyer. *The United States and Mexico.* Chicago: University of Chicago Press, 1985.

Verrier, Richard. "Cinepolis Plans to Expand Luxury Cinema Concept in Southland." *Los Angeles Times,* October 25, 2011.

Vialet, Joyce C., and Barbara McClure. "Temporary Worker Programs, Background and Issues." Congressional Research Service, 1980.

Villarreal, M. Angeles. "NAFTA and the Mexican Economy." Congressional Research Service, 2010.

Vitello, Paul. "Immigration Issues End a Pennsylvania Grower's Season." *New York Times,* April 2, 2008.

Vulliamy, Ed. "How a Big U.S. Bank Laundered Billions from Mexico's Murderous Drug Gangs." *The Observer,* April 2, 2011.

Wadhwa, Vivek, AnnaLee Saxenian, Ben Rissing, and Gary Gereffi. "America's New Immigrant Entrepreneurs." Master of Engineering Management Program, Duke University; School of Information, University of California, Berkeley, January 4, 2007, http://people.ischool.berkeley.edu/~anno/Papers/Americas_new_immigrant_entrepreneurs_I.pdf.

Walker, William O. *Drug Control in the Americas.* Albequerque: University of New Mexico Press, 1981.

Wallace, Edward S. "The United States Army in Mexico City." *Military Affairs* 13, no. 3 (1949): 158–166.

Walter McKay Consulting. "Narco Killings." http://sites.google.com/site/policereform/narco-killings.

Ward, Mike. "Lawmakers Discuss Deporting Foreign Convicts." *Austin American-Statesman,* 2010.

Warnock, John W. *The Other Mexico: The North American Triangle Completed.* Montreal: Black Rose, 1995.

Wasserman, Mark. "Foreign Investment in Mexico, 1876–1910: A Case Study of the Role of Regional Elites." *The Americas* 36, no. 1 (1979): 3–21.

Watson, Julie. "Drug War: Mexican Police Standoff with Mexican Federal Agents." *The Guardian,* June 9, 2009, http://www.guardian.co.uk/world/feedarticle/8549879.

Weldon, Jeffrey. "Political Sources of Presidencialismo in Mexico." In *Presidentialism and Democracy in Latin America,* edited by Scott Mainwaring and Matthew Shugart, 225–258. Cambridge, UK: Cambridge University Press, 1997.

White House. "National Security Decision Directive No. 221." 1986.

Wilkinson, Tracy, and Ken Ellingwood. "Cartels Use Legitimate Trade to Launder Money, U.S., Mexico Say." *Los Angeles Times*, December 19, 2011.

Williamson, John. "What Washington Means by Policy Reform." In *Latin American Adjustment: How Much Has Happened*. Washington, DC: Institute for International Economics, 1990.

Wilson, Christopher. "Working Together: Economic Ties Between the United States and Mexico." Washington, DC: Woodrow Wilson Center, Mexico Institute, 2011.

Wintemute, Garen J., Anthony A. Braga, and David M. Kennedy. "Private-Party Gun Sales, Regulations and Public Safety." *New England Journal of Medicine* 363, no. 6 (August 5, 2010): 508–511.

Wolfe, Alan. "Native Son: Samuel Huntington Defends the Homeland." *Foreign Affairs* (May/June 2004): 120–125.

Woolsey, L. H. "The Expropriation of Oil Properties by Mexico." *American Journal of International Law* 32, no. 3 (July 1938): 519–526.

World Bank. "World Development Indicators." 2011, http://data.worldbank.org/indicator.

Yanikkaya, Halit. "Trade Openness and Economic Growth: A Cross-Country Empirical Investigation." *Journal of Development Economics*, no. 72 (2003): 57–89.

Yockelson, Mitchell. "The United States Armed Forces and the Mexican Punitive Expedition: Part 1." *Prologue Magazine* 29, no. 3 (Fall 1997): 256–262.

York, Emily Bryson. "Sara Lee Bread Business Sale: Getting to Know Bimbo." *Chicago Tribune*, November 9, 2010.

Zarembo, Alan. "Coyote Inc." *Newsweek*, August 29, 1999.

Zepeda Lecuona, Guillermo. "Criminal Investigation and the Subversion of the Principles of the Justice System in Mexico." In *Reforming the Administration of Justice in Mexico*, edited by Wayne A. Cornelius and David A. Shirk, 133–152. South Bend: Notre Dame Press, 2007.

———. "Índice de Incidencia Delictiva y Violencia." Mexico City: Centro de Investigación para el Desarrollo, A.C., 2008.

———. "Mexican Police and the Criminal Justice System." In *Police and Public Security in Mexico*, edited by David A. Shirk and Robert Donnelly, 39–64. San Diego: University Readers, 2009.

Zogby Internacional and El Centro de Investigación para el Desarrollo, A.C., . "Encuesta CIDAC-ZOGBY de Percepciones entre Mexico y Estados Unidos." Mexico City, 2006.

INDEX